DEELEY

MOTORCYCLE MILLIONAIRE

DEELEY
MOTORCYCLE MILLIONAIRE

Frank Hilliard

ORCA BOOK PUBLISHERS

Canadian Cataloguing in Publication Data
Hilliard, Frank, 1941–
   Deeley

   ISBN 1-55143-025-8 (pbk.)
   1. Deeley, Trev, 1920–   2. Motorcycle industry—North America—
Biography.   3. Businessmen—British Columbia—Vancouver—
Biography.   I. Title.
HD9710.5.C32D43 1994   380.1'456292275'092   C94-910705-0

Publication assistance provided by The Canada Council.
Cover design by Christine Toller.
Cover photographs: Silverworks Studio (colour photograph);
   Trev Deeley private collection (black and white photograph).
Interior photographs: Trev Deeley private collection, unless
   otherwise noted.
Author photograph: Silverworks Studio.

Printed and bound in Canada

Orca Book Publishers   **Orca Book Publishers**
PO Box 5626, Station B   PO Box 468
Victoria, BC Canada   Custer, WA USA
V8R 6S4   98240-0468

10 9 8 7 6 5 4 3 2 1

To Pamela de Silva, whose good sense,
loving support and enthusiastic encouragement
made writing this book possible

INTRODUCTION

FREDERICK TREVOR DEELEY carries a lot of baggage for a man who has done most of his travelling on a motorcycle. As the leading motorcycle importer, distributor and dealer in Canada, a multimillionaire many times over, he is praised as a philanthropist, business visionary and motorcycle legend. Colleagues and competitors talk about his uncanny foresight in market trends, his thorough knowledge of the product and his charm, consideration and thoughtfulness, both unexpected and unrequested, to them personally and their families. Some of those interviewed for this book stopped just short of saying Trev Deeley can walk on water, feed fishes to the multitude and raise people from the dead. Others, less open, painted a more demonic picture, casting Trev as a cunning financial operator who always had more cards in play than his opponents saw on the table, a father who left his only daughter with his parents while pinching his best friend's wife, a man in love with toys, in league with the Hell's Angels and in thrall to a cold, autocratic, and often inebriated father. These contrasting pictures no doubt explain why people who know him have variously described Trev as aggressive, ruthless, impulsive, generous, charming, vindictive, fearless, underhanded, open minded, loudmouthed and polite, a jet-setting playboy and a contented husband, a brilliant businessman and a lucky son of a bitch.

These words don't just flow out of people's mouths in short descriptive Anglo-Saxon sentences. When asked to talk about Trev, everyone always starts to speak in warm generalities, as one would of the Pope in the presence of Catholics, noting how his manner is personable and warm, how he always has time for visitors and how he makes them feel important. His acquaintances then go on to say, very gently, how he tends to dominate a room when he enters it, like a celebrity, and how he can on occasion use that power to "speak his mind," "let people know what he thinks," and "be quite candid." Trev's friends and supporters leave it at that. The bluntness of his manner is seen as a sign of character, as if, in a world of liars and schemers, some honesty can be a good thing. Trev's critics view that same quality a different way. They say his candour sometimes comes in the form of merciless tirades in which individuals are verbally stripped and shredded in front of others, leaving them humiliated and bitter.

In general though, criticism of Trev Deeley is muted. Where lesser individuals might be attacked for style, personality, business dealings or even their married life, comments about Trev always sound muffled, as if delivered with feather pillows rather than rocks. Lengthy interviews with his bitterest critics are laced with compliments and praise, often repeated several times, before the slightest innuendo is revealed. It's as if they don't want you to notice what they're saying; as if they hope you won't consider what they've slipped into the conversation worth even a moment of your time. Finally you realize what they hope is that you will pick up on their comments, but that Trev, should he read them in the original, will not. No one, apparently, wants to pick a fight with a multimillionaire, no matter what his, or their, personality profile.

Trev's personal wealth is in excess of $20 million. It is a considerable sum, and it is this fact that makes all the other facts, opinions and conjectures about him so interesting. It is not so much whether Trev Deeley is described now as charming or overbearing by people who worked with him or knew him through the years that is important, it is what he actually was and did that matters, because of what he became. We want to know what factors, what mixture of intuition, intelligence and happenstance combined in one person to make him successful when so many other people in the same business were not. We want, in short, to know what we can learn from his life to teach ourselves how to live ours.

One way to understand Trev Deeley is to study the Trev Deeley myths. The positive one says he was poorly paid as a young man, that he bucked his father's and grandfather's wishes and imported a few Honda motorcycles into Canada, that his dealers didn't want them but the public did, that he sold the Honda franchise back to Honda, did an even better job of launching Yamaha across Canada, put his family life on hold while he built up prosperous dealer networks, introduced the Japanese to snowmobiles, bailed out of Yamaha prior to a disastrous slump in Japanese motorcycle and snowmobile sales in North America and joined Harley-Davidson just in time to help the company achieve the leading market share and overwhelming public acceptance it has today. It's a rags-to-riches story worthy of a Horatio Alger novel, a tale of vision, pluck, grinding work, and personal charm rewarded by financial success.

The counter-myth, one only hinted at by his critics, is of the playboy son of a millionaire car importer who used his money to buy friends and influence people, a racer who always had access to special factory machines, a motorcycle distributor who could call on what amounted to a family-owned commercial credit company to build his dealer networks, someone whose wealth impressed the Japanese more than his appreciation of their product, and finally someone who on three separate occasions divided his loyalties between his then current and future motorcycle manufacturing partners to their surprise and his financial gain.

The myths, both of them, have been created in response to a very remarkable life, one both more complex and more compelling than either viewpoint suggests. Trev has neither been entirely the saint of the first view nor the sinner of the second. He has, rather, been a combination of the two personalities and the two myths. You can go down each list in both paragraphs above and explain individual events from the other perspective. He was an heir but he was treated to the same poor wages as his father's employees. He did get good racing equipment but he earned it by winning races and making friends. He impressed Honda officials with his racing as much as with his connections. Yes he used his father's credit, but often he had to fight for every cent from the "old man."

Each of the potentially damning instances of conflict of interest can just as easily be read as astute business dealings, all technically legal, that provided an alternate growth path if the wheels came off the primary relationship. In all three cases—British bikes/Honda, Honda/Yamaha and Yamaha/Harley-Davidson—

those back-up plans had to be put into effect. To people who don't understand that strategy involves maintaining choices, this fact makes it seem as if Trev Deeley made the decisions to cut and run well before he actually did. For this flexibility he is damned for being insincere. One gets the feeling his critics would have been happier, indeed some far happier, if he had held on until the British motorcycle industry collapsed, until Honda cut off his distribution, or until Yamaha's snowmobile business went through the ice. Blindness to underlying trends is such a common-place in business, people practically expect it. Had this been combined with a dissolute and irresolute life, Trev would have satisfied his competitors and critics perfectly. They would have been able to repeat the old aphorism, "shirtsleeves to shirtsleeves in three generations," point to Trevor and smile knowingly.

He did not, however, oblige them.

What we have here is a man built in three dimensions, with an unhappy past and a punch-'em-up attitude, a rich man's son who had every opportunity to cave in to his father's narrow vision, but who did not; a father who was so devastated by the death of his wife he virtually gave up family life; a businessman who could see beyond brands and past traditions to the import-ance of product value, who looked over the broad Pacific when everyone else overlooked Japan. What we have, in short, is a life lived to success. Some might call it a life lived to excess, with as many new yachts as the rest of us have new shoes; with homes in Maui, Palm Springs and Vancouver Island; with planes and helicopters, and parties that make participants gasp with admira-tion, disbelief and even fear. If it makes us uncomfortable and maybe even envious to read about it, that is not Frederick Trevor Deeley's fault. It is his virtue.

One of the young men, now old, who raced against him on the small, dusty dirt tracks of the west coast after the war, to the cheers of his wife Vera, the jeers of the Indian riders and the smell of pungent Castrol R fumes, summed up Trevor's character by saying: "He was a good winner, but a poor loser." Another former rider, asked what he thought of that comment, said: "I don't know. I never saw him lose." Somewhere between those two memories lies the spark of the man.

What this book sets out to do is to find where that spark came from, what kept it alight and how it was used to ignite three major and very successful ventures. There are business lessons here that have meaning and value far beyond the specialized realm of motorcycling.

Perhaps it's worth taking time for a little reflection on history in general and the personal histories that are biographies in particular. Many people, perhaps most people, fall into the trap of assuming that events, once they occur, were inevitable. They think that because company X is successful and company Y fails, that it was somehow written in the stars or buried in the genes of the participants involved. They therefore assume their own personal fate is similarly locked into some cosmic order that can't be nudged or prodded in some other direction. Nothing could be further from the truth. Trev Deeley had ample opportunities to fail in life. He could have quit the family concern and his apprenticeship long before he grabbed the reins of power. He could have picked up the personality of his father and made enemies wherever he went. He could have taken a nose-dive into depression after the death of his wife, or decided against importing Hondas when all his dealers rejected them, or made any one of a hundred decisions that would have made his life into something less inspiring. The business world is replete with well-meaning executives who have driven family businesses into the ground, only sons who have turned a sure thing into a bust, and Canadian companies who have screwed up relationships with the Japanese and the Americans. Trev could easily have been among their number and for a time actually appeared to have joined the great list of Canadian business failures. That he did not do so is a tribute to choice, not chance; the choices he made firstly in his own personality, secondly in his relationships with his family and thirdly in his view of the business he was in and how to conduct it.

There was nothing in any of this that was a sure bet.

CHAPTER ONE

THERE ARE TWO things that can break a young man: having a rich father and not having a rich father. Boys burdened by wealth often tend to come unglued, squandering their patrimony on sex, booze and drugs, failing to catch the baton of energy and effort being passed by their parent because there is clearly no need to worry. Poverty can be an equally damaging environment. If a father fails to provide personal support and financial resources to his son, the boy can feel defeated in the game of life before he begins.

As the big 1941 Oldsmobile sped across the high Idaho plain on the second day of March, 1948, twenty-eight-year-old Frederick Trevor Deeley must have thought he had both kinds of fathers wrapped up in one. On the one hand, his dad, also named Fred, was the Austin car importer in Vancouver, the largest city on the Canadian west coast. The post-war market for new cars was still intense and imports from England were in great demand because the North American car plants couldn't turn out enough Fords, Chevrolets, Plymouths, Dodges, Hudsons, Nashes, Packards, Kaisers, Willys and Studebakers. On the other hand his father was a notorious tightwad. A contemporary said of him he was so tight with his money he would have used both sides of a piece of toilet paper if he could. This penny-pinching extended to his only son, now slumped in the front seat of the Olds half asleep. When Trev had been invalided out of the army five years earlier because of recurring bouts of asthma, he had been forced to go to his grandfather, Fred Sr., to ask if he and his young wife could live at the family cottage twelve miles out of town at Deep Cove because he couldn't afford to rent an apartment, much less buy a house, on the low wages paid by his father. The old man had said yes and so the young couple moved into the uninsulated building in its beautiful, remote setting on Indian Arm and scrounged driftwood from the beach to fire up the wood stove that kept it warm.

His wife Vera was driving the car now, a petite blonde with an outgoing personality from a large family of White Russians. She had fallen in love with Trev at a motorcycle race in 1939 when he was nineteen years old — a handsome, aggressive young man with curly black hair who beat her brother Len whom she had gone to see win. Len introduced them in the pits after the races and she invited Trev home to meet her parents. She had agreed to go on this long trip across the continent because she wanted to be with him on his first attempt to compete in the most prestigious motorcycle race in the United States, the 200 miler on the beach at Daytona Beach, Florida. She would simply have to deal by herself with the fact that she was three months pregnant.

Vera pressed her foot on the accelerator and the speedometer climbed to seventy mph. In the back seat, Reg Shanks was a little nervous. At thirty-nine years old, he had lived all his life on Vancouver Island, where his father and now he, ran the local Harley-Davidson dealership in Victoria, Brooklands Motors. He was unused to the long, straight stretches of highway in the American west and had never travelled so fast for so long in his life. If the truth be known, he was also a little uncertain, in those pre-liberated times, of being at the mercy of a feminine ankle in a two-ton automobile towing a trailer carrying a motorcycle on a two-lane highway bordered by three feet of snow. To calm his fears, he began to count the miles between curves in the road by looking over Vera's shoulder and past the large white steering wheel at the odometer in the dashboard. The road seemed to go on forever, mile after mile of sagebrush poking up through the crusty snow on either side of the bare pavement in the overcast light of late afternoon. As Vera began steering into a long curve, Reg leaned forward to her dozing husband.

"Hey Trev," he said, "that's a twelve-mile stretch that we're ending."

Before the whole sentence came out of his mouth, there was

an almighty CRACK!, the car swerved and Vera let out a cry.

Trev woke up and grabbed the wheel to help keep the car on the road. As he looked up he saw a wheel and tire fly over the car and land on the road right beside them, bouncing a couple of times before catapulting into the adjacent field. A sudden cloud of steam and pungent smoke filled the automobile and they could feel and hear the right rear corner grinding along the pavement. Finally the car and trailer stopped in a cloud of smoke from burnt hydraulic fluid that gradually began to dissipate in the clear mountain air. Vera leant over the wheel shaken by the experience and Trev put his arm around her. Reg, who had unconsciously been expecting something to happen, threw open the door on his side and leapt out. It was immediately apparent the axle had broken and the right rear wheel had come off the car. The fender was dented, the backing plate for the wheel had ground down to half its diameter and the wheel was nowhere to be seen. Trev turned off the motor and they were surrounded in complete and utter silence in the middle of nowhere with no other cars or signs of human habitation in sight, the sun getting low in the sky and the temperature already below zero.

Reg started walking back down the track made in the pavement by the backing plate. At first it was quite wide and then after a hundred feet or so it narrowed down. Trev finally got out of the car and walked back down the road to join him.

"Where's the wheel?" he asked.

"Don't know," said Reg.

What he was thinking was that the three of them had been damn lucky to get away without a scratch. Another few feet and the Olds would have been in a curve with a much greater possibility of going out of control, rolling over or even burning. He could just imagine what the headline would have said in the *Vancouver Sun*: "Trev Deeley, Wife, Friend, Die in Mystery Car Accident in States." Well, they hadn't died; Trev had steadied the steering wheel in time and they were all safe and sound. The pair started walking back towards the car. Suddenly they noticed a spot where the regular outline of the snowbank on one side had been punched down.

"I bet that's where the wheel spun around," Trev said pointing at the patch in question. "But where the hell is it?"

They stared all about.

"Look!" Trev shouted, pointing at a large black mark in the middle of the road. "That must be where it took off."

The mark was at an angle and so they set off across the snow in the direction it pointed. Sure enough, they came to a big swath of flattened snow, and then another. The wheel had obviously been bouncing through the sagebrush at sixty miles an hour. After five or six of these marks, by now well ahead of the stranded car, they found the tire, lying flat on the snow, still on its rim, still inflated, as good as new. The two men looked at each other and shook their heads. Trev pulled it up and started rolling the wheel back to the car where Vera had been wondering what the two of them had been doing so far off the road. After a few minutes of "rolling the hoop" they made it back to the car and began discussing what to do next.

Their conversation was interrupted by the sound of a car in the distance heading towards them from the east. A couple of men drove by, parked a little way past them and walked back.

"Hey, you having trouble?" one asked.

"Yes, we are." Reg answered.

"You're heading west," Trevor said, thinking it out. "The next town you'll come to a few miles ahead, maybe ten or twelve miles, is Rupert, Idaho. We just passed through it. Would you mind going to the GM dealer and asking him to send a tow truck?"

"Sure will, pal," said the strangers and off they went.

The three got back in the car and turned the engine on to get some heat. Vera had very little to say and neither man wanted to make her feel worse by describing what might have happened on the next curve . . . or worse, in one of the mountain passes they had gone over, many with no guard rails and hundred-foot drops. While they waited they turned on the radio for some distraction, not just from the experience, but from the thought that the accident might mean they wouldn't make it to Daytona, still thousands of miles away, in the time they had left. The brand new WR Harley-Davidson racing bike was still securely bolted to its trailer and the trailer was still securely hitched to the car, but the Oldsmobile, with all their spare parts, luggage and dreams was going nowhere. The radio didn't help much to calm them down; the hit song it kept repeating was "Hernando's Hideaway" with its references to sunny, and very distant, Mexico.

Just as it began to grow dark, the tow truck arrived, slid a dolly under the rear of the car and towed the car and trailer back to the Workman Brothers garage in Rupert. Trev and Vera sat in the truck with the driver; Reg rode in the back seat of the car where he'd been when the accident happened. It was a dejected trio that got out and stamped their feet on the pavement at the garage, but there was some good news almost immediately. One of the mechanics looked at the failed axle and said, "Yeah, we'll have you on the road by ten o'clock in the morning." They were obviously going to be staying the night, so the three carried their bags over to the local hotel and went looking for somewhere to eat.

Reg woke up with a start the next morning at eight o'clock. Trev was knocking on his door. He got out of bed and let him in.

"Hey," Trev said, "we've got a problem. Something about the axle. The guys want us to go down to the garage and talk to them."

Reg dressed rapidly and then he and Trev walked across the park which made up the town square to the garage at 5th and E street at the southeast corner. The Oldsmobile was up on the hoist with the trouble light hanging above the right rear wheel opening.

"There's something funny about this car," the mechanic said. "We've never seen a '41 Oldsmobile with a five-spline half shaft. They're supposed to be seven spline."

Reg and Trev looked at the damaged shaft and counted the splines with their fingernails. It was five all right.

"Well, where can you . . . " Trev began. The mechanic cut him off.

"Oh, we've already phoned," he said. "Salt Lake City just didn't believe us when we told them. This has got us beat. We don't know what to do."

The garage mechanics, Trev, and Reg looked back at the offending half shaft.

"You can't help us, eh?" Trev asked.

"Nope."

He then turned to Reg and said, "We'll have to phone back to Vancouver." Then it suddenly hit him what the problem was.

"It must be that this is a Canadian Oldsmobile, that's the difference," he said. "No wonder they've never seen it before."

Trevor went into the office of the garage and placed a collect call to his father's car dealership in Vancouver. The operator accepted the charges and buzzed Trev's father to pick up the phone. Trev told him what had happened and Fred Jr. said something that indicated he wasn't about to let the potential advertising benefit of a Daytona win slip through his son's fingers by default.

"Well," Fred Jr. said, "sit tight and we'll see what we can do and call you back."

A little more than two hours later there was a call from Vancouver. His father said a new part could not be found in the city.

He had obviously phoned all the local GM dealers looking for it. When that hadn't worked he sent one of his best mechanics, Johnny Buchanan, to a wrecking yard to have him pull a half shaft out of a scrapped '41 Olds. This had been done and he was just now sending a staff member in a company truck down to Bellingham, Washington, to take it through U.S. customs and send it by air express consigned to Deeley at the Workman garage in Rupert.

Trev went back out to the garage and said the part was on its way. The reaction of the mechanics to the young man who could get same-day air shipments of obscure automotive parts rustled up at a moment's notice from a foreign country must have been one of amazement. Any ordinary motorist in the same fix would have had to cool his heels for days if not weeks for a part to come from General Motors in Oshawa, Ontario. Trev might have looked like a brash young motorcycle racer doing things on a shoestring budget, but there was more to him than appeared at first sight. There was clearly some financial force, somewhere over the mountains, ready to step in with aid and assistance at a moment's notice.

The three Canadians went back out, had breakfast and then Reg and Vera lounged around in the park. It was a beautiful early spring day, with bright sunshine throwing shadows from the still bare trees across the grass. Vera, who was wearing a tight, white sweater and brown checked wool pants, threw her jacket over the park bench. She leaned back with both her elbows behind her, then got up and threw a broken branch farther into the park. There was no sign of the snow Reg and Trev walked through the day before out on the highway.

There was also no sign of the missing part until the next morning when the garage got a call from the railway express agency from a city further east saying the package with the part had arrived.

"Well, could you put it on the bus?" Trev asked the express clerk.

"No sir, we can't," he said. "We only work with the railroad."

Trev tried again, "Can't you put it on the bus as a special favour, we don't mind paying?"

"Well, I'm sorry sir," said the clerk. "But we only work with the railroad and the next train won't be through till tomorrow morning."

The conversation was going nowhere but somehow Trev turned it around. He kept talking to the clerk on the other end of the line with a combination of charm and persistence until he agreed to break company rules and personally put the package on the next bus. Sure enough he did and the part turned up in Rupert at two o'clock in the afternoon. Trev walked back from the bus depot with the package under his arm only to find another problem. The mechanics were busy and weren't in a mood to drop what they were doing to fix the Olds.

"Well, it's kinda late Mr. Deeley and we're very busy," said one. "I don't know if we can do this for you today."

Trev exchanged glances with Reg and then started to smile. The solution to this little problem was close at hand. He went to the back of the car, opened the trunk, and pulled out two bottles of Canadian Club whiskey.

"Would this help you get it done today?" he asked.

It did and within the hour they were heading back down the same road they had travelled two days before. Trev was driving because he wanted to make up some of the time they'd lost waiting in Rupert. Vera was beside him, happy to have someone else drive, and Reg was staring out the rear window looking for the place where the wheel had come off. When that passed and more miles went by without incident, everyone started to relax and put the experience behind them. About an hour later they were just coming into Pocatello, Idaho. The road went into a slight curve and a dip down towards some railway tracks. Trev put his foot on the brake and absolutely nothing happened. His foot went right to the floor. Fortunately no train was coming and they just bounced across the tracks and continued up the grade on the other side. There was nothing for it but to continue moving until they got to the next garage. Trev slowed to about twenty mph in second and crawled into Pocatello. It was a typical western farming community and a busy one at that. To the three of them in a car with no brakes there seemed an awful lot of traffic in Pocatello.

Finally Trev found the nearest GM dealer. It was now quite late in the afternoon and the mechanics obviously wanted to finish up and go home.

"No, we're sorry, sir, we're too busy," one of them said.

Reg was the older of the two men, but he usually deferred to Trev whose car it was and who had invited him on the trip. On this occasion, though, he had a suggestion.

"Trev, why don't we take the wheel off?" he said. "We'll get stuck and the guy won't be able to get out the car he's working on unless he fixes ours right away."

Trev smiled and said, "Good idea."

He then grabbed a portable hydraulic jack, lifted up the car and the two men started taking off the right rear wheel which was dripping brake fluid from where the previous mechanics had failed to attach the brake line properly. The mechanic in the garage realized he'd been outmanoeuvred. He came over muttering, pushed them aside and finished the job. When he got up from tightening the wheel nuts and wiped his hands on a rag, Trev handed him a bottle of Canadian Club with the money for the work. There being no need for a bribe, it was tendered as a kind of thank-you.

From Pocatello the miles flew, first Wyoming and on into Colorado. On one day they drove 601 miles, a respectable distance even today on the Interstate, quite an achievement in 1948 on narrow, two-lane highways. They stopped at Colorado Springs and the next day went over the 7,834-foot high Raton Pass, still banked high with winter snowdrifts. Vera was driving again, her nerves quite recovered from the wheel coming off and the brakes failing. They were all marvelling at the view when she came over a crest in the road and suddenly was confronted by a huge pile of snow that had fallen across the pavement. There was no time to put on the brakes and Oldsmobile ploughed into it and lurched to the side, completely stuck.

Everyone piled out to survey the damage. The trailer was jack-knifed and half buried in the snow and the trailer hitch was twisted from the impact. They couldn't even get at the trailer to see how the bike was. There they stood, in the brilliant, bitterly cold sunshine, stuck again and only days to go till the big race in Florida.

A few moments passed while they surveyed the scene. The snow, the car and the trailer were blocking the road so they all knew the very next vehicle would have to help them get out. Some minutes later a man in a pickup truck came along, stopped his vehicle at the snowdrift and came over with a shovel.

"Oh," he said, "we'll get you out of there."

The man set to digging them out and before long they had hauled the trailer around behind the car and pushed the Oldsmobile out of the drift.

"What's the next town?" Trevor asked the Good Samaritan.

"Clayton, New Mexico," he replied. "It's about ten miles on this road. Drive in and ask the first person you meet where Pat Reiley's blacksmith shop is. He'll straighten you out."

Trev was back at the wheel as the Olds with the dented fender and twisted trailer hitch rolled into Clayton, a little Spanish-American western town where mahogany-skinned cowboys played dominoes in the shade of round-arched adobe buildings. The Irish smithy used his acetylene torch to fix the trailer and Trev bought another bolt to fit through the bike frame. The existing one had broken from the impact with the snow. Fortunately there was no damage to the machine and it looked as if it was still possible to make it to Florida on time.

They were driving rapidly toward Amarillo, Texas, when Trevor suddenly put on the brakes, stopped the car and got out. Vera followed him off the road and across a field to a radial-engined biplane that was sitting beside a shed. To Reg's amazement, they both got into the forward cockpit, one after the other, and posed for his camera. They were in high spirits at the experience, while Reg was wondering what the owner would think if he saw them horsing around with his aircraft. It was not the first time Trev had been in a plane; as a child he'd been flown right over his father's house in Vancouver at low level. However, despite his subsequent love of flying, it was the only time Trev and Vera were to be in a light aircraft together.

By Vernon, Texas, it was starting to get warm, the first really balmy air the trio had experienced since leaving the west coast where daffodils were already in bloom. It was so nice, in fact, Trev decided to get the bike off the trailer and try it out. These days taking a full-blown racing bike, minus lights or mufflers, out on a public road is generally frowned on. At the time, on the nearly empty highways of the American South, it felt as natural as breathing. Vera drove and Reg watched as Trevor cracked open the throttle of the Harley, its booming motor soon making him a speck in the distance. After fifty miles or so he stopped, a big smile on his face.

"How's it running, Trev?" Reg asked.

"Great. It feels really good," he replied.

Shreveport, Louisiana, was next, then Monroe and across the Mississippi at Vicksburg. In the warm Gulf Coast air Reg drove through the evening hours, while Trev and Vera cuddled in the back seat, curled up like teenagers at a drive-in movie. The daffodils were in bloom as they travelled through Mississippi and into Alabama. Georgia pines gave way to palms and they were in Florida. Trev was doing much of the driving now, often over seventy mph, even when it poured rain. Vera was feeling unwell with morning sickness but was trying not to make a fuss about it and in the back seat, Reg had given up worrying about his safety. More than once he thought to himself there was no point asking a motorcycle racer to slow down going to a race.

In fact it soon became obvious they were in plenty of time, rolling into Daytona Beach three days before the American Motorcycle Association's 200-mile race on Sunday. Trev had travelled the full length and breadth of the United States, using his personality and persistence to get the Oldsmobile back on the road, and his driving skills to make up for lost time. The temperature was in the 70s under patchy clouds as they hauled their bags into the two-storey Friendly Hotel from the dirty and slightly battered car bearing British Columbia licence plate P-78. Vera was already doing her part to promote the cause. Under her cardigan she wore a T-shirt with the Deeley logo – "Fred Deeley Ltd." above a Harley-Davidson shield on a large winged crest with "Vancouver, B.C." underneath. No one would have any doubt where her heart lay in the days ahead. Nor would anyone remember until much later that same heart had been damaged by rheumatic fever when she had been a child.

Trev's bike was sponsored by the Northwest Harley-Davidson Dealers Association, so the first order of business was to find the service station that racers from the Pacific Northwest used as their base. They all knew each other because, over the years, all of them had competed in events in Washington, Idaho and British Columbia. Daytona was virtually the only motorcycle event that could draw these riders over the mountains to the east coast. As travellers from the farthest corner of the continent, they felt a kinship that must have been the envy of other contestants closer to the action.

One of the first people the three met was Norm Telford, a Vancouver boy who was being sponsored by Trev's father's arch rival, Bill Ablitt, the Indian motorcycle dealer in Vancouver. The rivalry didn't extend to the racers, though, because Telford was planning to compete in the Amateur 100-mile race on the Saturday, while Trev was gearing up for the 200-mile Expert event on Sunday. They agreed to help each other in the pits for the two big races.

While they were chatting, Reg had been looking over the WR, still on the trailer behind the car.

"Why don't you take a ride on the bike?" Trev suggested.

"Well, all right," Reg replied.

As a Harley dealer, Reg Shanks knew the make backwards and

forwards. Thus, it surprised him as he set off how high-geared Trev's racer was. Instead of just popping out the clutch in first, he had to feather it in until the motor came up to speed without bogging on the hard-packed sand. No matter, it was a glorious day, with the surf catching the sunlight out to sea, the pelicans cruising in line astern fifty yards out, and the local girls looking wonderful in their one-piece bathing suits as they rubbed Tartan antiseptic suntan lotion on their arms. Then, as now, Daytona Beach is a flat expanse of brilliant white sand that expands and contracts with the tide. The area between high and low water, the strand as the English riders say, was darker in colour, quite hard and usually very smooth. The only imperfections were the occasional small jellyfish dying under the noontime sun. Reg rumbled along, listening to the motor and breathing in the sea air. After about five miles, he suddenly thought, "Hell, I've travelled all this way to the sea. I should get off and paddle about in it." He stopped the Harley, put it on its stand, took off his shoes and socks, rolled up his pant legs and had a wonderful time splashing like a child in the warm, shallow water. After a few minutes of this he remembered that Trev would be wondering about the bike so he walked back, rubbed off the sand, put his socks and shoes back on and rode slowly back up the beach.

"How was it?" Trev asked when he got back.

"Fine," Reg smiled, "just fine."

Racing at Daytona is now done in a large purpose-built speedway and road course north of the airport. In 1948 the racetrack was nine miles south of the city centre, half on the beach and half on the road running parallel to it. The 1948 race was the seventh at Daytona and the tenth overall since national 200-mile racing began in Savannah in 1934. (It had been cancelled because of the war from 1942 to 1946.) The lure of Daytona was that it was far and away the biggest racetrack in North America. Because of the width of the beach, more riders could participate than at any other event on the quarter-mile, half-mile or mile-long tracks that dotted the United States and Canada. And because the straights were so long, much higher speeds could be attained by the relatively low-powered motorcycles of the day. Bill France, who was organizing the race for the Daytona Beach Motorcycle Club and the American Motorcycle Association (AMA), made certain the event would be pre-eminent by lengthening the course for 1948 by nine-tenths of a mile over the previous year, and by taking out a kink in the road portion that had marginally slowed riders in 1947.

For the contestants, race strategy stayed the same as before: go like hell in the straights and try not to fall in the corners. Riders would race north along the beach for just over two miles, brake hard for a skidding left-hand turn up onto the paved road and then blast down the road to the south turn and back onto the beach. The straight stretches each had their problems. On the beach side you had to be careful not to go too far to the right or you'd be into the water or too far to the left or your bike would sink into soft sand. The road side was dry and hard, but it was only eighteen feet wide and spectators continually walked across it during the race.

Fairings — metal enclosures that cut the wind — were not allowed, and so some riders adopted a "human bullet" approach to cut wind resistance on the two-mile straightaways, lying on the tank with their feet extended straight out behind them. Telford used the technique; Trev did not, preferring the normal crouch that had always served him so well before.

The real challenge of Daytona, however, were the two corners, built up by city works crews the week before using bulldozers. They were notorious for dumping bikes and riders, so much so that large wooden stands were erected to allow spectators to see the action. At the north turn, the sand from the beach covered the start of the pavement like miniature ball bearings, making tires spin and affecting steering. Riders would fight for control, accelerate hard through the gears, and then roar off to the south on what the rest of the year was Florida state highway A1A. After a minute holding the throttle wide open, they would have to brake hard in order to get set up for the left hander onto the beach. The faster the rider, the more likely he wouldn't be able to make the turn, and a surprising number went straight over the edge of the banking and landed in the sand and sea grass beyond. You can tell how important the corners were by looking at the lap times for the 4.1 mile course. In spite of two long straights that allowed extended periods of speeds up to 120 mph, the record was just over seventy-eight mph. The race itself would be forty-nine laps in all to make up the 200 miles. France announced 175 AMA "expert" riders, each with at least two years' racing experience, had qualified for the event. Among the favourites was Billy Mathews of Hamilton, riding a Norton. He had won the race in 1941 and this was his first return to Daytona since racing resumed the previous year. Trev Deeley, while a fixture on tracks in the Pacific Northwest, wasn't mentioned in the pre-race hoopla and wasn't pictured in the *Daytona Beach Evening News.*

In a remarkable parallel to the fact the race was half "dirt track" and half roadrace, the field competing for the $7,500 in prize money was also split between two basic design ideas, side valve V-twins made in the United States and overhead valve (OHV) twins and singles made in Europe. As might be expected, the field was dominated by American-made V-twins: eighty-eight Harley-Davidsons and forty-four Indians. But there were also seven British brands: twenty-one Nortons, seven Matchless, six Triumphs, three Excelsiors, three B.S.A.s, one Ariel and one AJS. The war had only been over for three years, but there was also a German-made BMW.

First though was the 100-miler on Saturday in which Norm Telford was entered. With low tide due for 4 PM, the 148 ama-teurs were flagged off at 2:30 PM in rows fifteen abreast at six-second intervals from the start/finish line on the beach just north of the south turn. The weather, as it often is in early March at Daytona, was uncooperative with a northeast wind blowing off the water and a temperature of no more than 60 degrees. As a result the crowd lining the course was estimated at only about 9,500. As usual the south turn was taking its toll, one rider after another slithering into the sand. Number 14, William Graves of Mansfield, Ohio, wasn't so lucky. When his motorcycle jumped the banking, he was hurled into the wooden judges' stand with a dull thud that could be heard by nearby spectators. Fortunately he escaped with just bruises. Meanwhile a tragedy was taking place a few hundred feet away along the pit straight. Armin Hostettler of Hanover, Pennsylvania, Number 78, slowed down and started to pull into the pits at the same moment that Charles McHale of Denver, Colorado, Number 155, was accelerating up the beach on the inside. The two bikes collided and McHale's machine whipped for seventy feet on its side into the spectators with a terri-fying roar, hitting four of them. Thirty-four-year-old Harold McKeever of Marion, Ohio, was killed instantly. His wife Margaret was knocked headfirst into the sand, unconscious and had both her legs broken. Two other spectators received lesser injuries. It was only the second fatality in the history of the 100-mile event – the previous year a novice rider, Porter Clark of Miami, had been killed in an accident. Trev and Vera soon heard the news. It brought home an appreciation to both of them this was not just a game after all, but a matter of life and death for racers and spectators

alike. For Trev the racer and Vera the spectator, it was a sober-
ing thought. Willie Telford meanwhile, oblivious to drama,
roared across the finish line in twenty-seventh place, satisfied to
have finished despite a fall and some fuel problems, but disappointed to have failed to get into the money.

That evening, on their way back to the hotel from the beach,
another event happened that, while apparently minor at the time,
gave a warning of two tragedies to come later in Trevor's life.
They were just crossing the wooden bridge between the beach
strip and the mainland when Vera shouted.

"Let me out! Let me out! Trev, let me out!"

Trev immediately pulled to the side of the roadway. Vera
jumped out, ran over to the bridge railing and began to vomit
over the side. Reg, realizing he was closer to her than Trev,
grabbed a large bath towel that was lying beside him on the seat,
got out and went over to where she was retching into the Inter-
Coastal Waterway. He handed it to her and she wiped her
mouth and tried to catch her breath. It was the most forceful
indication any of them had that Vera's pregnancy was not going
well at all.

Race day, Sunday March 14, dawned with this headline across
the Sunday *News-Journal*, "MOTORCYCLE KILLS SPECTATOR AT
RACE." Just below it was a picture of William Graves crashing
into the stand at the south turn. It was hardly an auspicious omen,
but everyone was too busy, and too excited, to let it bother them. Trev,
in addition to Willie Telford, was being helped by other mechanics and riders from Washington and Oregon, even though his
bike, which was practically brand new from the factory, hardly
needed any attention. He already had his number painted on
both sides — a large black 69 — so all that was needed was to
have his bike inspected and to make final preparations. He had
drawn position 85, about halfway back in the field, not as close to
the front as he would have wanted normally, but theoretically a
matter of little importance in a timed event. The temperature was
just touching 71 degrees, a warmer day than the day before, as
22,000 people crowded along the two-mile stretch of beach and
road for the main event. At the start line, riders were lined up in
rows behind ropes, each of them gunning the throttle to keep
their motors running. Then the first row was off, and the second,
and the third. Trev with his eyes on the starter waited impatiently
and then suddenly was off, accelerating hard in pursuit of the
specks in the distance that were the earlier riders.

From the start, the race was between Mathews and Floyd Emde, a twenty-nine-year-old mechanic from California riding an Indian. While they battled for the lead, the field rapidly began to thin out. First to go were twenty machines that scratched at the start, including one that caught fire and burned right at the line. Most of the spills were at the south turn, which accounted for Paul Albrecht of Sacramento, Ray Hyland of Eugene, Oregon; Putt Mossman of Beaver Falls, Pennsylvania; Ed Guill of Danville, Vermont; Bud Croy of Columbus, Ohio; Dowd Rozzelle of Alta Vista and Ernie Roccio of Los Angeles.

Trev, riding with his usual aggressive style, had started to move up on the leaders. Because position was based on individual total elapsed time, it wasn't always clear to spectators what was happening unless they paid attention to the race commentary being broadcast over loudspeakers. However, Trev had rapidly moved from eighty-fifth place to eighth and was charging hard to move up to seventh when he came up to the south corner on his eighteenth lap. Like so many others, he lost it in the loose sand and the WR Harley went down.

A photographer from On-The-Spot Photos in Daytona Beach captured the moment from the inside of the turn. Trev is less than an arm's length off the track as he hits the sand. The number 69 stands out clearly on his back and the cloud of sand is already engulfing the machine.

"Just going too fast," he says now, looking at the picture.

Trev had fallen many times in dirt track races and knew he still had a chance if he could remount the bike and get right back on the course. Although on its side, it was still running so Trev hauled it upright, gunned it through the sand and got back into the race.

Halfway to the north turn, with other riders blasting past him on either side, the WR's motor lost power and finally quit, leaving Trevor to coast to a silent stop. Its racing carburetor, little more than a bellmouth and a main jet, and big enough to see the backside of the intake valve, had sucked in a bucketful of sand, causing the pistons to overheat from the loss of lubrication and seize tight. When the motor was disassembled in Seattle later, sand was found to have penetrated right into the big end bearings on the crankshaft, the heart of the motor.

Trev said afterward he should have hit the kill button in the millisecond before he went down, saving the motor from strangling itself with sand. That's hindsight. All his dirt track training told him to let it run, so he could remount and resume the race as quickly as possible. Training wins over intellect every time when there isn't time to think of the consequences.

Racers continued to roar past him as he walked back to the pits to smile at Vera and the other racers from the Northwest and shrug his shoulders. Oddly, the pits were where Mathews was in the process of losing the race. Each rider anticipated he'd have to make one scheduled pit stop for gas. Emde came in and gassed up in thirty-one seconds. But when Mathews came in, a crewman spilled gas over his tank and it took one minute and five seconds for him to get on the track again. When Emde's time was computed, it was discovered his elapsed time of two hours, twenty-two minutes and fifty-six seconds was just eighteen seconds better than Mathews. Emde's average speed was eighty-four mph; he had also smashed Mathews' record from 1941.

Perhaps this was why, when Trevor ran into Mathews later after the race and introduced himself, the attempt led to a public humiliation.

Mathews was just coming down some stairs at a hotel when Trev stepped up and said, "Hi, I'm Trev Deeley from Vancouver." Mathews, the man many had tipped to win the race, replied: "Don't tell me your troubles, I've got enough of my own." The remark rankled the young Deeley, but he didn't show it. He vowed quietly to himself he'd make Mathews aware of the Deeley name just as he'd vowed earlier to make his father aware of his achievements, both at the store and on the track. Somehow, some way, his parents, his grandparents, the motorcycle community and eventually the world would hand some praise out to the little boy who so often was left at home alone or with a neighbour, who was so often ignored, countermanded or criticized, who was assumed by others to have a silver spoon in his mouth when he could hardly feed himself and his wife, put clothes on their backs and a roof over their heads.

As Trev, Vera and Reg drove home, through the red dirt of Georgia with the silent WR Harley behind them, Reg was thinking of the ocean and the race, Vera was thinking of the child she was almost certainly going to abort and Trev was thinking of how to make his life a success — what actions to take, what people to see and influence, what business decisions he would have to make first.

Unknown to him at the time, and for many years afterwards, he had already set the wheels in motion for one of his later business successes. Despite his failure to complete the race, his aggressive riding style and his even-tempered attitude to his problems impressed senior Harley-Davidson officials who were there. Unlike some other riders who badmouthed their equipment to make up for their own deficiencies, or who acted like prima donnas off the track, Trev was charming, philosophical and self-confident in addition to being a very hard competitor. At Harley-Davidson, the young Canadian's qualities were duly noted.

While the Oldsmobile's wheels are turning and the soft March air is blowing in the window, let's race ahead of Trev and his thoughts, in a kind of literary *Back to the Future*, and see how things look forty-three years later, on July 20, 1991.

The tires now are wider and lower. As we glance up we can see they're attached to a silver, four-door Rolls Royce Silver Spur sedan. Behind it is a long line of expensive cars, Mercedes, Cadillacs, Lincoln Town Cars and Audis, all travelling together in a convoy over the hills and curves of Landsend Road, a narrow two-lane thoroughfare at the extreme northern tip of the Saanich Peninsula on Vancouver Island. The drivers and passengers in the convoy, which also includes a shuttle bus, have all been guests at a christening ceremony for Trev's latest and largest yacht at the Canoe Cove Manufacturing Ltd. dock at Canoe Cove Marina a few hundred yards from the B.C. Ferry terminal in Swartz Bay. The boat is a stunner, a sixty-foot sports fisherman with an interior finished in light, matched bird's eye maple, with a silk headliner, taupe and pink Ultrasuede panels and deep ivory carpeting, and powered by two turbocharged V-12 V92TA Detroit-Allison diesel engines capable of speeds up to thirty-eight miles an hour. Like all his boats, except the first which was named *Blonde Lady* after Vera's cocker spaniel, it's called *Cove Lady*, named officially after his former home at Deep Cove north of Vancouver, but actually for the woman he fell in love with there and who became his third wife. Joyce Christopher, for twenty-two years Mrs. Joyce Deeley, is sitting turned towards him, relaxed but alert in the deep leather seat, watching Trev drive and looking back at the line of cars following. At sixty, Joyce is a slim, tall woman with a comfortable bearing, a ready laugh and a direct way of talking who looks fifteen years younger than her age, despite a skin darkly freckled from too many hours in the Maui and Palm Springs sunshine. Joyce is the other half of a happy and loving relationship, and her feelings on this occasion, as during other major festivities, are tinged with concern prompted by Trev's recent illnesses, especially his battles with pneumonia and arthritis. He has aged noticeably in the past few years, grown smaller, and slightly hunched by recurring pain. He now shakes hands with his left hand, upside down, to avoid having his right knuckles squeezed. She turns and smiles at her Pied Piper. None of the more than 150 people in the convoy knows where they're going; the destination, as with many Trev Deeley parties, is a surprise.

The road passes private driveways leading down to the waters of Colburne Passage and others heading left up past spruce and fir trees to homes with commanding views that stretch all the way to the Coast Mountains north of Vancouver and the Mount Baker volcano in Washington State. Eventually, it winds south around Moses Point and along a large bay facing west towards the Malahat promontory across the Saanich Inlet. Trev brakes the Rolls and wheels into the grounds of one of the most exclusive restaurants on the Island, the Deep Cove Chalet.

The Chalet consists of two large clapboard cottages surrounded by formal grounds with manicured lawns, rosebushes and hedges, all with a magnificent view over the water. As the motorcade continues to enter the driveway, guests emerge from their vehicles in the parking lot to see Chef Pierre Koffel greeting Trevor and Joyce, a marquee set up on the lawn, food set out on white tablecloths and a four-piece jazz ensemble. There is a sense, even among the well-to-do, of having lucked out. The Chalet is renowned for its food, and its prices. Hors d'oeuvres start at $6.50 for Pâté de Champagne, rise through $8.50 Boneless Pigs' Feet pan-fried with beer reduction to $15 local Prawns Provincial, and wind up with $30 Steamed Blinis and Russian caviar. The champagne on the menu is equally exalted: magnums of Mumms are available for $130, Don Perignon for $380 and Lois Roederer for $450. On this day, for these guests, it is all free. Trevor has taken over the entire chalet and its grounds for the boat-launching party.

The menu includes hors d'oeuvres, hamburgers and roast pork (both favourites with the host), chicken, lamb, lobster, prawns, filet mignon and much more. There is an ice sculpture of the name Cove Lady and a sugar sculpture of the boat. The guests, who are a cross-section of Trevor's acquaintances, employees, business colleagues and personal friends, attack the food in a kind of giddy disbelief. The sense of the theatrical is accentuated when the *Cove Lady* herself, piloted by a crew from the manufacturer, races into the bay at top speed and proceeds to do a series of power turns throwing up sheets of spray and even a rooster tail, just like the wartime PT boat it, in fact, resembles. While the guests, champagne glasses in hand, are taking this in a second sound blends with the throbbing of the *Cove Lady*'s powerful motors. This turns out to be a helicopter which descends over the party and starts dropping a cloud of small objects from above. Incredulity turns to squeals of delight from the ladies as it's discovered the objects are orchids. The frenzy is intense as people leap for them in the air and dive to pick up the exquisite flowers from the lawn. From the patio in front of the Chalet's open door, Trev smiles. It's been a long road from Rupert, Idaho, when the wheel came off his dreams or Daytona when his Harley pitched him into the sand. It's been a long road but it's ended up as a celebration of success, supported by his love, surrounded by his friends and even anointed from above. If there is any cloud in Trev's mind about this ritzy, over-the-top extravaganza, it is the sure knowledge that, if his father were alive to witness it, he would have said: "Well, it's not bad, but you could have done better."

CHAPTER TWO

TO FIND THE origins of this modern-day pot of gold, you have to wind the clock back the better part of a century to Edwardian England.

The death of Queen Victoria in 1901 came as the British Empire was at the height of its power and influence. The Union Jack, containing the crosses of St. George for England, St. Andrew for Scotland and St. Patrick for Ireland, snapped in the breeze over Government Houses in every part of the world. British soldiers kept the peace in India, Africa, the Caribbean and Oceania and the Royal Navy patrolled the sea lanes of the globe practising, from time to time, a little "gunboat diplomacy" to further Britain's commercial interests. Fifty years of peace and prosperity had resulted in a dramatic growth in England's coal, steel, and manufacturing sectors and the creation of a growing middle class of factory employees, office workers and business clerks.

For the first time in history, ordinary people in England, as opposed to the aristocracy then at its zenith, had enough purchasing power to buy more than just the absolute necessities of life. They used this money, in large part, to break the bond that for centuries held them locked in the almost feudal grip of the villages or towns in which they lived. Owning a horse and carriage was out of the question; the purchase price, stabling and the cost of feed continued to restrict this mode of transportation exclusively to the rich. What was both affordable and available was the "Rover" safety bicycle introduced in 1884 by John Kemp Starley, improved on by others, and by 1901 far and away the most popular mechanical device in history.

Bicycles created freedom, not just from the place of one's birth, but from one's station in life. No longer did the ordinary person have to leap onto the verge when a fashionable carriage thundered by. He, or increasingly she, could cycle right past the high and mighty and arrive at a destination before them. The new railways that criss-crossed the country were cheap enough, and for many, family outings to the seaside or "up to town," became a popular diversion. But the bicycle was paramount; it created fashions, aided women's emancipation, resulted in demands for improved roads, helped start the move to suburbia and provided a focal point for social and sporting activities.

Bicycle club members went on day trips, longer holiday tours and competed with each other in endurance, point-to-point and match racing events. Bicycle racing was popular because it was egalitarian, local and exciting. Anyone could afford to enter, and if they practised diligently and strove mightily, anyone could be a winner. The bicycle racing craze expressed exactly the common yearning for equality of opportunity that had for centuries been denied by the English class system.

Alfred Deeley entered life in 1881 right in the middle of this social and mechanical ferment in Bromsgrove, thirteen miles south of Birmingham. The "Penny Farthing," so named because its large front wheel looked like an English penny and small trailing wheel like a farthing, had been invented by James Starley in 1870 and was at the height of its popularity. Birmingham was one of the centres of the English bicycle industry and scores of local factories had sprung up to satisfy British and overseas markets. As a toddler of three or four, he would also have seen the first safety bicycle — the diamond-framed design with two equal wheels and chain drive we take for granted today.

It was just as well the local economy was booming, because his father died while Alfred was still young and he had to leave school and go to work. Weekends, however, were another matter. The young man, filled with enthusiasm and energy, took to the new machines like chain oil to a pant leg. Starting with local races in Birmingham, he began peddling farther afield to compete in club races in neighbouring towns. Many of the contests were endurance events. On one occasion he travelled thirty or forty miles, competed in an endurance race, and then peddled all the way home with the prize, a heavy marble clock, on his shoulder. Other weekends Alfred would start Friday evening, ride 100 miles to Lincoln for a Saturday race meet, and then cycle home Sunday for a second club meet in Birmingham. Increasingly, he was successful in these events, establishing a name for himself as a top bicycle racer in the city. It was of more than just academic interest to bicycle fans, because betting was allowed at the weekend race meetings, and many a local punter wound up with a few extra bob as a result of a Deeley win.

His fame was also instrumental in starting his first business. Shortly after he married his sweetheart Elizabeth, "Lizzy," in 1903, he approached the local manager of the Rover Cycle Company in Birmingham and asked if he would provide stock and credit to allow him to set up a bicycle business in a small garage in Bromsgrove. The manager agreed, and a few days later the sign "Fred Deeley-The Cycle Man" went up over the garage entrance.

Business boomed right from the start. Thousands of people already knew of him from his racing victories, and patronizing a shop owned by a winning bicycle racer seemed an excellent idea for both competitors and ordinary bicycle riders alike. A year later, the young family, with their new business, was able to celebrate the birth of their first child, whom they named Frederick Granville Deeley. The proud father was twenty-three.

This could easily have been the end of the story. Most new businesses fail in the first couple of years, and Alfred Deeley had started his with essentially no capital at all. Fred Deeley-The Cycle Man however, just wasn't about to let that happen.

For one thing, he kept tight control of the finances, always working within his cash flow, and always keeping overhead to a minimum. Secondly, he almost immediately branched out into handling motorcycles, then little more than a bicycle with a motor attached, but clearly to Deeley the coming thing in popular transportation. This was not a very big step for someone familiar with bicycles, and many other bicycle dealers across the country were doing the same thing, but all the same it showed a remarkable willingness to identify and respond to a future market. Alfred Deeley may have loved bicycling, the physical exhilaration of peddling over hill and dale or pumping across the finish line as a winner, but he loved business success more. If strapping hot, noisy, smelly internal combustion engines onto his beloved bicycle frames was what it was going to take, so be it.

Nor was he irreversibly committed to two wheels in an era that was beginning to see more and more horseless carriages with four. By a happy coincidence the English industrialist Herbert Austin lived in Northfield, five miles away, where he began to build automobiles in 1905. Alfred Deeley, who found himself selling motorcycles to Austin's employees, went to see Lord Austin and negotiated a sales agreement in the very first year of production for Austin's new cars. The retail purchase price was £110, a considerable sum at the time, more even than the relatively well off professional classes could afford. Alfred Deeley's solution to this problem was to rent his new Austins when he couldn't sell them. He found his best customers were doctors who needed speedy transportation in all types of weather and who were, even then, upwardly mobile. The new line, however, meant new responsibilities. Often he had to get up in the middle of the night and travel ten miles to service one of his livery cars that had broken down.

As the decade progressed, so did the business. Alfred continued to sell bicycles and motorcycles and both sell and rent Austin cars. At home, in 1907, Lizzy presented him with another son, whom the couple named Ray.

Perhaps he was working too hard, or at least worrying about it too much, because by 1912 Alfred had developed a severe stomach ulcer. Renting his vehicles to physicians meant he got a lot of free medical advice, and one of his doctor clients prescribed a sea voyage and an all-meat diet to cure the condition. Given that suggestion, many people would have considered a day trip from Southend to Calais. Alfred Deeley, however, decided on the North Atlantic instead of the Channel.

The exact reason was a chance remark of a friend who turned up one day on a new motorcycle and explained he had just spent three years in British Columbia.

"You could make a killing out there selling cars," the friend insisted.

That prospect, plus the pain in his stomach, was cause enough to get going. To make certain he could continue moving on the trip, he acquired letters from a number of local manufacturers, including the Birmingham Small Arms Company, appointing him as a travelling salesman for their bicycles, motorcycles, rifles and other products. That done, he was off to Canada, seeking his fortune, as so many had done before him.

If you have ever been to Regina, Saskatchewan, in the dead of winter you have probably asked yourself why. Alfred Deeley sat in the warmth of his hotel room in the city named after his late Queen in 1913, watching a snowstorm howling outside, and asked himself the same question. He observed the population of Regina had remained static at 10,000 from 1902 to 1911 and resolved to find a place that was growing, and grow with it. Climbing back on the train, he travelled west to Vancouver and Victoria, and then eastward across the United States, paying expenses by selling goods from the companies that had given him their catalogues and authorization.

The following year, with war drums beating in Europe, the Deeley family, Alfred, Lizzy, Fred and Ray, were on the journey familiar to so many immigrants to Canada, the long trip across the Atlantic and the even longer trip across the country on the plush velour seats of the smoky, swaying carriages of the CPR. The Maritimes, the St. Lawrence, Northern Ontario, the Prairies all eventually passed before ten-year-old Fred and seven-year-old Ray staring out the window in wide-eyed amazement. Compared with the orderly, compact, busy and industrialized country of their birth, Canada felt as raw and untamed as a sleeping grizzly. Alfred told his wife the city he liked the most was Victoria, which, he said, was very much like England, and certainly a lot more civilized than what she could see out the window through the billowing smoke from the steam engine at the front of the train.

When they stepped off the train in Vancouver and Alfred said they had another boat trip ahead of them to get to Victoria, Lizzy, who had been in charge of two young children in confined spaces for the better part of three weeks, put her foot down. "Not another step further," she exclaimed, and refused to budge. Alfred acceded to his wife's demand to calm her down, then decided it was a good idea anyway. Victoria had clear air, sparkling sunshine, warm temperatures, a military garrison, Royal Navy ships in the harbour and the Union Jack flying from every flagpole, but it was not a rapidly growing city with a large business community. Vancouver, on the other hand, was Canada's only western gateway and already had a population of 110,000. It was certain to grow larger still, and any new business would grow with it.

Alfred had sold his business in Bromsgrove and had brought a nest egg of $2,000 to Canada. He now used this to open a bicycle store at 1078 Granville Street at the edge of the city. The sign over the door was the one that had worked so well before: "Fred Deeley, The Cycle Man." He was still a representative of the

Birmingham companies he had represented before, so the first bicycles he put on sale were Raleighs and B.S.A.s from the Birmingham Small Arms factory.

The times could hardly have been worse. Vancouver was suffering from a building and real estate boom that had gone bust in 1912 and 1913. Logging had hit a slump, unemployment was growing and there was a depression atmosphere. All the same, the bicycle wasn't then the high-tech luxury it is today; it was basic transportation for the common man. Alfred figured no one would be without a bicycle who could possibly pay for one. Bankers, businessmen, doctors, lawyers, clerks, secretaries and seamstresses; everyone travelled on two wheels.

Suddenly, tossing all his plans into the air, Canada was at war. At first the public expected a speedy victory in Europe and young men flocked to the colours while peacetime commercial life went on. The supply of bicycles from Britain continued and was augmented in 1916 when Alfred moved to 968 Granville Street and began importing B.S.A. motorcycles. Then in 1917 the supply stopped. The grinding, bloody conflict in Flanders was demanding an ever higher price in British blood and steel and nothing was left over to supply the colonies with non-essential consumer goods. Alfred looked for alternate sources in the United States to fill his store, and from scores of potential manufacturers picked the then fourteen-year-old firm of Harley-Davidson in Milwaukee, Wisconsin.

For the former bicycle racer, the choice was obvious – Harley-Davidson had won the three big races in the States in 1915: the Venice International Grand Prize, a 300-mile race at an average speed of just over sixty-eight mph; the Oklahoma City Road Race, 150 miles at nearly sixty-five mph; and the Phoenix 200-mile race at an average speed of just over sixty-four mph. In 1916 it continued its winning streak with fifteen victories, on board tracks, flat tracks and in the FAM Nationals, more than a couple of which were complete sweeps. A brochure at the time offered 11-horsepower, twin-cylinder racers that were capable of up to seventy-five miles per hour, direct from the factory. Optional equipment included different oiling systems, seats, tires and gas tanks, including a sleeker rounded version introduced that year. The price of all this excitement was $250 F.O.B. Milwaukee.

Just as important to Alfred was the fact that H-D motorcycles could be ordered with heavy-duty sidecars, or even delivery boxes that could be interchanged with sidecars on the same three-wheel frame. There were no lightweight pickup trucks available for small businesses and motorcycle sidecars of the type made by Harley-Davidson were priced right to fill this growing need.

He wrote to the company and was rewarded with the third dealership agreement in Harley-Davidson's history, and the first one in a foreign country. When the war ended, Alfred, now called Fred because of the name of his company, was ideally placed to take advantage of the boom caused by returning servicemen and the growing population of the British Columbia lower mainland.

Things were going pretty well by 1919, when he had to turn his attention to a crisis in his own family. His son, Fred Jr., aged fifteen, announced one night he was quitting school and was going to pack up and see the world. He had already figured out how to do this, having obtained a job as a cabin boy on one of the Canadian Pacific Steamship passenger vessels that ran out of Vancouver to Japan. We don't know how Fred Sr. and Lizzy reacted to this announcement, but they clearly didn't block his plan because both of them went down to the dock to see their son off on his first voyage.

They were joined by nineteen-year-old Islay Jeanne Segwick, Fred Jr.'s girlfriend, the daughter of a motorman on the B.C. Electric street railway system that serviced Vancouver. She proceeded to burst into uncontrollable tears as the *Empress* slipped its hawsers and moved away from the pier. Lizzy tried to comfort her, but Islay was inconsolable, creating a scene that had Fred Sr. genuinely concerned. Eventually Lizzy pried it out of the pretty little girl with the tear-stained face: she was pregnant.

What Fred Jr. thought of this little vignette on the dock, what he did on the trip, how he found Japan or what he expected on his return is a mystery. What we do know is that the Deeleys and the Segwicks had him promptly in front of a minister on December 20, 1919, pledging to love, honour and obey. Frederick Trevor Deeley was born to the newlyweds on March 15, 1920. The mother was delighted, the father was anything but.

Fred Jr. had been trapped by parental pressure, the strict morals of the time and no doubt by a guilty conscience but he was not an enthusiastic bridegroom. At sixteen years old, he was in the first blush of manhood, with a whole world of personal and social options suddenly cut off at the start. Even his career path had now been mapped out. To support his new-found family, he would be joining the family firm immediately, helping with the motorcycle side of the business rather than in bicycle sales. Although he didn't know it at the time, and probably didn't appreciate the decision for many years, Fred Sr.'s determination to point Fred Jr. at motorcycles would have a profound effect on him, the family business and the squalling infant that was his son.

Fred Sr.'s decision to go with Harley-Davidson was already proving well founded. In just three years it had become the largest motorcycle manufacturer in the world, both in floorspace and the number of machines produced, and had expanded its dealer network to sixty-seven countries. British machines were also back in stock, so Deeley's entered the decade well placed to take advantage of the public's need for personal transportation.

It's worth taking a look at photographs of North American cities at the start of the '20s to see what a significant role motorcycles were playing. Unlike today, when many street scenes have no motorcycles at all, urban views at the time almost always have motorcycles in them, many with sidecars. The fact was, that even while Henry Ford continued to lower the price of his cars, it was still far more economical to buy a motorcycle than an automobile. So many people owned or rode motorcycles that they were a normal part of everyday life, with no stigma attached and no special cachet given. A modern comparison would be the econocar. In the 1920s families who bought motorcycles and sidecars – called "combinations" – were the kind of people who today would buy a Chevy Sprint or Honda Civic for good basic and affordable transportation.

Understanding that makes it easier to understand Fred Sr.'s business success. He continued to sell bicycles, but most of his energy was now in promoting motorcycles, especially combinations that could be afforded by small families or small businesses. The Vancouver police were resisting his efforts, but he was doing well with stores, contractors and tradesmen who needed transportation to move goods or provide services, but didn't want to put up the cash for a new automobile. Motorcycles were also growing in importance as recreational vehicles as people developed more leisure time. Hillclimbs and flat track racing were popular as was the simple pleasure of riding out into the countryside and enjoying nature.

For Fred Jr., Sunday was riding day when he and a couple of his friends would go into the country, usually for a picnic at some spot at the end of a gravel road up the Fraser Valley. These trips soon became popular as other riders joined them, so they decided in 1922 to organize themselves into the Lions Gate Motorcycle Club. They met every Friday, which was payday, in a room above the entrance to the Deeley shop. Many good games of poker were played, often well into Saturday morning.

With wages at a few dollars a week, the weekend camp-outs were fairly simple, starting after work on Saturdays. Club members would ride out into the country, pitch tents and come back on Sunday. One of the members with a sidecar outfit would take a load of steaks and buy some corn on the way. When the cost was shared, it only came to about a dollar each.

Despite this bare bones approach, or because of it, the club continued to grow in size. Photographs of the period show turn-outs of thirty-five machines, including up to ten sidecars, many with families. The Lions Gate wasn't the only club of course; there were the Kit Kats from Kitsilano who didn't get on well with the local police, and the Flying Thirties with their club house out in the boonies in New Westminster, who were considered a bunch of rang-a-tangs.

By 1925, Deeley's had expanded to two locations, a bicycle store and a motorcycle shop. Fred Sr. was also doing a lot of travelling, visiting other Harley-Davidson dealers, such as Richard Shanks in Victoria and Elfred Leo "Pop" Place in Bellingham, both of whom became close personal friends. In addition, he was building a dealer network for B.S.A. motorcycles in the B.C. interior and Alberta, as well as servicing his competitors as an agent for Castrol Oil.

Two years later there was so much activity on the motorcycle side, Fred Sr. decided to move to a new location at 561 West Broadway and discontinue retail bicycle sales. Fred Deeley was still "The Cycle Man" but from here on it was to be mostly motorcycles. Because they took less time and effort to look after, and probably because he just couldn't part with the product that had been instrumental in getting him started, he continued to be a bicycle wholesaler from a store at 639 Hornby Street.

The following year the motorcycle business was doing so well he decided he could afford to build a shop of his own. As he considered the possibilities, his eye ran straight up West Broadway, a long straight street on the south side of False Creek that ran east-west on the crest of a rise and looked back across the water to the city centre. The first vacant lot he could find was at 901 West Broadway, located between Oak and Laurel streets, just a block north of the Vancouver General Hospital. Doctors had been some of his best customers in the past; he would make certain they'd have no trouble finding his shop now. He would not be selling cars for two more years, but already he had a location nailed down right next to a proven automobile customer base, the medical community. The only problem was that the street was still "paved" with wooden blocks which stank when wet and had the habit of floating away when there was a bad rain.

The choice of location was inspired. Fred Sr. could just as easily have gone east on Hastings to find reasonably priced property near the docks, or picked a north-south thoroughfare in the east end such as Commercial Drive. Instead he chose what was a suburban street up on a hill. Today, more than sixty years later, east Hastings is still resolutely working class and Commercial Drive is struggling with graffiti and the urban poor. Nine hundred block West Broadway, on the other hand, has moved upscale, with attractive, multi-level condominiums rising on the streets to the north, fashionable restaurants and coffee houses and increasing numbers of professional and business offices.

Unknown to his sons, his workers or his competitors, Fred Sr. was also starting to back his hunch on this location with investments in the immediate area, buying property on either side, behind his store, and across the street when it became available or was needed by his business. The value of these relatively modest landholdings, and the borrowing power they represented, were to provide much of the financial stability the company was to count on through the Depression, the Second World War, and the postwar boom of the late '40s and early '50s.

The move to the new shop in April, 1929, created the need for a new, more formal, arrangement of the company's structure. Accordingly, Fred Sr. incorporated the firm as Fred Deeley Limited, giving himself eighty-nine percent of the controlling shares, Fred Jr. ten percent and Ray one percent. Fred Jr. accommodated himself to the new reality by buying a house at 843 West 19th Street, ten blocks directly south of the new motorcycle store. Ray, by now also married, marked the occasion by fathering a son, who in the Deeley tradition of keeping one name going as long as possible, he also named Ray.

Fred Deeley Limited was in the perfect position to handle continued growth when the North American economy crashed and motorcycle sales crashed with it. The start of the Great Depression is popularly thought of as one shattering event before which everything was rosy and after which everything was a disaster. In fact, the economy ratcheted down in stages over the next three years while business people of all types did everything they could to turn it around. The motorcycle industry generally reached out to stimulate sales. The American Motorcycle Association staged a nation-wide Gypsy Tour, a longtime motorcycling tradition, to keep enthusiasts involved in the sport. Most dealers in the U.S. and Canada held some kind of event – including tours, rallies, polo tournaments, races, hillclimbs, field meets, rodeos, picnics, jamborees or anything else they could think of. Turnouts were tremendous, but sales continued to decline as potential buyers simply ran out of money.

In British Columbia, Fred Deeley handed the task of generating enthusiams over to his twenty-six-year-old son who came up with a New Year's Day run and a rally called the "300 Miler" hosted by the Lions Gate M/C club. The latter was modelled on events in the States such as the Jack Pine Tour in Michigan which had been running since 1924, and which was won in 1930 by Bill Davidson, son of William Davidson, the vice-president of the company. The 300 Miler (renamed the Caribou Trails Rally in 1948) was laid out over gravel roads up the Fraser Canyon to Yale or Boston Bar and back down to Vancouver. Riders started from Stanley Park and were given general directions as to where the course went and a schedule to maintain. Checkers at various stages would deduct points if they were late, which they often were because of the roughness of the terrain. The winners were generally young men with a lot of brawn and good luck.

Often they were Americans, because the Lower Mainland (Canada) and the Pacific Northwest (the States) were then much more of a connected area, because of their mutual isolation, than they are now. Riders from Vancouver were regularly joined by others from Bellingham in the 300 Miler, just as they regularly travelled south to compete in rallies, races and hillclimbs in the United States. There were so many events taking place that overlapping dates became a problem for organizers on both sides of the border.

There was also another racing issue that bedevilled Fred Jr. Nineteen thirty had seen a big influx of 500 cc overhead valve (OHV) machines from England in the United States and these were cleaning up in races with the side valve V-twins made by Harley-Davidson and Indian. As a result, the American Motorcycle Association, which was dominated by the big two, outlawed OHV machines from most events. Fred Jr. could see half the bikes he carried would be shut out of any AMA-sanctioned races. The solution to both the overlapping schedules and the new AMA regulation was discovered by his friend "Pop" Place. He found a clause in the AMA rulebook that said there were no restrictions on any class of machine providing it was run in a closed club event. Place suggested the formation of a "club of clubs" so that events on both sides of the border would all be under one club umbrella. Fred Jr. readily agreed and so the Pacific North West Motorcycle Association was formed in 1931 to both coordinate events and allow racing between English and American machines. This cross border sporting activity would later help the career of Fred Jr.'s son Trevor who, because of it, was given a larger canvas on which to paint his reputation.

The Vancouver riders, meanwhile, were also getting better organized. George Pinchin, a city policeman who rose to become a detective inspector, built a club house the same year on the rear of his parents' farm on Quesnel Drive and started The Big Four motorcycle club with three of his friends: Bill Ablitt, Jack Waterfield and Bill Hayes. The Lions Gate M/C decided to join forces with this group, changed both names to the Vancouver Motorcycle Club and started to meet at Quesnel Drive. Originally the colours of the Lions Gate club had been scarlet and black, later changed to maroon and green. When they joined forces with The Big Four, who used black and orange with four bands on the sleeve, these were adopted as the offical colours of the combined organization. Fred Jr. was now a leading member of the largest motorcycle club in the city. By coincidence, its colours were the same as those Harley-Davidson would eventually adopt.

In a way it was symbolic. The local Indian dealership run by Kenny and Jimmy McPhee had gone bust the previous year and so Fred Deeley Ltd. had the motorcycle market on the lower mainland pretty much to itself. Even so, sales were poor and customers scarce.

The economy was worsening in Canada, the United States and Britain when the Austin Motor Company dispatched its ace salesman, George H. Crane-Williams, on his forty-second trip around the world. His target market this time was Canada and his product was a remarkable little car, the Austin Seven. It was popularly called the "baby" Austin because, although it looked more or less like a Model A Ford, it was hardly larger than a baby carriage. Arriving with two dozen of these little vehicles, Crane-Williams set to work to establish distributorships across the country. It wasn't easy. Few people had any money to invest and many potential distributors laughed off the tiny little car as too small for Canadian drivers and too flimsy for Canadian roads. Even so, he succeeded in dropping off pairs of Austins all the way to Vancouver.

What happened next almost defies belief because of the degree of happenstance and coincidence.

Crane-Williams drew a blank canvassing his usual prospects until someone suggested he contact Fred Deeley, the largest local importer of British motorcycles. He arrived at 901 West Broadway and proceeded to talk Fred Sr. into taking the cars on consignment, apparently without knowing he had been a successful Austin dealer in England seventeen years earlier. Going back to his hotel and still uncertain about the wisdom of the move, Crane-Williams suddenly realized that he was dealing with the same Fred Deeley on whom he had placed bets as a bicycle racer at the turn of the century. He reassured himself with the thought that since he had backed Deeley before, he should do so again, this time the bet being two cars.

Fred Sr., meanwhile, was wondering what he had got into. "We took up the line, but not with a great deal of confidence," he recounted years later. "It was not a suitable product, largely because it was a right-hand drive and had a small amount of horsepower."

If the salesman was reluctant to drop off the cars and Fred Sr. was reluctant to have them cluttering up his shop, the cement that sealed the deal was Deeley's history as "The Cycle Man." Crane-Williams knew Fred Sr. was a successful competitor and reassured himself with that thought. Fred Sr., on the other hand, knew Austin made good cars because he had sold them from his bicycle store and knew some of the workers personally. Without this unlikely conjunction of past history and mutual regard, it's unlikely the Deeley empire would ever have become as large as it eventually did.

There it sat in the Deeley showroom, like a miniature of a real car, the baby Austin convertible, sale price $655. The coach, with an enclosed roof, was a hundred dollars more at $755. The big question as the Depression worsened was, would anyone be interested in it at any price?

As it turned out, some people did fancy an Austin Seven. Despite its size and right-hand steering, the little car started to sell to people who wanted basic transportation. It was cheaper than a Ford or a Chevrolet and it appealed to women a lot more than a windblown motorcycle combination. Trying to boost sales further, Fred Sr. wrote to Sir Herbert and asked that future models be converted to left-hand drive for the North American market. Austin agreed and a little over a year later, the 1933 models arrived with steering wheels on the correct side for the Canadian road.

Sales started to pick up, sometimes as many as one a day. Then in 1936 Austin came out with an improved model that had more horsepower. Austins continued to sell, even with a price tag of $995 or more. Volume was growing enough that Fred Sr. decided to move the car division next door to 901 West Broadway and the motorcycles again had the original building to themselves. Altogether, in the eight years from 1931 to the start of the Second World War in 1939, Fred Deeley Ltd. put about 2,000 Austins on the road in B.C. and Alberta, an average of 250 a year.

While the automobile sales increased, motorcycle sales remained slow, except for some good news provided by the Vancouver Police Department. The VPD was in the habit of buying Indians and their continued interest in the brand helped a new Indian dealership, Haskins & Elliott, start up in 1932. Four years later, however, the City of Vancouver became dissatisfied with their service and approached Deeley's, who had been trying for two decades to get them to buy Harley-Davidsons for the police force. Instead, they bought six V-twin B.S.A.s and proceeded to run them into the ground in a matter of six to eight months. Going back to Deeley's, no doubt very unhappy at the experience, they provided Fred Jr. with the exact argument he had always made to them — that they should buy the more robust Harley-Davidsons. They agreed, and the City of Vancouver still primarily buys Harley-Davidsons today.

With the increased importance of automobile sales, the responsibilities began to split three ways among Fred Sr. and his two sons. While Fred Sr. was spending most of his time in the car showroom, Fred Jr. was largely taking care of the motorcycle operation and Ray was working in the bicycle store down on Hornby Street. Fred Sr. was still very much in control of all the finances, but it was clear his heart and his interests were now primarily attached to the automotive division. This was probably because cars were beginning to eclipse motorcycles as profitmakers for the company and Fred Sr. wanted to be where the action was.

The division of effort was a lucky break for Fred Jr. and subsequently his son. It meant that, unusually for a family company controlled by a powerful figure, the motorcycle division had more autonomy than it would have had if the car division hadn't been there to keep Fred Sr. occupied. This change of focus would eventually open up some running room for Trev, the third Deeley to bear Fred's name. It would provide him with space to grow, think and mature that would never have been possible under the direct gaze of the old man in the automotive showroom on West Broadway. The split, however, also opened a schism between Fred Jr. and Ray that was never healed and, in fact, grew worse as the years went on. Fred Jr., the first born, was being given the lion's share of the extra responsibility and control and Ray was left with the crumbs.

As the economy continued to pick up amid worsening news from Europe, the Deeley shop windows were rattled by the sound of renewed competition in the motorcycle business. Bill Ablitt, one of the founders of The Big Four club, had started a motorcycle and car repair business out of a backyard garage. He was approached in 1939 by Ray Garner, the Indian factory representative for the West Coast, to reopen the Indian franchise in Vancouver that had been inactive for several years. Bill was excited at the prospect and jumped at the chance, riding with Garner in his big Packard down to Portland to pick up his first demonstrator. On the way back that evening he fell asleep on a long, straight stretch between Tacoma and Everett. Fortunately the section was an early example of a divided highway with a median and smooth ditches on either side. The new bike gradually slowed, ran down into the ditch, and up the other side into a grove of trees. Bill woke up some hours later on the ground with his bike propped up beside him against a tree without a scratch on it. It was a lucky break for Indian, but a new concern for Fred Jr. The Indian Four, based on a design the company got by purchasing the ACE factory in 1927, was smooth and powerful, and Harley didn't have anything like it on the market. To make matters worse, Ablitt was planning to open his new shop right down the street at 561-577 West Broadway in the same building Fred Sr. had been in himself.

Young Trevor, meanwhile, was no longer the innocent little bundle in Islay's arms that he had been in 1920.

CHAPTER THREE

THERE IS A delightful picture of Trev Deeley at the age of two on one of his father's motorcycles. It is a large, shiny Harley-Davidson with two-tone fenders, a V-twin motor and running boards, sitting on a rear-axle centre stand. Trev looks like a cherub, chubby with baby fat, his hair tousled and his legs so short they don't reach the barrels of the cylinders, much less the running boards or the ground. He is neither smiling nor crying, but has an air of calm self assurance.

That's probably too much character analysis to read into one snapshot, but what is clear is that there are no adults in the immediate vicinity to catch him if he should start to fall three feet to the ground.

In a larger context, that was the story of his childhood. Young Trevor was given the comfort and security the motorcycle business provided — eventually even given his own motorcycle — but he was often left physically and emotionally alone, propped up as he is in this picture on the family business, but not held onto by anyone in the family. In response to this lack of personal support, his little hands are firmly grasping the handlebars. It is as if, in the motorcycle, he has found something real to hold onto, something he can trust with his life.

Trev doesn't remember much about his childhood. His memory has selectively removed any references to feeling hurt or upset by the absence of his parents. Others, however, do remember. What they recall is a domineering father who was jealous of any competition for Islay's affections. Austere and aloof to his son, he would regularly take Islay away for a night or a weekend with his motorcycle buddies, leaving Trevor with Islay's best friend, Bea Saunders, or her brother Harvey Sedgwick.

Fred Jr. would ride his motorcycle over to the Sedgwick home, pick up Harvey, and bring the older boy back to look after Trev at his and Islay's apartment. It's not clear when exactly the practice began, but Harvey was certainly looking after his nephew by the time Trevor was four. Fred Jr. would have been twenty at the time, Islay, twenty-three. The baby-sitting continued later when the family moved to their first house on 19th Avenue, the only change being that Harvey would ride his bicycle and Fred Jr. would follow along behind on his motorcycle to make certain he arrived safely. Typically, Harvey would be picked up on a Saturday, stay overnight and return home on Sunday.

Trev's other main baby-sitter was Islay's girlfriend, Bea. She would come over, or Trevor would be dropped at her home, and Fred and Islay would take off for a summer weekend of camping or visiting the family cottage in Deep Cove.

There is only one quote from this period, but it speaks volumes on how the little tyke felt about these regular absences of his parents. Bea recalls, "I can remember Trevor's little face so many times saying to me, 'Auntie Bea, aren't my mummy and daddy ever going to come home?'" It was a good question. While most of his parents' absences were for one or two days, on one occasion they went off on vacation and didn't come home for three weeks. It was such a long period, Trev was transferred to Florence Nightingale school at 12th Avenue and Kingsway to be closer to his baby-sitter. Not surprisingly, given all this, he suffered throughout his childhood from asthma.

If Trevor often cried himself to sleep at night, he was a feisty little boy the rest of the time. Sometimes when Harvey was looking after him, Trev would insist on playing catch on the laneway behind the Sedgwick home on 15th until it grew dark and Harvey's palms were smarting from Trevor's hard pitches. Other times the two of them would play pickup games of touch football, sandlot baseball or practise punting and catching a pigskin. Rain wasn't a problem; if it started to pour and the other kids went home, Harvey and Trev just kept on practising.

Playing sports was easy to do because there was a city park a half block to the east and a second larger park a block south of the Deeley home. The area today is still well kept and middle class and the two parks look as inviting now as they did then. Both are well away from main roads and Trev's parents, whether at home or away, would have had no fear of letting him run freely through the neighbourhood. As a result, young Trev could be found most summer evenings and every weekend playing soccer, baseball or football with other youngsters from the area.

His first public school was Edith Cavell on Tupper St., two blocks east and two blocks south of his home. Its location meant he had to pass one or the other of the neighbourhood parks on his way to or from school. It was certainly no hardship for the young Deeley who, it was generally agreed, was getting pretty good at catching, kicking and throwing footballs, playing baseball and taking part in soccer.

He was also greatly attracted to the motorcycles he saw every day because of his father's business. Ironically, it was not a Harley-Davidson, but an Indian Scout on which he took his first ride. A family friend, Fred O'Neal, put seven-year-old Trev on his machine at Hastings Park and the young man successfully rode around the track by himself. Since he didn't know how to stop, bystanders had to grab the bike while it was still moving and disengage the clutch to bring it to a halt. It says a lot for Trevor's nerve as a child that he was prepared to set off on a motorcycle before he knew how to stop it. It also says something about fate that the experience took place on a racetrack, the same kind of track he would dominate twenty years later.

In time there was an apparent improvement in Fred Jr.'s treatment of his young son. In 1930, Fred Jr. and Islay piled Trev, Harvey and Harvey's sister Millie in the back of their Essex and set off down the Oregon coast to California. It was the first long trip for all three of the children, now aged ten, nineteen, and seventeen, and they had a wonderful time. When they weren't looking out the window at the magnificent scenery, Trev and Harvey would throw a football back and forth in the back seat past a resigned Millie, who would occasionally intercept the ball to stop play. The destination was the home of one of Islay's uncles who had grown wealthy in the sheet metal business. He indulged his young guests by showing them his factory and then taking them to football games at the local high schools. In retrospect, the inclusion of Trev's young relatives on the expedition was obvious. Because the three kids played together as a group, there was little need for the kind of personal contact that would have occurred if Trev had been in the back seat by himself.

At age eleven, with Trev revelling in his prowess at sports and getting along well in school, the family moved up in the world, both literally and figuratively. Fred Jr. and Islay exchanged their modest two-bedroom bungalow on 19th Avenue for a larger home well to the west on Quesnel Drive, two houses north of 25th Avenue. It was quite an accomplishment, given that the Depression was worsening and many people were losing their homes, rather than buying new ones. Combined with Fred Jr.'s new thirty-two-foot cabin cruiser, the *Sea Belle,* tied up at the Burrard Yacht Club, it was clear evidence Fred Deeley Ltd. was doing very well and Fred Jr. was taking home a larger portion of the company's profits in salary. The house had a commanding view to the north that extended from English Bay on the west, past Stanley Park and the downtown core, to Burrard Inlet on the east. At night the view was spectacular with the lights of the city glowing against the darkness of the mountains like diamonds on mahogany.

Trev didn't realize it at the time, but he had just joined the upper middle class. His home and surroundings were now clearly a cut above the average and the people he ran into began to be aware his father had money. What he did notice were the sports facilities at his new school, Lord Kitchener at 25th and Blenheim, and at the high school he would soon attend, Lord Byng at 3939 West 16th Street. One day after he moved in, he set off on his bicycle and rode it out to Sea Island, the site of Vancouver Airport, then just a field with a collection of huts. When he arrived, he discovered a friend of his father's, Gordie Bulger, working on a biplane with an open cockpit. Trev asked if he would take him up for a ride and Bulger agreed.

"Where do you live?" he shouted as they bucketed along.

"Twenty-fifth and Quesnel Drive," Trev replied.

A few minutes later the wings dipped and the plane dived over a residential section of the city. Trev looked down and there, just below, was his house. It was an experience of pure joy he put in the back of his mind to savour. Decades later he would draw on that memory to sustain himself at a time of personal anguish.

The next four years raced by, a blur of school, sports activities and a growing interest in motorcycling. If Trevor felt any angst about his home situation, he didn't brood over it but worked it off physically playing sports. He was a friendly youngster and a good team player. Older kids didn't mind him hanging around them because he acted more mature than his years; younger kids looked up to him because he spent time with them and treated them as equals. In a way, Trev was more like his grandfather than his father, as if Fred Sr.'s charm had leapt one Deeley generation and landed on him. Today we would call these attributes "people skills." At the time, Trev was just called a nice kid.

Christmas 1934 was a turning point in Trev's life. His present under the Christmas tree was a box with a card reading, "From Mom and Dad." It turned out to contain a set of keys to a black, single cylinder 250 cc Francis Barnett Cruiser motorcycle in the garage. Trev was ecstatic because the bike signalled his parents' recognition that he was maturing and could be trusted with more responsibility. Because it was partly from his father, it also created the possibility he could please him by showing a greater interest in motorcycling.

The way he did this, after riding to school to the envy of his friends, was to ask his father if he could quit at the end of the school year and start an apprenticeship in the motorcycle shop. Today the average parent would squelch that idea between forkfuls of potatoes. A university education is now considered by many to be the minimum needed to succeed in the world. In 1935, however, the *School Act* only required children to be educated to the age of fifteen. There was nothing unusual about a fifteen-year-old quitting school after grade ten, particularly if there was a family business he could go into. Fred Jr. said yes and so in the spring of 1935, a somewhat nervous, 5'6", 145 pound third generation Deeley presented himself at Fred Deeley Ltd. on West Broadway for his first day at work.

He needn't have worried. The employees, many of whom had worked at Deeley's for years, welcomed him with open arms. Some of this was a natural desire to get on the right side of the boss' son. But most of it was simply a response to Trev's pleasant personality and dedication to hard work.

For Trev, it was almost the first time any male adult had paid attention to him and he thrived on the companionship. Trev's choice of words remembering the period makes it plain how he felt: "I got a lot of help from the boys in the motorcycle shop at 901 West Broadway when I first started there," he says. "They took me in as if I was their own son."

His first job was to drive "the wrecker." This was a motorcycle with a big sidecar that was nothing but a flatbed with pipe rails around it. In the mid-'30s there were hundreds of combinations being used for delivery jobs in Vancouver and they, naturally, got into accidents, broke down or needed help of one kind or another. Trev would be dispatched with the wrecker to pick these bikes up. This was easier to say than to do because of Trev's relatively small size compared to the weight of the average combination. If the bike had a smashed front wheel, he would drag it up onto the wrecker bed and tie it down, leaving the sidecar wheel or the rear wheel on the ground. If the rear wheel had the problem, he had to haul it in backwards. It was a heck of a job but it was fun too and Trev enjoyed doing it, except when it was snowing or raining.

Some of the jobs weren't wrecks, but repossessions. In the midst of the Depression, Fred Deeley Ltd. was increasing its sales by offering credit terms to make it easy for potential customers to afford the motorcycles they wanted. Invariably, a few of these buyers couldn't keep up their payments, and Trev would be sent out to pick up their bikes. Of course the customers knew they were going to be repossessed so they tried to hide them. Trev would go into apartments and up and down stairs searching for the elusive machines and try to get the owners to sign them off.

"I think I was so small in those days, everybody was afraid to hit me," he says with a laugh. "But I usually came back with the goods."

The only problem was when the unpaid bike was on an Indian reservation. Band members would promptly kick him off tribal land, often with the motorcycle sitting right there in full view. The buyer hadn't paid, and Trev couldn't touch it. The solution was to wait off the reservation until the purchaser rode it out and then nail him.

In effect, Trev was unwittingly continuing his schooling by other means. If life can be said to be a series of lessons waiting to be learned, Trev had learned three business principles by the end of his first year on the job. Having witnessed the result of poor riding he had been taught to ride safely. He had been taught the importance of service to a business selling a product. And he had been taught that making certain a product is paid for is just as important as making the original sale.

The next stage of his education was learning how motorcycles are built from the inside out. Working under the direct tutelage of the best mechanics, Trev spent two years "on the bench," learning how to disassemble and reassemble transmissions and engines. To anyone who hasn't seen an exploded diagram of a typical motorcycle motor, this may seem a minor affair. In fact, hundreds of parts are involved, and a mistake at any stage in the process can easily ruin the whole thing. Many business lessons were thus learned, including a respect for methodology, exactness, and cleanliness, as well as an admiration for mechanics and an appreciation for their importance to the organization.

At about this time, Fred Sr. moved the Austin cars next door to another building and Harley-Davidson came out with a revolutionary new bike. This was the 61 cu. in. overhead valve "EL" model of 1936, the original "Knucklehead," so called because of the rounded shapes of the polished rocker boxes atop its cylinder heads. The EL boasted a number of improvements, including a double-loop truss frame, a welded teardrop gas tank, integrated teardrop instrument cluster, dry sump lubrication and a new hand-shift, four-speed transmission. Most important, the OHV engine produced almost double the horsepower of the side-valve 74.

Given their interest in this model, the mechanics could have narrowed Trev's perspective by indicating Harleys were always better built than other makes or that V-twins were the only proper type of motorcycle engines. Instead, because Fred Deeley Ltd. also sold British bikes, such as B.S.A. and Ariel, Trev got to know the strong points and weaknesses of a wide number of makes with all kinds of configurations. The experience left him remarkably open minded years later on the issue of motorcycle brands when most dealers and a lot of customers were convinced their brand was best.

The next step was the parts department. Fred Jr. had organized the shop so his parts people were also responsible for selling bikes on the floor. There were three counters. One long counter looked into the showroom, the second went down the side of the building where customers drove their bikes in to get worksheets made out, and a third, smaller counter at the back supplied parts to the mechanics in the shop. This set-up gave Trev a chance to try his hand at retail sales. All he had to do was to hop over the counter when a likely prospect walked in the door. Gradually, he started to sell a few bikes and then eventually to outsell the other men in the department. The difference wasn't that Trev was a better salesman, it was that he didn't pigeonhole himself in his own mind to one specialty.

"They thought they were partsmen; that was all they were going to do. I thought I was everything," he recalls. "I'd be out in the shop buggering around if there wasn't something else to do."

This hyper-kinetic energy also came out in his spare time as Trev began to play amateur baseball and football at a more senior level. He was especially good at football, making up in speed and dexterity what he lacked in weight. He was skilful at throwing and catching, but especially at punting, or kicking the ball on the run. Trevor's ability at this manoeuvre earned him a position on one of the major city teams of the day, the Meralomas, where he was a standout player.

At one point, Trev seriously considered a professional career in football and many of his friends, including Harvey Sedgwick, urged him to do so. However, he continued to feel a love for motorcycles and motorcycle sports. There was also a growing appreciation in the back of his mind that he had a good shot at inheriting at least half of the Deeley fortune if he stayed with the motorcycle business. The clincher appears to have been the role played in the background by his father. Starting in 1936, Fred Jr. helped his son, directly or indirectly, get the best motorcycles available. Everyone remarked on the quality of Trev's bikes, before during and after the War, some of them specially prepared models unavailable to the general public. Obviously Trev wanted the best he could get, but it's clear these were also Fred Jr.'s wishes, and that the resulting success Trev had on the track contributed to him sticking it out with Fred Deeley Ltd. Whether Fred Jr.'s motivation was to increase publicity for the company or ensure the line of succession, motorcycle racing appears to have been the only cusp on which his self-centred world and Trev's interacted.

To Trev, who both loved motorcycles and wanted to impress his father, joining his dad's motorcycle club was a natural, and he did so in 1937, the year before it changed its name and incorporated under the Society Act as the Greater Vancouver Motorcycle Club. This immediately got him interested in hillclimbing because, in addition to its club house on Quesnel Drive, the club had a site at Booth's Hill in Mallardville that it used for these events. Hillclimbing, in turn, led to short track racing which was taking over in popularity because it could be held at any fairground that had a harness racing track. When closed circuit events weren't scheduled, there were always illegal drag races between the area's Harley-Davidson and Indian riders. These would take place early on Sunday mornings on the main road towards Mission or another stretch near White Rock. The problem with the second location was that there was a church half-way along the drag strip and if the racers started later than usual, irate parishioners would call the police.

Among the other new members at the club was an old pal, Willie Telford. William Norman Telford, as a boy of twelve, used to hang around the Deeley motorcycle store on Friday nights until the meeting was over so he could get a ride home with one of the members who was dating his sister. Naturally he ran into Trev, who was then nine, and the two boys hit it off right away. He was by now a keen motorcyclist of twenty who usually rode Indians, so he and Trev were natural competitors, as well as good friends. Eleven years later they would both be at Daytona riding factory machines, although not in the same race.

For the two new club members, one of their first tasks was helping to build a new clubhouse. The Pinchin farm site had been sold and members gathered at Deeley's while they looked for another location for a building of their own. They eventually found an industrial lot they could buy for fifty dollars on Melbourne Street near the Kingsway. Members volunteered their time, scrounged lumber from building sites and took most of 1938 erecting the new clubhouse. When they finished they were inordinately proud of the building with its excellent hardwood floor, wall pennants and shiny club trophies. It was home but it was just twenty by twenty-eight feet.

Back on West Broadway, Trev was moved into the parts department at the Austin dealership to help keep up with the increasing business. He hated it. Selling car parts held no appeal and he continually agitated to be moved back next door to the motorcycle store. Eventually, even though cars were making more money than bikes and his help was certainly needed, Trev got his way and was transferred back to the area he loved. It was another crucial turning point in Trev's life. Had he stayed in cars he would have tied his wagon to a rising star in the boom years after the war and then seen it gradually decline. By sticking to what he liked, he isolated himself from that business cycle and positioned his career for an even bigger one in motorcycles.

Trev's long-term view, as opposed to the short-term thinking of his father, was becoming apparent in another way as well. Every winter, the mechanics in the motorcycle shop were sent down to the basement to root out old customer machines and wrecks that had been gathering dust for three years and cut them up for scrap. Fred Jr. had written them off and was selling them for fifty cents a pound. Trev was horrified at the waste. Classic machines, some made by companies no longer in business, were being torched for peanuts. Someday, he thought, these are going to be worth a lot of money, so they had to be preserved.

Fred Jr. was very much against saving them. If the company had a motorcycle it could sell, he wanted it sold right now. Trev could see there was no use talking to his father on the subject, so he began working behind his back. With the help of the mechanics and the company bookkeeper who let some of the bikes go for scrap prices, he began to squirrel some of the better machines away in a secret location. It would be many years before Trev had the nerve to show the treasure trove to his dad.

The secret bike collection was a milestone for another reason. It was the first occasion on which Trevor was faced by a stone wall in business and instead of quitting, went around it. The stealth was necessary because Trev was intimidated by his father; it was possible because he had the support of practically everyone else on the staff. There would be occasions in the future when Trev's ability to run covert business enterprises, much larger than his nascent motorcycle museum, would pay off handsomely.

CHAPTER FOUR

THE YEAR 1939 was a turning point for the world in Europe, for Canada as a member of the British Commonwealth and for Trev Deeley personally.

The nineteen-year-old by now had a large number of motorcycle friends in the GVMC. He got along well with everyone, was a go-getter, and accepted responsibility, so it was not surprising he soon wound up as the club secretary with Willie Telford as president. It was also not surprising that he now began his racing career, given his competitive nature in sports and that of the other club members on the track. The prime venue for this was Con Jones Speedway, located near the Pacific National Exhibition grounds.

It was here, mingling with the other riders before a race, that Trev ran into Lenny Wasilieff. He was a good competitor, but that wasn't what caught Trevor's eye, it was his younger sister Vera. She was a cute blonde with a soft voice and a bubbly personality who looked like a cheerleader. Trevor had never had a serious romantic relationship before and was swept off his feet. Not only was she a knockout, she came from a family of seven who all seemed to be interested in motorcycling. Her father Timothy, for example, had been a motorcycle dispatch rider in the First World War. Vera was with a B.S.A. rider, Jimmy McGowan, but she was impressed by the handsome young man with the Deeley name, and they soon began dating. Often these would be on club runs into the country which continued much as they had always done with barbecues and camping at the end of the road. It was on these excursions, and at dances at the new clubhouse, that Vera and Willie Telford's girlfriend Marie became friends.

Trev, meanwhile, was developing some friends of his own that would prove to be lifelong companions. One evening when he was racing at a harness track at White Rock, Trev noticed a young man talking to Vera in the stands. The fellow was obviously trying to make some points with his date, so every time he came around the track Trev glowered at the stranger to try and get him to go away. When this didn't work, Trev rode harder to get the race over with and wound up winning it. Finally able to get off his Harley, he stormed over to Vera and her companion.

"What are you trying to do, steal my girlfriend?" he asked.

"No," said the stranger.

Fred Pazaski, a seventeen-year-old from a Polish family in Bellingham, Washington, was lying – in fact he had been trying to score with Vera – but Trevor let it pass and listened while Fred explained that he had always wanted to meet him. The reason was that when Fred was five, his family had moved next door to the local Harley-Davidson dealer. This was "Pop" Place, who created the PNWMA with Fred Jr., and so Fred Pazaski had heard about the Deeley business and a young Deeley named Trev, just two years older than himself.

"It's a pleasure to finally meet you," he said, holding out his hand.

Whether Fred's fast talking worked, or his obvious interest in motorcycling got through, Trevor and Fred soon became very good friends.

One reason was that they kept running into each other at the local racetracks. Fred's brother John, who had a tremendous sense of balance and was a really good racer, turned out to be Trev's toughest competitor. John had a hot 1931 Harley DLD that had been specially built by Place at Northwest Cycle Company, and Trev just didn't have the horsepower to catch him. Trev told his father that John Pazaski was beating him on a hot bike, and the news got the competitive juices flowing in Fred Jr. As soon as he could, he presented Trev with a carefully prepared 1937 WLD, a predecessor to the later Harley-Davidson WR factory racing machines. Among other things, it had aluminum heads and racing cams.

"It was fixed up with gearing and everything," Pazaski recalls.

"On the racetrack at Con Jones nobody could beat him. He was just phenomenal. I mean he was just a crowd pleaser."

This was literally the truth. In three years at Con Jones, except for his first two events, Trev never lost a race, no matter if it was a heat race, a time trial, a pursuit race or a Class A main event.

Another fan of Trev's at the time was Bobby Dawe, a fifteen-year-old who used to pedal his bicycle down to Con Jones to watch the races, and especially to watch Trev and his WLD whip round the track. He would sit there entranced at the spectacle of Trev beating one big-name competitor after another, little realizing fate would soon bring them together, first as friends, and later in business. One spectator who didn't stay was Trevor's mother. One night, Fred Jr. brought Islay down to see their son, who by then was developing quite a name for himself. Halfway through the event she got up and left. She just couldn't stand watching, it looked so dangerous.

It was clear the big guns would soon be barking and woofing in the hayfields of Europe. Great Britain, in an effort to rally patriotic opinion in its oldest Dominion, dispatched King George VI and Queen Elizabeth to Canada for a coast-to-coast tour. The Vancouver police, who normally used motorcycles for crowd control during parades, realized right away they had nowhere near the manpower needed for an event of this magnitude. They looked around for help and decided to ask the Greater Vancouver Motorcycle Club.

The members of the GVMC were touched. Usually sneered at as a scruffy bunch of joy riders, they were now being asked by the authorities to help control the thousands who would jostle to catch a glimpse of the King and Queen. They were delighted to help out. There was just one catch. In order to be part of the security service they would have to take the Oath of Allegiance and to do that they would have to join the militia, or army reserve. That was still no problem, so most, including Trevor, did. On Monday, May 29, and Wednesday, May 31, the GVMC members, their machines polished to perfection, each wearing a red armband, helped control traffic as their Highnesses sped through the city to open the Pattulo Bridge and inaugurate the King George Highway.

They had been told signing up was purely a formality and that if war broke out they would not have to go overseas, but when the Declaration came the following September most went anyway. Willie Telford, for example, formed a team of dispatch riders and later joined the armoured corps where he became an instructor.

Trevor was in a more complex situation. Because he was working in the parts department of Fred Deeley Ltd., a motorcycle distributor, he was in a reserve industry and thus initially exempt from being called to active service. What he got, instead, was a deferment. This meant that while many of his friends were forming up and marching off, he was still working at 901 West Broadway, racing at Con Jones Speedway and dating Vera. There was nothing he could do about it, so he made the most of the situation, racing wherever he could, particularly against the Americans who still weren't at war. Sometimes the races were at White Rock, the Chilliwack Fair or the Western Washington State Fair at Lynden. Wherever he went, accompanied by Vera in a sidecar with the race bike trailed behind, he did very well.

Club events also continued. One Sunday he and Vera were late getting to the clubhouse and when they rolled up they found everyone had left except a young man vainly trying to start his 250 cc B.S.A.

"Where are all the guys?" Trev asked.

"I don't know," answered the youth, who turned out to be Bobby Dawe.

"And they left you here?"

"They sure did,"

It was obvious Trev wasn't impressed with the other members leaving the newcomer to fend for himself, so he helped Bobby get his machine started and accompanied him on the ride. It was just as well he did, because the little B.S.A. burnt out its clutch and he and Vera had to tow Bobby home. When the same thing happened again on another run, Trev helped Bobby get a 500 cc B.S.A. so he could reliably keep up with the rest of the club members. Trev's generosity and attention was deeply appreciated by Dawe who began to look at Trev almost as a brother.

Finally, in 1941, the army called him up and Trevor found himself in the Royal Canadian Ordnance Corps in Calgary. Amazingly, the military had put a round peg in a round hole because his specific job was to look after motorcycle parts, the same thing he'd been doing at Fred Deeley Ltd. Not only was it the first time Trev had been away from home, it was also his first separation from Vera, and it made him realize he didn't want to lose the little beauty he'd fallen in love with. The only thing to do was to get married and so he wrote to Vera and proposed and she wrote back and accepted.

When he told his parents, they were very unhappy. Islay, in

particular, was furious Trev hadn't consulted her beforehand and she accused him of marrying beneath his station in life. Fred Jr.'s reasons were more general; he thought his son was too young to get married, even though Trev was four years older than he had been when he marched up the aisle with Islay. Despite the negative reaction, Trev was adamant and his parents finally consented to help in getting the nuptials arranged.

A marriage licence was obtained and Trev applied for and got a week's leave to go home and get married. When he got back to Vancouver he got his motorcycle out of storage and went to see Vera, leaving the wedding arrangements up to his mother. This proved to be a mistake. Not only did Islay not organize a church ceremony – the dream of every new bride, then and now – she excluded potential attendees by holding the service in her living room at 2897 Point Grey Road. Trev and Vera only discovered the final indignity two hours before their wedding: Islay had deliberately not invited Vera's family.

The young couple were beside themselves. If they cancelled the wedding Trev would have to return to Calgary alone. If they went ahead with it, Vera's parents, brothers and sisters would be devastated.

Swallowing hard, hoping they could make it up to everyone later, they went through with the ceremony, packed their bags and boarded the CPR for the overnight trip back to Calgary. There, lying in the lower berth, with the moonlight shining on the Rockies far above them, they held onto each other and tried to put the insult to Vera's family out of their minds. They had each other, they had their freedom and they had a wedding certificate. Islay couldn't take that away from them now.

Over fifty years later, the surviving members of the Wasilieff family still remember the insult. "Maybe we were a lower class," Nick Wasilieff says. "I really don't know why we weren't invited."

As a married man, Trevor was eligible for a subsistence allowance and could live off the base at 7th Street and 10th Avenue Southwest. He chose an apartment as far away as possible in the city's north end. It was an idyllic time. Trev's responsibilities were hardly onerous, and the couple had a chance to get to know each other on a daily basis for the first time. They even were able to do some motorcycling, riding a borrowed machine on Trev's days off in the surrounding countryside. One weekend he decided to take things a step further, entering a hillclimb sponsored by the Calgary Motorcycle Club and the Ace High Motorcycle

Club in a gravel pit west of the city. Things, however, didn't go as smoothly as they had back in Vancouver. An armourer upstairs at the same Depot, Walt Healy, was the local Indian dealer and quite a hot shot at hillclimbing. Much to Trev's surprise, Healy won the event on his Indian with a faster time. It was a unique occasion. In all their subsequent encounters in flat track racing, Trev showed Healy the way to the finish line.

As is usually the way in the army, once you're nicely settled down, it's time to move on. Trev was transferred to London, Ontario, and the newlyweds decided to separate while he found an apartment in the forest city. Vera went back to live with her family and Trev went on to his new posting. It turned out to be a long separation, five or six months, before she travelled across Canada and joined him at an apartment near the base. It also wasn't a very happy time because Trev found the job boring and repetitive and was starting to experience renewed bouts of his childhood asthma.

Finally his breathing difficulties became so bad, they began to interfere with the performance of his duties. He was sent to the medical officer, diagnosed and told he was being given a medical discharge. It was 1943. In Europe the war would take another year to head towards climax, but for Trev, the war was nearly over.

Trev and Vera returned to B.C. with virtually no money. They hadn't saved any before they were married and they had just been able to get by in the army. Going back to his old job at Fred Deeley Ltd. meant Trev would earn less than he'd been getting in army pay with a subsistence allowance. His father was now a wealthy man, but Fred Jr., whether out of animosity or indifference, offered Trev just twelve dollars a week, about half what was paid the other employees. Trevor appealed to his grandfather to let him and Vera live out at his cottage at Deep Cove because he had nowhere else to go. Fred Sr., who'd always had a soft spot for Trevor, agreed and the couple moved out to the cabin in the woods.

The saving grace in all this, for commuting, work and pleasure, was Trev's Harley 45. Although Deep Cove seemed as if it was in another world, it was only twelve miles from the city across the Second Narrows Bridge on the west side of Indian Arm off Burrard Inlet. This meant that if he wound open the throttle, he could leave work at noon, get home in twenty minutes, have a quick lunch, and return by one o'clock. There were two roads to the cottage on the north shore; one along the water, and a second farther up the mountain called the high road which was unpaved. One day Fred Pazaski was visiting the shop and Trev asked if he'd like to join him and Vera for lunch. Fred agreed, much to his regret, because Trev rolled out an OHV Harley 61 and proceeded to gun it all the way home, power sliding around the gravel corners on the high road just as if they were part of a flat track racecourse.

On other occasions, Trev was so broke he didn't even have a nickel for the toll on the Second Narrows Bridge. To get home, he would ride around the barrier, curve over some railway tracks and scoot by without paying. There was no other way.

The motorcycle helped Trev and Vera socialize because they used it to attend the regular GVMC meetings and go on runs. Shortly after getting demobilized, Trev drove down to the Tudor Inn on the Pacific Highway Truck Route in Blaine, Washington, for a meeting of the PNWMA. He walked in the door, still wearing his big army greatcoat, and was greeted with a round of laughter from the forty or fifty motorcyclists from both sides of the border gathered inside. Still just five-and-a-half-feet tall, he looked ridiculous in the outfit, like a child dressed up in his father's clothes.

"You can laugh," Trev remarked smiling, "but you'll be in my shoes some day."

The third benefit from the bike was a second income. By 1944, Trev and Vera had managed to rent a duplex on 7th Avenue, just east of Main Street in Vancouver. The cottage at Deep Cove, while a godsend initially, had proven to be bone chillingly cold, even when heated with the driftwood Trev found on the beach. The duplex was usually warm and cosy and even had a garage out back in which Trev could work on his racing motorcycle. The only problem was paying the rent and buying food for the table.

At 2:00 PM, May 24, 1944, Bobby Dawe was discharged at the Little Mountain army camp following a serious bout of scarlet fever. He was given a new uniform, new shoes and $125 mustering out pay. Since he only lived three blocks from Trev and Vera's duplex, he dropped in on them on the way home. They were both sick in bed. The doctor had called and left two prescriptions, but neither of them had the seven dollars needed to get the prescriptions filled. Bobby took the scripts to the drug store, got them filled and took the pills back to the invalids. He then lit a fire in the kitchen stove to get the house warm and went on his way.

To make ends meet, Trev got two evening jobs, one with the

Canadian National Telegraphs, the other with Reed Prescription Pharmacy. His job at CN started at 6:00 PM and involved delivering telegrams. The war was in high gear and there were a lot of messages from every part of the country. Trev would get a stack four or five inches high and would go out and deliver them until around nine o'clock. Then he'd ride down to Reed's Pharmacy in the Birks building, pick up the prescriptions that had to be delivered and get them out by midnight.

Winter weather on the west coast is often just above the freezing mark, with weeks of rain and rolling fog interspersed occasionally with snow. Bobby Dawe liked Trev's company and would frequently accompany him in the sidecar to tell him what address to go to next. Trev would pull up to the house, Bobby would hand him the telegram and Trev would run up to the door, deliver it and get the signature of the recipient. That kept Trev warm, but it was so cold for Bobby sitting in the sidecar, the pair started to carry a hot water bottle to place on his knees. About the time they got to the Shaughnessy area after leaving downtown, the water bottle had cooled down, so Trev would stop and knock on a door and ask the lady of the house if she would fill the hot water bottle for him. He was never refused. Thanking his unknown benefactor, he would run back to his bike, give the water bottle to Bobby in the sidecar and finish his deliveries.

Most of the telegrams were routine, but some contained tragic news of someone wounded, missing or killed overseas. These came in a different envelope and Trev would have to stay at the door while the people read it in case they fainted or needed medical assistance. There weren't many of this kind, but Trev never forgot the ones that there were. The rate of pay for delivering telegrams was forty-two cents each and Trev would get thirty or forty telegrams to deliver every night. It was more than a week's pay at his dad's shop and Trev really enjoyed doing it. He was helped by the girl in the telegraph office who would sort them all out in the right order, so when he delivered one he could go right on to the next without doubling back.

"That was a good time," says Trevor remembering. "When we got home we'd always have something to eat. Vera was a great cook and she was always baking cakes and pies. I don't know why I didn't weigh 400 pounds, but I guess I mostly ran it off in those days."

Bobby's interest in motorcycling and his enjoyment of Trev's company were such that he began playing hooky from his job at an optical factory just to hang out at the Deeley motorcycle shop.

Finally Trev asked him since he was spending so much time there, why didn't he come and work for them? Bobby jumped at the chance and joined Fred Deeley Ltd., rising through the organization until he became general manager of retail sales years later.

Now that they were back in Vancouver, Trev and Vera began working on repairing the bridges between them and Vera's family, visiting her brothers, and especially her parents. They were all pleased Vera was back in the area and, while perplexed about the wedding snub, held no grudges against Trevor personally. It was natural, therefore, that Trev and Vera travelled out to the Wasilieff homestead on Father's Day, 1944, to pay their respects. By now, Trev had his hands on a hot Harley 61 that had been bored out to 68 cubic inches and tuned for racing on the track. When he and Vera showed up at the Wasilieff's on this gleaming sports bike, her father Timothy decided he wanted to try it out for himself. The sons tried to stop him. They knew their father hadn't ridden in years and, since it was a fast bike, they weren't sure he could handle it.

Timothy would have none of it. Stubborn as a mule, he insisted he wanted to ride Trevor's bike himself.

Reluctantly the family agreed, but Nicholas was so concerned he said he'd follow along behind in his car. Timothy got on the bike, wheeled it out onto the road and headed for the nearby King George Highway. After a few miles speeding along, he turned around and headed back along the Serpentine Flats. He was two miles from home when suddenly a truck pulled out of Clearbrook Road right in front of him. Timothy wrenched the handlebars to one side and stood on the brakes, but the big Harley hit the corner of the truck and he went down. Nick, right behind, saw the whole thing. He was on the scene in seconds, bundled his father into his car and sped off to the nearest hospital. Timothy, gravely injured, died before they got there.

When Timothy and Nick didn't return, Trev and Vera jumped in a car and retraced the route, finding the accident scene almost immediately. Surprisingly, the motorcycle was scarcely damaged and Trevor was able to ride it home.

The tragedy struck him like a hammer blow. The bike he was so proud of had killed his father-in-law right in front of one of Vera's brothers. Through the shock, embarrassment and grief he vowed to never let anything like that happen again. No more would he allow a member of his family to ride a motorcycle. They were too dangerous. The Wasilieff family, on the other

Endless miles of Idaho stretch ahead; the view from Vera's seat in the Oldsmobile.

Broken down in the middle of nowhere. Note the gouge in the road.

Trev and Vera wait for a half shaft in the park at Rupert, Idaho.

The Oldsmobile after Vera hit the snowdrift in New Mexico.

Reg Shanks (left) and Trev Deeley with two Oregon riders at Daytona Beach, Ray Hyland and Red Rice.

Daytona Beach racetrack from the air in 1947. The kink in the road was removed for the 1948 race.

Racing north on the beach side.

Racing south on the road.

Trev goes down on the south turn.

Trev, aged two, on his father's 1920 Harley-Davidson.

Fred Deeley Jr. and Islay in their kitchen about to go out to a formal party.

Trev poses with his racing trophies
outside his parent's house on
Quesnel Drive in 1939.

Vera appears to be part of the family in 1940.   Trev just after the war.

Trev competing in a field meet at 54th Street in 1940.

Well in front of the pack at Con Jones Speedway, 1940.

Trev racing an Ariel Red Hunter, 1938.

GVMC members in their clubhouse in 1938. Trev and Vera are second from left. Club members are a well-scrubbed group of young people compared to what riders looked like fifteen years later.

Trev racing his father's temperamental H-D hillclimber on Enderby Hill before the war.

Vera's brother Lenny hands off to Trev in a motorcycle relay race at 54th Street.

A publicity shot after a winning season in 1948.

Trev poses before a race.

Vera watching Trev race.

Trev crouches low to overtake the rider in first place.

Trev hugs Vera before a race, the most emotional picture from this era.

Trev and Vera at a typical dirt track with Trev's bike on a trailer.

Fred Deeley staff outside the store at 915 West Broadway in 1948. From left are Lloyd Perry, Phil Walker, Bobby Dawe, Vic Smith, Bob Grant, Bob Rutledge, Trev, Fred Jr., Bill Goldfinch and two others. Behind them in the window is a new Harley Knucklehead (photo courtesy of Don Doody).

Trev on a 1948 WR Harley 45 with a special Max Bubeck engine (photo courtesy of Don Doody).

The consummate dirt track racer.

The usual view other racers had of Trev.

Triumph and tragedy: Trev wins the Alcan Cup in Edmonton in 1948 while his son dies. Bobby Dawe on the left, Fred Boyd behind, Vic Smith at right.

A party at Trev and Vera's house on East 4th. Most of those in the picture are GVMC members or Deeley employees. Interestingly, Fred Jr. and Islay are also present.

Trev in the army in London, Ontario with an unidentified friend.

Trev and Vera in Kamloops on their trip through the Interior.

The Princeton-Hope trail with Trev's H-D on its side.

A log bridge on the trail.

Vera and the H-D beside one of the many steep canyons.

The final hurdle, a locked gate.

hand, was remarkably composed considering what had happened. Once they were over the pain and the tears, they held no animosity towards Trev or even towards motorcycling in general. The head of the household had rejected their advice and had died doing what he enjoyed. It was God's will.

Little did they know fate would have another tragedy in store just thirteen years down the road.

CHAPTER FIVE

THE END OF the war in Europe and the Pacific released a pent-up wave of consumer demand unlike any seen before in Canadian history.

Returning servicemen wanted homes, cars, clothes, consumer goods, university educations, vacations, families – and, yes, motorcycles. Rationing and enforced savings had built up a huge backlog of purchasing power and just about everyone wanted to start spending. The only problem was that European and Japanese industries were devastated and Britain, Canada, the Soviet Union and the United States had totally converted to a wartime economy.

While they were converting back to peacetime, the only goods that were readily available were war surplus items from Crown Assets Disposal Corporation. Amazingly for someone as astute as Fred Sr., Bill Ablitt beat him to the punch in putting in a request to purchase some of the thousands of British- and American-made motorcycles that were now surplus. The Crown Assets people contacted Ablitt and he ordered two rail carloads of Royal Enfields and Harley 45s sight unseen. It didn't take long for that news to filter back up West Broadway to the Deeley shop at 901. Fred Sr. picked up the phone.

"Bill," he asked. "Would you mind bringing in a third carload for us? We'd get a better price on freight if we brought them in under your shipment."

"Okay, that's fine with me," Ablitt replied.

The shipment showed up and Deeley's, as good as their word, paid for the third carload of army bikes. They did not, however, pay for the freight charges that went with it, which were in Ablitt's name. Fifty years later he still shakes his head at how he was outmanoeuvred.

Perhaps he shouldn't have been so surprised. The level of competition between Ablitt's Indian dealership and Deeley's Harley shop was close to becoming a blood feud. Both sides were continually thinking up policies, marketing schemes and dirty tricks designed to boost their profits and reputation at the expense of the other's.

On one occasion Fred Jr. decided to sponsor a novice hillclimb in Kamloops and put up a large silver cup as a prize. Ablitt tuned one of his Indians and rode it up to Kamloops to take part. In his one and only run, the bike went up the hill like a rocket and he won the event. After returning to Vancouver with it on the back of his bike, Ablitt placed the cup in his window for all to see – a Harley cup won by an Indian.

Another incident involved Ablitt's decision to stay open longer hours than Deeley's. Fred Sr., who always closed his shop on Saturday afternoon, told Ablitt he should do the same or he'd call the Labour Board and have him ordered closed. Ablitt's response to that was, "To hell with you, I'm going to stay open." The inspectors from the Board showed up, but took no action, presumably because he was doing nothing illegal. While this was going on, Fred Sr. was trying to re-establish his distributorship with Triumph, which had been interrupted by the war. Letters were exchanged and the matter seemed a foregone conclusion when the Triumph agent arrived in Vancouver to inspect the shop at 901 West Broadway and get Fred Sr. to sign a new contract. By mischance, he happened to arrive on a Saturday afternoon and the doors at Deeley's were closed. Not having time in his schedule to stay over the weekend, he proceeded to walk four blocks east to Ablitt's Indian dealership and asked him if he would carry Triumphs. Ablitt didn't really like English motorcycles – he liked Indian and that was it – but the chance to twit his larger rivals was too good to pass up. The following Monday he announced he was the new Triumph dealer in town, much to the annoyance of Fred Sr., Fred Jr. and Trevor, and the amazement of everyone else.

The mood up at 901 was vitriolic. Ablitt had lost an eye years previously in an accident and was referred to by Fred Sr. and Jr. as "that one-eyed son of a bitch" whenever his name came up. Bobby Dawe, newly hired, knew Deeley employees were forbidden to go into Ablitt's store, unless on official business, but had never taken the injunction seriously. He went into the Indian shop and expressed interest in an Eaglet leather helmet priced at $4.95 which was a bit more than he could afford. Ablitt marked it down to $3.50 and the sale was made. A short while later Dawe walked into Deeley's wearing the new cap.

"Where'd you get the helmet?" Trev asked.

"Down at Bill Ablitt's," replied Bobby.

"I told you never to go in there again," Trev exploded. "If you like that guy so much, go down there and work for him."

One of the reasons for Trevor's sensitivity was that this was exactly what had happened with three of Deeley's mechanics. Ablitt had offered them more money and they had quit en masse and gone to work for him. They didn't last longer than six months, but Ablitt had made his point and caused Deeley's some headaches.

Another incident involved a show bike. Harley-Davidson resumed peacetime production in 1946 with the 1947 models. These were basically updated 1941 machines, but they featured significant improvements, such as a new taillight, redesigned instrument panel, hydraulic shock absorbers and more chrome and accessories. Deeley's put one of these beauties in the window where it was a star attraction. Ablitt, down the street, brooded about what to do. Finally, he got some money together and gave it to a young man with instructions to go up to Deeley's and buy the bike in the window. At first Fred Jr. didn't want to sell, but the eager customer had cash, and the temptation was too great to resist. The "customer" wheeled the new machine out onto West Broadway and right down to Ablitt's, who put it in his window with a "for sale" sign. Walk-in visitors were then told it had been traded in on an Indian because the purchaser was disappointed with its performance.

These escapades were little more than marketing gimmicks. Beneath the surface, a far more serious competition was underway, one that posed a direct threat to Deeley's Harley-Davidson business.

The challenge began when Ablitt snared the first batch of war surplus bikes. This not only gave him stock when Deeley's was short, it gave him Harley-Davidson motorcycles he would never otherwise have been able to obtain as a dealer for Indian. For a time, Ablitt's actually had more Harleys for sale than Deeley's, an intolerable situation to Fred Jr. and Trevor alike.

A second element involved staffing. When Bill Ablitt had gone out to the War Surplus office in Richmond, he had noticed one of the attractive young women working in the motorcycle area and had offered her a job. Vera Kachaba was happy to leave the large Crown corporation, which was obviously going to shrink in size, for a position on civvy street, particularly because at Ablitt's company, Motor Cycle Sales Ltd., she'd be involved with the same products she was familiar with. He immediately put Vera to work answering the scores of responses generated by his advertisements of war surplus Harley-Davidson 45s.

Among those who became aware of the sell-off was the H-D district manager for the Pacific Northwest who showed up at Ablitt's to see what was going on. While the sales were interesting, he found himself more attracted to Vera than the war surplus business and made a point of dropping by the Indian shop every time he was in Vancouver. These visits eventually put the thought in his mind that there was room for two H-D dealerships on the lower mainland and he recommended to Milwaukee that Ablitt be allowed to open a dealership in New Westminster. When Fred Jr. was informed of this move, he threw the Harley representative bodily out of his office and dispatched Trevor to Milwaukee to straighten things out. Trev flew to Wisconsin — his first commercial flight — and had a meeting with Bill Davidson and the Harleys to discuss the issue. He told them that one way or another there was only going to be one Harley-Davidson dealer on the lower mainland; either Fred Deeley Ltd. or Ablitt's, because if they appointed Ablitt, Deeley's was quitting. The threat, plus the long years of service, won the Harley-Davidson owners over, and they cancelled the idea of a second dealership in the Vancouver area. As a sop to Ablitt, they gave him instead an outlet in Prince Rupert, hundreds of miles away on the remote northwest British Columbia coast.

The key factor in Ablitt wanting a H-D outlet was that he had trouble getting parts for his war surplus bikes. If Ablitt had a Harley-Davidson in his service department, Deeley's refused to wholesale him the H-D parts he needed for the repairs. Trev would sell them at the full retail price, so that he, and not Ablitt, would pocket the profit. Ablitt, blocked by this policy, began ordering parts from H-D dealers in Bellingham, Portland and Seattle. Fred Jr.'s response was to form the Northwest Harley-Davidson Dealers Association comprising all the H-D dealers in B.C., Washington and Idaho. Members agreed not to sell bikes or advertise in each other's territory and not to sell wholesale parts to Indian dealers.

"Fred (Jr.) was very, very competitive as far as I was concerned," Ablitt recalls. "His idea was that all Harleys should be repaired at a Harley dealership, and no Indian dealer should have anything to do with them. He wanted to keep the business to himself."

This desire to hold onto the parts, repair and aftermarket business was hardly exclusive to Fred Deeley Ltd. Walter Davidson had stressed the importance of accessory sales as early as a dealer meeting in November 1920, and throughout the '30s Harley-Davidson was well ahead of the competition in promoting aftermarket sales of H-D approved products. What made the Deeley attitude stand out, was that they took every lost sale extremely seriously, almost as a personal affront, and instituted measures wherever possible to make sure it didn't happen again. Whether it was a leather helmet or a gearbox, they wanted the business to stay at 901 West Broadway, nowhere else.

The thrust towards monopolization has been a successful one for many large businesses. Standard Oil, General Motors, and U.S. Steel were all built up through the creation of trusts or the acquisition of competitors that had the effect of monopolizing their respective industries. In a smaller way, this is what Fred Deeley Sr. had always believed in. Operating a bicycle, motorcycle and car business at the same time, he had integrated sales vertically by price; and by offering different motorcycle brands, he integrated them horizontally by make. The key goal he was aiming for was to reduce the amount of choice between himself and other dealers and to increase it internally between products and brands. In the same way that General Motors utilized different car divisions to compete with Ford at every price point, Fred Deeley Sr. sought different makes to battle single-brand competitors.

The multi-product, multi-brand approach to doing business had a number of advantages, the most important being the maintenance of a source of supply. Fred Sr. never forgot the fact B.S.A. supplies dried up in the middle of the First World War and had to be replaced with machines from Harley-Davidson. Never, he told his son Fred Jr., get yourself into a position where you only have one source, or country, of supply. Fred Jr., by osmosis apparently, passed the same message onto his son Trevor. Staying in business was a lot more important than brand loyalties. Let the customers drool over this or that make of machine, let them buy pins, pennants and leather jackets with company insignia, let them be as loyal as they wanted to a particular motorcycle brand; the golden rule in the back office at Fred Deeley Ltd. was cover the market with whatever sells.

The second advantage was that multiple brands created the marketing image of one-stop shopping comparable to warehouse outlets or auto malls today. Motorcyclists knew if they went to Deeley's they could browse a number of makes and numerous models all at one location. The simple fact that more people walked in the door, meant that more bikes were sold out the door. Combined with the Austin distributorship next door and a new used-car lot beside that, and you had the beginnings of a critical mass in transportation sales.

The validity of this philosophy was soon apparent in Deeley's long-running competition with the Ablitt shop down the street. Two years after he obtained the Triumph dealership, Ablitt lost it, mostly because he was more committed to selling Indians than selling motorcycles, and Deeley's, just as quickly, picked it up. Now if prospective purchasers wanted to settle a dispute between which was faster, B.S.A. or Triumph, there was no need to visit two motorcycle shops to do so.

There was one danger in Deeley's handling both English bikes and Harleys — it irritated Harley-Davidson and almost cost Fred Sr. his franchise. Throughout the '20s and '30s, Harley regularly asked Fred Sr. to drop his English lines and concentrate on their products. He regularly refused, annoying Milwaukee, but not angering them enough to do anything about it.

The Deeley balancing act between English bikes and Harley-Davidsons now came under a new strain, competition dressed up as Canadian nationalism.

The problem actually had its origins in England in the '20s when dirt track motorcycle racing there split into two streams, speedway racing which continued on small dirt ovals and road racing which took place on public roads or paved racetracks. In North America, where there was ample space for large dirt tracks, and little money for paving them, this division didn't occur until much later. The result was that by the late 1930s, British factories were developing lightweight, high performance machines with big brakes and better handling frames while in the United States, Harley and Indian continued to concentrate on heavier V-twins that worked well in the dirt. Within this context, there was a second issue relating to tooling costs, reliability and performance.

Horsepower, essentially, involves getting as much air/fuel

mixture in and exhaust gas out of an engine as quickly as possible. In the conventional four-stroke piston engine, a camshaft opens the intake valves, the air/fuel mixture enters on a downstroke, the cam allows the valve springs to close the intake valves, the piston compresses the mixture on the upstroke, the spark ignites the compressed mixture sending the piston down again, the camshaft opens the exhaust valves and the piston forces the spent gasses out the exhaust ports. For maximum efficiency, the route the air/fuel mixture travels should be as direct as possible and the gas should be as dense as possible.

The problem engineers faced in the traditional flathead, or "side valve" design, was that the intake was at the top of the motor and the valves actuated by the camshaft and driven off the crankshaft, were at the bottom. Not only did the air/fuel mixture have a long way to go, it got warm on the way there, reducing the volume that actually arrived. The first step they took, therefore, was to move the valves to the top of the engine, the so-called overhead valve or OHV design. This was much more efficient, but it introduced a new level of complexity because the valves were now separated by about five inches from the camshaft and so had to be driven remotely by pushrods. The pushrods would expand and contract quite a bit as the engine warmed up and cooled down, so much so that if enough slack wasn't left between a cold pushrod and its rocker, the pushrod would expand too far when it was hot and the piston in a high compression engine could actually come up and smack the head of the valve still protruding into the combustion chamber. The result, if this happened, was total engine failure. The whole process was also counter intuitive for the user because it meant that an engine with a lot of valve noise at idle was probably about right, while a quiet engine, with very little valve clearance, was in danger of self destructing.

To overcome this problem, and reduce the amount of inertia caused by so many bits of metal moving up and down, the designers decided to put the camshaft on top of the engine too, along with the valves. This concept, not surprisingly, was called an overhead cam (OHC) engine. To transmit the necessary rotary motion to the camshaft, they used a bevelled gear shaft or a train of idler gears running up the side of the cylinder. The cam could now work directly on the valves, or through short, stiff rockers; the pushrod expansion problem was eliminated and the amount of valve train inertia was significantly reduced. On the test stand

and on the track, the result was even more power than an OHV design.

Unfortunately, the trade-off for this greater power was a much higher cost for the motorcycle manufacturer.

For both Harley-Davidson and Indian there was also a marketing problem. Throughout the '30s both factories had kept themselves afloat by selling to police forces and to businesses who used their machines as delivery vehicles. Civic administrators and company purchasing agents alike were adamant they wanted reliable machines at the lowest possible price. Since OHV machines could be unreliable if they weren't properly maintained and since OHC machines would be more expensive than the market could bear, both companies took the only other low-cost route to additional horsepower; greater size. By 1940, Harley's largest motor had grown from sixty-one cubic inches to a gigantic eighty. Of course a larger motor meant the bike itself was both larger and heavier and its tires, once not much bigger than those for a bicycle, were now the same size as those on a car.

It was just as well the English motor engineers went down the track they did, because when the war came they had already designed the magnificent OHC V-12 Rolls-Royce Merlin aero engine that went into Hawker Hurricane and Supermarine Spitfire fighter aircraft that won the Battle of Britain. This combat-winning technology was exported to America, where it was built under licence by Packard and mounted in arguably the best piston-engined fighter ever built, the North American P-51 Mustang. The Mustang, in turn, wrested air superiority from Germany over Europe and did much to contribute to the Allied victory in 1945.

When the hostilities were over, there was a lot of new technology in engine design for motorcycle manufacturers to pick up, including supercharging, fuel injection, and liquid cooling. Once again, however, there was little inclination to do so, either in England where the factory owners were extremely conservative or the United States where both Harley and Indian were selling everything they could produce with the designs they already had.

Of the two countries, it was England that picked up the technology challenge first, not from the war, but with the advanced designs they were working on before the war began. By the late '40s, British motorcycle companies were producing OHV and OHC machines that, pound-for-pound, were better all-round racing bikes than the side-valve machines coming out of Springfield and Milwaukee. It was a gradual process that began in 1941, when a Norton ridden by Billy Mathews humbled Harley and Indian at Daytona, and continued into the '50s when the smaller Nortons beat their larger competitors four years in a row from 1949 to 1952. The difference was most apparent in road racing, where light weight and maximum horsepower were more important than torque, and less apparent in flat track racing where torque was king and engines never had the chance to run out of breath.

To Harley and Indian, the inevitable domination of OHV and OHC motorcycles was a fact they hoped they could conceal as long as possible. Working through the AMA, they banned them entirely in 1930 at the start of the Depression when both factories were looking for ways to stem the flow of English bikes into the United States. This produced such an outcry from English bike dealers and riders, the rules were changed again and a new formula, Class C, racing began to emerge in 1932. This allowed OHV machines, but limited them in size to 500 cc, while side valve motorcycles made by the big two were allowed up to 750 cc. In addition, the rules stipulated Class C machines had to be "of catalogued design," meaning they had to be stock production motorcycles. It was a brilliant piece of rulemaking, because the one-third difference in size made up for the better efficiency of the English OHV motors and the series production requirement eliminated the OHC English race bikes entirely. Together, the two regulations would keep side valve Harleys and Indians competitive for two more decades.

Like most good arguments, there are two ways to look at the Class C rule. While the English bike riders thought it was discriminatory, the AMA said it was exactly the opposite. Their position was that Class A and B racing, with its factory specials and exotic fuels, had become too expensive for the average motorcyclist. Class C, on the other hand, was open to everyone. Indeed, one of its requirements was that riders had to own the bikes they raced. The AMA said the capacity difference allowed between side valve and OHV machines was simply to promote better competition for riders and fans alike.

"While it may not have been as glamorous as the old Class A and Class B factory racers," says AMA president Ed Youngblood, "it provided opportunities for grass roots racing throughout the United States and became very popular among everyday motorcycle owners. Consequently, during the 1933 season, AMA and the supporting factories decided to totally abandon Class A and

Class B racing, and announce that effective with the 200-mile season opener at Jacksonville in 1934, American racing would become strictly Class C."

The AMA argument, in essence then, was that Class C was democratic and egalitarian, while unlimited racing was narrow and elitist. In a larger sense, it was the New World's values against those of the old, honest torque vs fancy horsepower, simple dirt versus sophisticated pavement, humble colonists against the King's mercenaries, good against evil. All this would be easy to sneer at, except for the fact it became demonstrably true as the '30s drew to a close. In Europe, BMW, in furtherance of the Nazi dream of world domination, developed a supercharged OHC twin that captured the world land speed record at 173.6 mph, won the 1938 European Championships and came first and second in the 1939 Senior TT on the Isle of Man. Six years later, Harley-Davidson side valve 45WLA military motorcycles would ride through the rubble of the BMW plant in Munich, a surreal testament to the AMA's racing position.

The argument of Harley racers was blunter and to the point. These were American races and if anyone else wanted to compete, they could damn well play by the same rules. They suggested, by way of contrast, if Harley-Davidson had gone to the Isle of Man and asked for a rule change that would have given it an advantage, it would have been laughed at. Trevor, himself a member of the AMA racing committee, put it succinctly:

"If there are rules, you gotta follow them."

In Canada before the war the Class C restrictions hadn't mattered much. Most Canadian racers were members of the American Motorcycle Association and the English bike dealers simply accepted the AMA rules as a fact of life. In Vancouver, Fred Jr., one of the very few dealers with both English and American machines, had finessed the issue by helping form the PNWMA which established club rules of its own. After the war, however, his west coast solution was presented with a new problem, the formation of a governing body for Canada, the Canadian Motorcycle Association.

The issue, as is usual in sports, was business, not sport.

The man pushing the CMA on the west coast was Frank Carr, the owner of British Motorcycle Sales, besides Ablitt, Deeley's only other competitor. He used the argument that if Canada ever wanted to be recognized in world racing by the International Federation of Motorcycling (FIM), it had to form its own national organization and adhere to FIM rules. These were much more advantageous to European machines, because they contained no special benefit for side valve engines. The AMA, who didn't want to see a form of racing in which Harleys and Indians would regularly lose, countered by announcing that any riders racing in CMA-sanctioned events would be automatically suspended from AMA membership and prohibited from entering AMA events.

To Fred Jr., who was happy with things as they were, the CMA was nothing more than a device to damage his Harley-Davidson sales, then increasing rapidly because of a growing number of wins by Harley-Davidson in flat track racing. Not incidentally, one of the most successful local racers was his son Trevor.

Trev Deeley's racing career, which had been doing well before he went into the army, now really took off. His new mount was a Harley-Davidson WR race bike, the successor to the famous WLDR sports model that had won Daytona three times, in 1938, 1939 and 1940, and that Trev had used with such success before the war. With a roller bearing crankshaft and ball bearing camshaft, it was more powerful than the WLDR, but it was still basically a side valve design, used a foot-operated clutch and had so-so brakes.

Even so, Trev on the WR was virtually unbeatable at Con Jones and, as he travelled to tracks in the Interior, Alberta, Idaho, Washington and Oregon, he proved a very tough competitor away from home as well. Bob Harrison, a racer who rode a B.S.A. Gold Star, competed with him on the half-mile track in Penticton and was very impressed.

"In fact," he remembers, "Trev was so far ahead of everyone, he made us all look bad. He was one of the best one-mile flat trackers there ever was, right up at the top with the best."

By now he had a 1937 Chevrolet and a trailer to take his bike to the races instead of the motorcycle and sidecar outfit he had used before. Vera would usually accompany him, and one of his friends, such as Bobby Dawe or Fred Pazaski would often come along as well.

On one occasion, Trev didn't get away early for a Sunday race in Washington, and by the time he and Vera in one car, and Bobby in another, showed up at the racetrack, the Saturday night practice was over. That would have been reason enough for most people to find a bar or a place to bunk down for the night. Instead, Trev waited for everyone to leave and then broke into the stadium. After getting his racer off its trailer, he positioned Vera at one end of the track and Bobby at the other so their car lights would illuminate the surface. Then, in the middle of the night, he began practising, checking his motor and tires and gauging the coefficient of friction on the track. The next day, he won.

Another time Trev won despite the rules was at the Bob Knox Memorial Races on Memorial Day, 1946, at Puyallup, Washington. The main event was a forty-lap "TT" style of race. This was a dirt track type of event modelled on the famous Tourist Trophy race on the Isle of Man, with both right and left-hand corners and an elevation change. Trev was lapping the field when he came up on Fred Pazaski on a 1935 VL Harley-Davidson. Going into a right-hand corner, Trev cut inside him and the two bikes collided, clipping the right side of the VL and breaking off its cast iron brake pedal, and knocking Trev past the wrong side of the marker. Pazaski, more dazed than annoyed, continued to go round the course, now without a rear brake. Trev, who normally would have had to turn back and head around the marker on the right side, decided since he had lapped the field, to just carry on and accept the penalty. When the race was over, there was an immediate protest. A spectator, Johnny Martinolich, contended Trev should be disqualified for cheating.

Trev responded angrily, "What the hell does that matter, I went one lap farther than you guys."

In the end, Trev was awarded the win and got the trophy. He immediately handed it to Vera for safe keeping. "If anyone comes after me for this, I'll hit them over the head with it," she announced, just as feisty as her husband.

On a third occasion, Trev's problem was again lack of time to get to a race in the United States. The Mount Baker Motorcycle Club had organized a race for Saturday afternoon at the Lynden, Washington, fairgrounds and 3,000 people had shown up to see the competition for $600 in prize money. To qualify, Trev had to make it to the track by noon to enter the time trials. Washington was on Standard Time while British Columbia was on Daylight Savings Time, which allowed Trev an extra hour to make it, but even so, he rolled up five minutes after the cutoff. Too late, said the officials. Pazaski, who was a club member and had urged his friend to attend, got the racers together and appealed to them to let Trev at least make one timed lap of the track. They agreed, overruling the officials, and Trev set off, taking a warm-up lap, and then the single timed lap of the kidney bean-shaped half mile track. Roaring down the straightaway, he appeared to be going too fast to the crowd, which instinctively stood up to see him crash. Instead, Trevor laid his Harley into a power slide and threw a huge rooster tail of loose dirt over the spectators, covering them in dust. The one lap was certainly enough to qualify — it was the fastest time recorded. Trev then went on to win all the expert races that followed.

This pugnacious attitude extended off the track as well. One weekend Trev went to the States for a three-day PNWMA field meet and rally near the little resort town of Point Roberts. He was drinking with his friends outside a bar when someone in a Model A Ford drove up on the sidewalk, apparently with the intent of running the motorcyclists down. Trev went berserk. He rushed over to the car, ripped open the door and hauled the driver out onto the road where he proceeded to pound him with his fists. One of the friends, Russ Martin, fearing Trev was going to kill him, went over and tried to pull the two men apart. Trev swung round and started fighting with Martin. At this, Fred Pazaski rushed over:

"Knock it off," he shouted, "he's my friend."

"Oh, is he?" Trev asked, his fist still cocked.

"Yeah, I'm Fred's friend, I'm Fred's friend," Martin hollered.

That ended the fight and the driver was let go with nothing more than a bloody nose.

Another time Trev let his fists do the talking was on the way back from a baseball game in Vancouver. Vera was driving home in an Austin A40 with Trev dozing beside her when another car came up alongside her several times and finally cut her off at a traffic light at 4th and Alma. Trev jumped out of the car, went forward to the other vehicle, pulled the driver out and punched him. The incident was observed by a druggist at a nearby store who called the police. They duly arrived and threw Trev in the back of the squad car. He immediately got out the other side, ready to continue the fight, when the cop pulled his gun out and arrested him. He was then hauled off to jail and put into a cell. Vera, distraught at what had happened, called Fred Jr. to get her husband bailed out. Trev, meanwhile, became irritated at the light left on in his cell because it was keeping him awake. Taking off his shoe, he threw it at the offending bulb, the light went out and Trev went to sleep. By two o'clock in the morning, Fred Jr. and Vera got him out of jail and the potential charges were dropped with an apology and a payment for the damaged property.

The willingness to put in an elbow, cut off an opponent or

ride another competitor into the rail became one of Trevor's characteristics. The anger inside him came bursting out when he got on the track in a take-no-prisoners attitude. This could be called aggressiveness, or poor sportsmanship, depending on your point of view. To young Nick Wasilieff, watching in the stands, it seemed more of the latter than the former, so he used to yell at Trev when he came round the track.

"Poor sport, poor sport," Wasilieff shouted.

Of course Trev couldn't hear him, but at one race another member of the family did, turned around and began talking back. Nick told him to forget it.

"I can say what I like," he said. "He's my brother-in-law."

Trev's response to criticism about his riding style and racetrack manners was that he was forced to be tough. "I always fought like hell if I felt I was being screwed," he said, "and it was easy to be screwed in the States, especially in the Seattle area."

It didn't really matter what anyone said, fair or foul, Trev was on a winning streak wherever he went. In 1946, in one week alone, he won the Alberta championship in Lethbridge, the Montana state championship in Great Falls, Montana, before a crowd of 10,000 people, and the Bob Knox Memorial Race in Tacoma, Washington. The trophies continued at the Western Canada Championships organized by the Canadian Athletic Association in Edmonton. The races September 2 were run on a loosely-packed, half-mile track at the Exhibition grounds and consisted of a number of events in different classes. Trev won the preliminary event, followed by Bobby Dawe, and another Deeley employee, Vic Smith. He then came roaring back to win the feature ahead of Jack Ripley of Regina, with Dawe coming in third. The prize was $300 and a handsome cup put up by the Aluminum Company of Canada Ltd. Some of the local riders didn't even finish. Herby Cartwright of Calgary was knocked out when his machine threw him into the air. Another Calgary rider, Bud Johnson, suffered facial lacerations when his bike skidded out of control.

The next year Trev skipped the Edmonton races, but made it to Tacoma where he won again. He also took part in a unique Northwest racing fixture, the Death Head Derby, organized by the Olympia Motorcycle Club. This TT-style event was held on a dirt track at Hawks Prairie in Lacey, Washington. The track featured a long straightaway, an easy sweeping left, a short straight in the backfield to an overhead ramp – at this point many riders became airborne – a right loop under the ramp, then a right-hand dog-leg followed by a left-hand carousel turn to the start/finish line. What made the event truly extraordinary, however, was the trophy, a human skull. This object, dug up when the track was being built, was the head of a native American female. When they found it, club members immediately mounted the skull on a block of wood, named it *Annabelle* and turned it into the perpetual trophy of the Death Head Derby. If this seems remarkable to you now, even bizarre, ask yourself how many skulls you've seen on biker paraphernalia over the years. Now you know where it all started. Trev, racing in the expert event, came in fourth, after Cliff Steering of Seattle on a Harley-Davidson, Jack Colley of Seattle on an Indian and Red Rice of Portland riding a Matchless. While that was a disappointment, he managed a second in the three-lap Helmet Dash, again behind Red Rice.

Back in Edmonton, the winner of the Alcan Cup in front of 8,000 fans was Jack Ripley riding a Triumph twin. Ripley's victory photo shows a mud-spattered machine with open pipes, girder forks, sprung seat and a solid rear end. He is wearing jeans with wide turn-ups, what looks like a football helmet and is holding the cup with a shy smile on his face. One assumes Trev's reaction, on seeing the picture, was that he wanted to remove both the cup and the smile. He now had an extra incentive to do so because Harley-Davidson was giving him official factory sponsorship, something it would continue to do for the next six years.

At work, Trevor was by now virtually the acting manager of the motorcycle division, but he was still on a very short rein from his father. He would regularly come up with new ideas for marketing motorcycles only to have them rejected by Fred Jr. Some of his actions were countermanded and more than once he was given a public dressing down in front of the other employees. The situation was so humiliating and frustrating he announced his desire to quit to several people, including accountant Lloyd Perry, service manager Jack Wilkinson, and his friend Bobby Dawe. To a man, they advised him against doing so.

"One time he got a job offer to sell cars for somebody," Dawe recalled, "and he was all set to quit and give it all up. I told him 'Use your bloody head. Suck up to the old bugger if you have to, but Christ don't just tell him to stick it because there's too much at stake.'"

Trev, as much as he didn't like it, took the advice and continued doing whatever he could to promote motorcycling, in the office or after work. One of his ventures was to begin, with the help of a Sgt. Cookie Ryan, a regular training program for the Vancouver police motorcyclists who had, up till then, been learning how to ride their bikes on their own. This led Trev to suggest the formation of a police drill team which proved a boon for internal morale and public relations. Trev came up with the routines, organized the practice sessions and joined the policemen in staging demonstrations. Deputy Chief Gordon Ambrose was so grateful, he proposed to his boss that Trev be sworn in as a policeman. Unfortunately, police chief Walter Mulligan was forced to quit and was replaced by a retired head of the RCMP, George Archer.

"When Archer arrived on the scene in Vancouver it was thought by everyone he would not even tolerate that an outsider like myself could be part of the police department," Trev recalled. "However, they presented the idea to him and he agreed. I was paraded before him by Gordon Ambrose and sworn in with the bible and the whole bit in the police chief's office."

The department made him an honourary cop and gave him a uniform and a badge, but knowing Trev's hot temper, they thought better of giving him a gun.

Another project was the creation, through the GVMC, of a small club track on city property at Boundary Road and East 54th Street in Burnaby. This could be used freely at any time and was perfect for field meets in the summer and "mud races" in the winter.

Actually, some Canadian roads were a mud race at any time of year. Trev found this out when he and Vera set off on a Harley Knucklehead for a holiday trip up the Fraser River to Kamloops and through the Interior. The usual route back to the coast would have been over the Cascade mountain range in Washington state, but in Penticton Trevor discovered that it might just be possible to ride his bike over a logging trail between Princeton and Hope in Canada, the route later taken by the Hope-Princeton Highway. The first part of the trip from the Okanagan was easy, but from Princeton onwards, the track degenerated into a slippery, washed-out obstacle course that got progressively worse the higher it went. Several times the heavily laden touring bike slithered to the ground and Vera was forced to nimbly leap off the rear to avoid being crushed. At one point Trev had to manoeuvre the Harley across a log bridge; at another they slithered along mere feet from the edge of a precipitous canyon; at other times, he and Vera forded a number of mountain streams. As darkness fell they met a final obstacle – a gate barring the way and a government employee who refused to open it. Going back over the pass was out of the question, so Trev simply said that if the fellow didn't open the gate, he'd come crashing through it. The gate was opened.

As a test of fate, manhood and love, the trip was a resounding success. Trev had met the challenge of the unknown, he had muscled his huge bike over the worst road in the country and Vera was still talking to him at the end of the journey, despite the very real threat it had posed to both their lives.

The year 1948 began with Trev's spirited but unsuccessful effort at Daytona and continued with numerous local races on the lower mainland, including events at a new Vancouver track, the 4,000-seat Digney Speedway on McPherson Ave. just off the Kingsway. Trev was so intent on racing, he felt stifled in the relaxed atmosphere of the GVMC, whose members were more interested in touring than racing, so he and some of the younger riders split from the main group and formed the 21 Rebels, taking over the track built the previous year at East 54th for regular races.

Not all his appearances were successful, especially when he went hillclimbing on a temperamental 1930 Harley-Davidson hillclimber purchased by his father and grandfather before the war. At one meet near Bellingham, Trev shot up the hill, couldn't make it, and hit the kill switch. This was a simple affair made out of a piece of hacksaw blade that grounded the ignition circuit to the frame just beside the left-hand grip. The engine stopped and Trev turned around and starting back using engine compression to slow his descent. Suddenly, the switch failed, the engine fired up again and Trevor found himself racing down the hill at full throttle. The crowd scattered and Trev, seeing no other way to stop the runaway bike, threw it down on the ground and slid the full distance of the run-up area, into the parking lot, and under a car. When the dust settled, Trev was only shaken up. In retrospect, it's clear the Deeley heir came very close to killing himself and an unknown number of spectators.

Instead of being fazed by the experience, Trev picked the bike up and went on to win the hillclimb.

At home, Vera's pregnancy, which had caused both Trev and Reg concern at Daytona in March, was difficult right to the end. When the baby suddenly arrived September 1, it was four weeks premature and a Rhesus baby with severe anemia due to an RH factor mismatch between its blood and Vera's. Hoping for the best, and fearing the worst, they named him Timothy Trevor, after his maternal grandfather and his father. Trev, who was again entered in the Western Canada Championships, stayed with Vera and Timothy until the last moment before catching a flight to Edmonton on Saturday, September 4, for the Labour Day races September 6. There was concern in his mind for Vera and the baby, but they were getting the best possible care and his father, his friends and his fans still expected him to show up in Edmonton.

In the Alberta capital, the build-up for the race was prodigious. The *Edmonton Journal* headline when he arrived said, "Motorcycle Thrills at Exhibition Track, Big Crowd Expected, Star-Studded Entry List For Championship Events." The accompanying article made clear he was one of the stars. "The entrant considered likeliest to walk away with first prize money," it reported, "is Trevor Deeley of Vancouver. He is among the top motorcycle racers in North America." Then, in what sounds like an attack on Trev's lifestyle, the paper added: "In contrast to most of the competitors who will be riding their machines to the meet, Deeley, because of business commitments, will ship his and fly out in time for the race." The attack on the wealthy Vancouverite winging in to steal the prize from the humble hometown boys was off the mark. The local racers were trailering their specially prepared bikes, not riding them, and Trev's "business commitments" were his wife and new son.

The sarcasm hardly mattered, because the publicity for motorcycling, Fred Deeley Ltd. and Trevor personally was wonderful. Trev's picture, charging around a corner on his Harley-Davidson with both feet on the pegs, was the illustration used by the race promoters in their official advertisement. The event carried the highest rating of the American Motorcycle Association, five stars, and would contribute points to his ranking in the United States. In addition, the chance of a Deeley machine winning was pretty good because Trev was accompanied by two of his employees, Bobby Dawe, who had started to win a few races on his own, and Vic Smith, who could not only race with the best of them but was a top mechanic.

Surprisingly — it was certainly news to Trev — parimutuel betting was allowed on the race and so Trev put fifty dollars down on himself.

The competition began at one o'clock. Six thousand spectators were in the stands as the first of ten races got off to a roaring start. Almost immediately there was trouble. George Bass, one of six Calgary competitors, suffered a broken leg in a three-way spill at the start of the first amateur heat. Two races later and Fred Elgert of the Edmonton Motorcycle Club, the winner of the second amateur heat, lost control in the backstretch and crashed without injury. More races followed and then came the expert heats. Trev won the first heat, waited patiently, and won the final. Then it was time for the feature, a twenty-lap expert race for the Alcan Cup and the prestige of being called Western Canada Champion. The flag dropped, there was a roar and a cloud of dust and the six qualifiers in the race were off.

Trev grabbed the lead on the inside turn of the first lap and never looked back. He was so fast, that before the ten laps were over he had lapped the fourth and fifth place riders once and the sixth place rider twice. At the finish, Trev was a quarter of a mile ahead of the previous year's winner, Jack Ripley, of Regina, who had to scramble for place position. Third was Rob Flack from Great Falls, Montana. For his efforts, Trev won the cup, $400 for the feature and $200 for the expert events.

Trev was such a favourite the odds were no good, and he only collected fifty-two dollars when he went to the betting window with his ticket.

Unknown to him getting the congratulations of his fans, Timothy was about to die in Vancouver.

Trevor returned home both exhilarated and distraught. He had once again become Western Canada Champion, adding that title to the Pacific Northwest Motorcycle Championship he already held, but no sooner had he arrived than he lost his only son. The funeral the next day was a private, heartbreaking affair at the Forest Lawn Memorial Park and Mortuary on Royal Oak Avenue. It was made even more barren by the cemetery's policy of not allowing gravestones and not planting many trees or shrubs, a rule which give the area the appearance of a vacant field, rather than a place of rest. The exact spot chosen for the little casket was in an area known as Babyland, close to the Crescent Wall of Memory. The small bronze marker, which was not ready until later, would read, "Our Baby Timothy Trevor Deeley Sept. 8, 1948." Entwined on one side of the plaque were four gardenias. Years later, recounting this period in his life, Trevor would skip right over his son's birth as if it never happened, the memory of that moment clearly too difficult to bear.

Racing didn't seem much fun either after that. Trev still competed locally and in the States and helped organize spring field meets, mud races, and rallies, but he seemed to lose the aggressive edge that had done so well for him in the past. Among other things, he decided against competing at Daytona, just five months away. Vera needed nurturing at home and the business was getting more and more demanding as the post-war economic boom got into full stride.

For Fred Deeley Ltd., this was the period of its greatest growth in sales, highest employment and most activity. The basic reason was that Britain, desperate to earn foreign exchange, had told its automakers to produce new models for export before satisfying the home market. This meant that foreign car distributors such as Deeley's in Vancouver, could get supplies while the dealers of North American-produced automobiles were still scrambling to catch up with their orders. It also helped that Austin had come out in 1948 with the A-40, an attractively packaged car that appealed to Canadian consumers, both for its low cost and upscale appearance. The combination of push/pull in supply and demand worked its magic at 901 West Broadway, turning the quiet street into a hotbed of automotive activity. Sales for 1948 were 1,250 cars, sixty-three percent of their sales for the entire 1930s! For several consecutive months in 1949, Fred Deeley Ltd. outsold every make of car, including Canadian and American models, by a large margin. By year's end, the company had moved 3,274 vehicles compared to its next closest competitor at 2,443. With thousands of cars on the docks, over 230 employees and buyers lined up at the door, it was time to think about expansion.

There was another reason as well. The Austin company had taken one look at the adjoining motorcycle shop and had told Fred Sr. it had to go. The image the company wanted to cultivate was not helped by the working class aura given off by motorcycles, no matter where they were made. Fred Sr. and Fred Jr. protested, but Austin was adamant, and they eventually gave in.

Given that they had to expand, and move the bike shop, the Deeley's made the best of it, building a new 20,000-square-foot building on the west side and remodelling the 14,000-square-foot building on the east side, creating a three-building complex of 81,000 square feet. At the same time they drew up plans and began construction of a new motorcycle shop one-and-a-half miles east on a 66 by 122 foot lot at 606 East Broadway. Built on the corner of Carolina Street by the Dominion Construction Co., this 10,527-square-foot building was the last word in motorcycle facilities with two mezzanine floors and more space to sell, service and supply motorcycles of all kinds. Significantly, none of the new constructions carried a mortgage. Fred Deeley Jr. paid for it all in cash.

Trev, writing in a magazine-type advertising flyer he had started called "Deeley's Dope," was effusive in his praise for the new structure even before it was completed: "It is undoubtedly Canada's largest, finest and most modern motorcycle shop. Our new show room has been doubled in size over our present show room, and our stock room has been more than tripled in size with the twenty-five- by sixty-six-foot mezzanine over the stock room for our surplus and large parts. Our work shop too has been enlarged approximately 2,000 square feet and the used machine display department has also been enlarged. We will have a modern wash and steam cleaning department, and our new heating system will be by an oil furnace. Every modern convenience has been installed to make your visits to our store more pleasant." The most important reason for Trevor's enthusiasm, however, wasn't mentioned. This was simply that because 606 East Broadway was quite a hike from 901 West Broadway, and since his father was up to his ears in Austins, he, Trevor, would have the place all to himself to run. More than leaving school, his army career, his marriage and his racing, this was the moment Trev began life as an independent person. It was only a measure of independence – his father and grandfather still held the purse strings tightly in their own hands – but his role as manager was tangible and physical. When Trevor walked in the door at 606, there would be no question in anyone's mind who was the boss.

There was also no question it was a significant business all on its own. Besides Trev, the motorcycle department had nine employees and annual sales in the hundreds of thousands of dollars. It handled Harley-Davidson, B.S.A., Triumph, Ariel, Norton, Francis Barnett and Sunbeam motorcycles, some scooters and even the Cyclemaster, a $115 power unit anyone could add to a bicycle to turn it into a motorcycle capable of going twenty-five miles an hour while getting 250 miles per gallon. In addition, the shop acted as the dealer for Harley-Davidson on the lower mainland; and the dealer and distributor of B.S.A. and Ariel in B.C. and Alberta, and Triumph and Norton in B.C.

The cost of a new Harley Model 74 OHV machine was $1,195; a 1,000 cc Ariel Square Four touring machine, $875; 500 cc Norton International club racer, $825; 500 cc B.S.A. Gold

Star club racer, $775; Triumph Tiger 100 sports bike, $680; and a 125 cc B.S.A. Bantam economy bike, $265. Most of the marketing push, however, was for machines with the larger English capacity of 650 cc. "The new B.S.A. and Triumph 650 cc vertical twin models will definitely change the motorcycle picture," Trev wrote. "They weigh practically the same as the 500 models, but develop far more horsepower and at a lower rpm. The high rate of cruising speed available with these models and their ability to 'take it,' carry two people without effort, will make every enthusiastic rider want one." The Triumph 650s were priced only a few dollars more than the cost of the traditional 500 cc twins, so they were very good value.

While Trevor was juggling all the demands on his time caused by the planning of the new buildings, the increased level of sales and the needs of his dealer network, he was also desperately trying to lose weight. During Christmas 1949, he had received a telephone call from Walter Davidson, the President of Harley-Davidson, a rough, tough guy with a no-nonsense attitude.

"How are you?" Davidson asked.

"Fine," he replied.

"How much do you weigh?"

"What the hell difference does that make?"

"Answer my question," Davidson pressed Trev.

"Walter," Trev responded, "I haven't got a clue, but I guess around 158, 160 pounds, something like that."

"Well," said Davidson, "we're going to send you tickets. We want you to ride for us at Daytona next year. We'll get the bike ready here, you come to Milwaukee, we'll make it fit and then we'll ship you off to Florida."

"That's great," Trev said.

What he thought was another thing. What with his improved income and lifestyle, his weight had shot up to 212 pounds. Davidson had obviously known this and was providing Trev with the ultimate slim fast reduction plan, the chance of a factory ride at Daytona.

Trevor immediately became a man possessed. He cut out the beer, began eating steak and grapefruit, went running, played basketball at the local high school gym and put away his car to toughen up riding his motorcycle. Some nights after work he would ride all the way to Hope and back on a solo Harley 45 or sometimes a 61, even if it was below zero. On arrival in Milwaukee, in early February, he weighed 158 pounds.

What the factory had waiting was another new WR. Since its introduction in 1941, it had not won at Daytona and Harley-Davidson was starting to become anxious about the company's historic racing reputation. Perhaps "Daredevil Deeley" could push the WR to its full potential. The H-D executives had every right to be worried. Norton 500 cc OHC singles had shut Harley and Indian out of the top three the previous year, and the word was that Norton was making a major effort to repeat their success by again sending over their famous race director, Francis Beart.

Race day dawned with the smallest crowd since the war, down from 16,500 the year before to a mere 8,000 fans. Trevor was fit and in shape, his bike was as sharp as it could be and the weather was sunny and warm. More important, Trev wasn't the aggressive youngster he had been two years earlier. Now almost thirty, he vowed to avoid his mistake of 1948 and ride a consistent, intelligent race, especially in the difficult north and south corners. It was a good plan, because when the flag went down, the corners were still as treacherous as ever. Ted Totoraitis of Grand Rapids, No. 25, and Bob Mertens of Milwaukee, No. 116, came broadsliding into the north turn together on lap four and collided. Mertens went cartwheeling off his machine, breaking his nose, wrist and finger. Bill Huber from Reading, Pennsylvania, No. 7, had an even worse record at the north turn, dumping his bike on laps twenty-six, twenty-seven, twenty-eight, and twenty-nine, making it on laps thirty and thirty-one, and crashing for good on lap thirty-two.

The early lead went to Triumph, as it had in 1949 when Jack Horn led for most of the race. This time a Triumph 500 OHV twin was being ridden by Ed Kretz Sr., No. 38, of Monterey Park, California. Right behind him was the slight, boy-like Dick Klamfoth of Groveport, Ohio, on a Norton and a little farther back a determined Billy Mathews, the stubby 5'4", 150-pound Canadian with bull shoulders and ham-like hands who had lost to Klamfoth the previous year by sixteen seconds, also on a Norton.

Trevor, meanwhile, raced up the sand and down the road with skill and determination. He knew he could never catch the Triumphs and the Nortons, but he hoped he could work his way up the standings by riding consistently and relying on his Harley's motor to keep going. The secondary goal he set himself was to be the first of the sixty-seven Harley-Davidsons entered in the race to cross the finish line. Unfortunately his transmission was not cooperating, occasionally jumping out of gear when least expected.

Reliability was also the Triumph problem. Kretz Sr., an experienced rider who won the race in 1937 on an Indian, led until the halfway mark, then developed engine troubles and had to make the first of four pit stops. It was not a concern, however, for the Nortons, as the thirty-seven-year-old Mathews gradually reeled in Klamfoth and passed him, to win the race in two hours, fifteen minutes and two seconds, one minute and forty-five seconds ahead of Klamfoth. Next was a B.S.A., a Norton, two Harley-Davidsons, another Norton, two more Harley-Davidsons, and, in tenth place, Frederick Trevor Deeley.

It was a very creditable performance. Of the 124 expert riders at the start of the race, only thirty-seven finished, and of the Harley-Davidsons, only four crossed the finish line ahead of him. Many riders had wound up in the sand, many more had dropped out when their engines died, but Trevor had made it into the money for a share of $8,000 in prizes, despite a bad gear in his transmission. The WR Harley had shown its motor was reliable enough to last the 200 miles, but it simply didn't have enough speed to win. For Trevor, the feeling was one of satisfaction rather than elation. He hadn't won, but he had done well, far better than most, and he felt energized by the results, almost ready to go another 200 miles. It proved a major psychological lift and he returned home with a new sense of optimism and self confidence.

He would need it. The situation at Deeley's was like a madhouse because of the increased business, the reallocation of space among buildings, and the construction of the new headquarters for the motorcycle division which was just about to start, and for which he would be the project manager.

Ironically, his first step on returning home was to blow the horn for Norton, the motorcycle brand that had showed its heels to his Harley-Davidson. As the Norton distributor for British Columbia, he was free to take advantage of the Daytona win through his dealers, newspaper advertising and in-store displays. Indeed, had Triumph or B.S.A. won, he undoubtedly would have done the same thing because of his across-the-board line-up of manufacturers. Sometimes acquiring new brands hadn't panned out, such as with the Salisbury scooter. It had a large single-cylinder engine with remarkably quick acceleration that could be tricky in the wrong hands. One day a passerby went for an unauthorized spin on a Salisbury, let it get away from him, crashed and was killed. The family sued and Trev settled out of court. He also ditched the killer scooter pronto before anyone else did the same thing. Despite this, the Deeley philosophy was to throw every available brand at the market, from the German NSU and the Italian Ducati to the French Manurin scooter. If it rolled, it sold, was the motto.

Down the street, meanwhile, Bill Ablitt was causing problems by changing his mind. Since 1948, when it prepared fifty special 648 Sport Scouts and saw one of them ridden by Floyd Emde win at Daytona, the Indian factory had been experiencing financial difficulties and had been unable to match the new models from Harley-Davidson or the flood of street bikes from England. Ablitt, who must have seen the writing on the wall, decided, after twenty years in the business, now was as good a time as any to get out of motorcycles. Accordingly, he announced a Going Out of Business Sale. The response from loyal Indian owners was amazing. They descended on his store and began cleaning it out. Business was so good in fact, Ablitt then announced he wasn't going out of business, and ordered in more stock. This caused the rush to die down, leaving him with an excess of inventory. The only solution was to really go out of business! Up at Deeley's, the turnaround was giving Trevor conniptions. He pondered what he could do to put Ablitt out of business for good and decided to buy up all of Ablitt's stock. Unfortunately, he couldn't convince Fred Jr. to put up any more than $2,000 and Ablitt turned the offer down and salted his hoard away in a warehouse to await further developments.

The new Deeley motorcycle shop, in contrast, was the toast of the town. When it opened July 2 – conveniently on a long weekend – 300 motorcyclists showed up for the ceremony and then proceeded to Lulu Island for a field day with free Coke and ice cream for the kids. That wasn't the end of it though for the company's dealers who had travelled to Vancouver from around the province. They were invited back to the new building for a cold plate dinner, some films and a dance on the waxed workshop floor. When it was over, and the doors were locked, Trev and Vera went home proud parents at last, if not of a family, at least of the latest offshoot of the family business. The struggles of the early years were behind them. Islay had accepted that Vera's bubbly personality was more important than her working class background, Vera had got over the death of her father and her son, and Trev had temporarily come to terms with himself and the role fate had carved out for him in the family business.

It was, in a way, the end of Act One in Trevor's life. Act Two was about to begin, a curious replay of the opener in which a business triumph would replace Trev's sporting achievements, but where he would once again find himself standing on the barren fields of the Forest Lawn Memorial Park and Mortuary staring through tear-stained eyes at freshly dug earth.

CHAPTER SIX

IF YOU LOOKED south from downtown Vancouver in 1951, you could see a sign on the horizon that was as famous locally as the "Hollywood" sign in Los Angeles. It was even more concise, just the single word "AUSTIN." Because he had chosen a hillside location twenty-two years earlier, Fred Sr. now had the perfect spot to erect one of the largest advertising signs in the city, the roof of his store at 901 West Broadway. Unlike every other sign on the street, it faced north to the commercial heart of Vancouver several miles away, not south to the passing traffic. In a way it was symbolic. Fred Sr. and Fred Jr. hadn't turned their back on local customers, they had raised their sights in the search for wider markets.

This optimistic, outward looking, salesman's approach to business had always been part of Fred Sr.'s thinking. But now, in his seventieth year, and at the height of his success, it was obvious there was much more to his business philosophy than simple optimism. There were basic principles and business methods that permeated every part of the Deeley empire and that now spanned three generations.

The first principle was to locate in a growing population centre and grow with it. That's why he had emigrated to Canada and that's why he chose Vancouver over Victoria. In such an expanding community he could grow easily, without having to capture market share from his competitors. The fact Vancouver had the mildest climate in the country and was the only place in Canada where bicycles and motorcycles could be used year round, was the icing on the cake. He would have more customers every year without lifting a finger and they would buy product all year round instead of just eight months out of twelve as in the rest of Canada.

The second principle he followed was to define his business broadly within a specific market. Thus, Fred Sr. didn't just think of himself as "the Bicycle Man"; in his own mind he was selling personal transportation. This flexible definition allowed him to move from bicycles to motorcycles and later from motorcycles to cars, as the personal transportation market matured and developed. Many bicycle and motorcycle dealers defined themselves more narrowly and thus did not catch the crest of the next wave of transportation devices. Many others limited themselves to one marque and rose and fell with its fortunes. Fred Sr. did the opposite; he averaged his risk by covering the market with brands, backing winners and pruning losers as he went along.

A third principle was a belief in the leveraging power of wholesaling. Fred Sr. realized if he could get other people to open up shop and sell his products, he would make more money on the lower margin of a wholesaler than if he tried to keep all the business to himself as a retailer. It takes a lot of nerve to set up new dealers in your own product lines, hoping you'll make more on less, but Fred Sr. never doubted it was the way to go, setting up dealer networks for bicycles, motorcycles and cars just as soon as he could find the people and make the arrangements.

And then there was finance. Of all his achievements, financial management is the one of which the least is known and for which the most praise should be given. There are passing references to it in the stories written about him during his lifetime, but he never gave the gameplan away, and since Fred Deeley Ltd. was a private company, he never had to. Fred Jr. had very little to say on the subject, and Trevor too, has kept the family's financial manipulations very much to himself. Nevertheless, the broad outline of what was going on can now be made out, even if most of the detail is missing. Basically, Fred Sr. set out to use money as a lever, just as he used population growth and dealer networks to boost his profits. To do this he had to first turn himself from a borrower into a lender, so the leverage of interest would work for him instead of against him. His method was a concept familiar to anyone who's ever bought a house and then seen it rise in value; Fred Deeley bought property, turned it into rental income, and then bought more property with the new asset value and cash flow. Profits from his bicycle business were used to prime the pump, as were profits from his Austin distributorship. By 1951, Fred Sr. was able to make the remarkable claim there was no mortgage on any Deeley building.

That wasn't the end of it of course. Fred Sr. soon realized there was a profit to be made in money itself, in the financing of everything he was selling in his stores. The way one story about him put it at the time was that Deeley's "carry all their own 'paper,' which is a very large figure." In fact, besides operating what amounted to a real estate development company, Fred Sr. was also running his own commercial credit company, financing motorcycle and car sales just as the charter banks do today.

Nor was that all. The Deeleys were running a Home Oil service station at the corner of Broadway and Oak, a used car lot across the street and a U-Drive business with a fleet of forty rental cars, in addition to the original wholesale bicycle business.

There is no record of how much money was involved in these various activities, but you can get some idea from the sales figures for Austin alone. In 1950 Austin sales in British Columbia rose to 5,186 units, bringing to $15 million the amount grossed in the province by Austin in the previous four years. About two thirds of that total went through Deeley's network of forty dealers, with the remaining going through Fred Deeley Ltd.'s retail sales showroom.

The way Fred Sr. managed his empire will surprise today's business school graduates who think the following concepts are new ideas: zero-based budgeting, profit centres, no frills, employee flexibility, personal service, and professional standards. He also had some old ideas, chief among them being benign paternalism.

The organizational chart was straightforward, because it was just about the same as Fred Sr.'s genealogical chart. He was the president of the company in charge of real estate and finance, with sons Ray and Fred responsible for, respectively, bicycles and cars, grandson Trevor for motorcycles, and managers in charge of the U-Drive and used car operations. Fred Sr. was supported by three long-time assistants, his accountant Lloyd Perry, auditor Jack Waters and lawyer Harvey Sedgwick.

Every year, the head of each department, was called in and

asked to do a sales projection for the following twelve months. When Fred Sr. agreed with the figure, the manager would then place orders for the cars, motorcycles or bicycles he wanted with the various manufacturers and get the accountants under Perry to develop a cash flow that would show the income from sales and financing, minus the cost of the product, borrowing and overhead. There were never any budgets as such, just the annual, zero-based cash flow projections. Meanwhile, the money for all this was the bank's. Fred Sr., while not a believer in mortgages, was a firm believer in using the bank's money rather than his own to finance operations, and did so through a commercial line of credit at the Bank of Commerce, later the Canadian Imperial Bank of Commerce. Vehicle purchases and consumer financing were done through this LOC, which expanded over the years into the millions of dollars.

To make money, you have to keep expenses down, and at this, Fred Sr. was a master, as was his son, Fred Jr. The original motorcycle shop was functional but stark, with bare floors and bare walls that wouldn't have been out of place in a saddle shop a hundred years earlier. Routine purchases were rigorously controlled and questions asked if even a spare elastic band were thrown into a garbage can. Employee tardiness was not tolerated, work breaks were monitored, and workers' personal lives had to be exemplary. The same rigour was applied to customer service, to the confirmation of appointments and the avoidance of over-booking. As early as 1950, all the shop staff had to wear white coveralls in addition to keeping their work areas spotless. They also had to be ready to do different jobs if there was a greater need in another area, or two jobs at once. For example the motorcycle parts people were also salesmen and Fred Jr.'s secretary was also the receptionist and the office switchboard operator.

Some young people today might find the rules and regulations at Deeley's unduly restrictive, some did so at the time. But there was also a remarkable degree of employee loyalty and even pride in working at Deeley's. Partly this was a response to high standards, partly it was knowing they were working at the largest bike shop and imported car dealership in western Canada and partly it was a simple matter of indebtedness. Fred Sr. frequently loaned employees money for personal expenses, car purchases or even the down payment on a home. If they left his employ, however, they would have to pay the debt off in full, a difficult task even in good economic times.

It was just as well that Deeley's was a tightly run ship as it closed out the best year in its history, because heavy weather lay ahead.

Two things happened in 1951 to rock the boat. Automobile manufacturers on both sides of the Atlantic caught up with the demand and produced a glut of new cars. At the same time governments in both Canada and the United States imposed credit restrictions to check inflation, sharply curbing sales. The standard terms of sale, one third of the purchase price in cash, and the balance payable over two years, were ended by government order. To buy a car, you had to pay half in cash and the rest in twelve months. At Deeley's, where the showroom had looked like the waiting room at the city's CPR railway station, things were suddenly quiet. It was the first in a series of shocks that would hit, one after another, for the next four years.

The motorcycle business, at its new location and under its newly revitalized manager, was thriving. One reason was that Deeley's was now offering two remarkable little machines for new riders produced by its two major suppliers, B.S.A. and Harley-Davidson. These were the B.S.A. Bantam and H-D 125, both a direct copy of the RT125 produced by DKW and picked up as war reparations by the victorious allies. Fred Sr. returned to England for the first time in 1950 and rhapsodized over the Bantam. "Undoubtedly the B.S.A. company has made a killing on this model," he wrote. "It is by far the most popular motorcycle on the road today in England. It seems to be the utility machine, the machine that would impress me as replacing the bicycle for the average working man getting to and from his work. It is not uncommon to see a man with a flowing beard riding one. There are quite a few elderly ladies too using the new Bantam." Given what happened nine years later, it's worth noting that Fred Sr., the original bicycle man, was bowled over by a small, lightweight machine that could "replace the bicycle for the average working man." It is also worth noting it was smack dab on the cusp between bicycles and motorbikes and that it came from a country defeated in the Second World War.

Other English bikes were also doing well, far better in fact than the larger Harley-Davidson models which were now the most expensive in Trevor's lineup. As a result, motorcycle sales in 1952 were greater than for both 1950 and '51 and the staff had to be increased to thirteen, nine full-time mechanics and four men in the stockroom. The boom in sales was fuelled in part by the fact that the 650 cc English bikes were remarkable value for money. For about $800 you could buy a machine that would accelerate you and a passenger to over 100 mph, or carry you and 250 pounds of camping gear all the way across the country at between fifty and sixty miles per gallon. It would also run rings around the mostly anemic automobiles of the day, had a delightful burbling exhaust note while cruising and produced a relatively low level of vibration.

For young men especially, they, and the smaller 500 twins, were perfect vehicles for sporting activities. A review of the events held by just one city motorcycle club, gives an idea of just how much of an impact English machines were making on the marketplace. The Royal City Rockets had been in existence for fouteen years and had thirty-five active members, who besides riding their bikes, also held numerous dances, parties, weiner roasts and crab feeds. Their first event of the year was a "50 Miler" cross country enduro which was won by John Peters on an Ariel with Forbes Donald, on a B.S.A., second. The next event was a closed club field meet and TT race. This was won by Dawn Clark on a Norton with Rhys Hull on a B.S.A., second. Number three was a big one, the 1952 PNWMA field meet, which included riders from the United States. It was won by Percy McGowan on a B.S.A. Empire Star with Hull, also B.S.A. mounted, second. Perhaps the most important event for the club was the Chick Fredag Memorial Run, named in honour of the founder of the Rockets who had been killed in an industrial accident. This was laid out over forty-three miles and included six timed sections and five observed sections, starting and finishing at Central Park and taking about four and a half hours to complete. Thirty-four riders entered and the event was won, for the second time, by Trev Deeley. Like other top riders, he was now mounted on a B.S.A.

Club runs were fun, but Trev was bridling at not being able to participate in the increasingly popular events organized by the CMA. He was now a member of the competition committee of the AMA, the only Canadian appointed, but the enforced inactivity on his home turf was getting under his skin. "It bugged the hell out of me," Trev says. "The CMA would sponsor a half-mile race at Ladner and I had to go and sit in the stands and watch these guys go around at about half speed. I was just boiling." Finally he got hold of the head of the AMA, E.C. Smith, explained how anxious he was to compete, and asked if he could be given a six-month suspension if he joined the CMA and went racing. E.C. agreed. The timing was perfect: if he stopped riding in September, his suspension would end just before the Daytona 200 the following year. Entering Daytona was something he wanted to do one last time, both for himself, and to show the lads around the shop there was still some daredevil left in his somewhat overweight thirty-two-year-old body. In the meantime, there were a few points to prove closer to home.

The CMA racing season had begun with a hillclimb on a one-mile section of Grouse Mountain won by Bob Harrison of the Victoria Motorcycle Club on a stock B.S.A. Golden Flash, and followed by a July 1 roadrace on the Abbotsford Airport won by Teddy Hilton from Vancouver on a Triumph. The next roadrace, the following Saturday, was on a real road through a nice section of South Burnaby. Trev rolled a new B.S.A. 500 Star Twin out of his showroom, slapped his AMA racing number, 22, on the front and sides, put on a set of straight pipes, joined the CMA, and proceeded to run away with the event.

Satisfying as that was, even better was to come. The British Columbia half-mile dirt track championship was scheduled for Labour Day in Penticton, the "Peach City" at the south end of Lake Okanagan. Trev had not been there in several years, and had not raced there at all under CMA sanction, and so was a surprise entrant to the hundreds of spectators when he turned up on September 1. It made no difference, as Daredevil Deeley raced off to win both the senior three- and six-mile events.

Trev's success filled him with a renewed sense of confidence. It also prompted the B.S.A. company to offer him a factory sponsorship to ride one of their machines at Daytona. Trev was torn. Although he was a B.S.A. distributor, he had developed a deep loyalty to Harley-Davidson through his racing career and to the company's senior officials, many of whom he had met personally as a factory rider. To try and square the circle, he picked up the telephone and called Walter Davidson in Milwaukee. He said he had an offer from B.S.A. that was too good to refuse, and he hoped Walter wouldn't mind if he raced for the opposition.

Walter didn't mind, perhaps because he had a secret weapon. This was a new side valve V-twin 750, the KRTT model, which he hoped would end Norton's domination of the famous race. With a power output of fifty horsepower, a weight of only 320 pounds and a top speed of 125 mph, the *KR* was going to be a potent threat to the British invasion no matter who rode it.

The event was, as ever, historic. Indian, the nemesis of Harley-Davidson for so many years, had finally sputtered out of existence, to be replaced by the Indian Sales Company fielding a huge team riding English-made Nortons. B.S.A. was also primed for its first win and Harley-Davidson had high expectations for its new KRs. At the start, Paul Goldsmith, No. 3, on a KR got a great start and narrowly led a pack of four down the beach to the first turn. Trev's B.S.A. competition Star Twin got away nicely as well, and felt strong underneath him as he blasted down the sand after the leaders.

When the racing gods decide to frown, trouble comes in a hurry. On this afternoon, it was all over for Norton in a matter of minutes. Dick Klamfoth, the previous year's winner, went out in lap nine. Bobby Hill, who finished second in 1951, went out in lap ten. Clifford "Red" Farwell, who was second in 1952, was on his eleventh lap travelling at over 100 mph when a spectator, forty-seven-year-old Charles Gerrard of Cocoa Beach, Florida, walked onto the course directly in front of him. Both men were killed instantly. Farwell's Norton went straight up into the air, landed and smashed into the crowd, striking Joseph Stahle from Macon, Georgia, injuring him critically. It was the first fatality in the 200-miler since it began in 1937, but it was bound to happen. The great length of the course and the lack of any kind of crowd control, meant riders often found themselves dodging suicidal, short-sighted or drunken spectators. Indeed, only two laps earlier, veteran rider Jimmy Chann, had also connected with a spectator darting across the track and had sustained critical injuries.

Trevor's race continued unaffected by events, but increasingly jinxed by his motor. The Star Twin had began leaking oil past its mag seal and into the magneto due to the high temperatures caused by the long straightaways. The result was that the motor began to miss, fouling the plugs and backfiring as it accelerated away from the corners. Trev's lap speed went down, but the problem didn't seem to be getting any worse, so he pressed on as best he could, ear piercing bangs and unburned hydrocarbons behind him as he went.

Goldsmith, firmly in the lead from lap twenty-three, rode flawlessly to a win in two hours and seven minutes at an average speed just over ninety-four miles an hour. The KR had won its first major victory, and Harley-Davidson had won for the first time since 1940. While the cheering went on in the Harley pits, Trevor banged across the finish line with a rattle of misfires in thirteenth place. Whatever disappointment he felt, was instantly removed by the devastating news of Red Farwell's death. Trev had known him very well, knew his wife, had raced against him and drunk beers with him. In fact, the racers from the Pacific Northwest had planned a party that night after the race to celebrate their successes. The tragedy left Trev numb with shock. It could just as easily have been him.

Red, interviewed before the race, was quoted by the *Seattle Post-Intelligencer* as saying, "You never think of danger in this business. If you start thinking about getting hurt, you had better quit racing. A fellow has to have confidence in his ability and his machine." That's exactly what Trev had always felt, but now he could no longer put the danger out of his mind. The more he thought about it, the more he realized it was time to quit. It had been a glorious, mad run, from the age of eighteen to thirty-two, with the elation of victory more than the agony of defeat, but now it was over. Times had changed.

Times were changing too for motorcycling, and especially Harley-Davidson. The company's victory at Daytona was about to be swept away by a public relations calamity of nuclear dimensions. The origins of the disaster went back to the post-war boom that had seen Fred Deeley Ltd., and all the other car dealers in America, sell just about every vehicle they could get their hands on. The people they were selling to were, by and large, families who wanted a car, even a small car, to carry themselves and their children to work, shopping, and the grandparents' place at Christmas. By 1951, this segment of the population had deserted motorcycling en masse for the chance, as the jingle said, to "See the U.S.A. in a Chevrolet." What was left in the sport were mostly young men who, not coincidentally, had some trouble connecting with the opposite sex. Most of these were just normal kids, but a minority were angry, disaffected youths on the very fringes of society. Unfortunately, in motorcycling's annual field days, rallies and club events, there were now a lot fewer of the sensible, well-behaved, average citizens who had kept the sport on an even keel since its inception fifty years earlier. The rowdies, as a result, began to take over.

A number of incidents had occurred on the AMA's Gypsy Tours over the years, but the one generally identified as the turning point happened when a motorcycle gang called the Booze Fighters descended on the small California town of Hollister on July 4, 1947, for a dirt track race and wound up terrorizing the local citizens for several days. The incident made the cover of a national magazine, but otherwise passed without much notice from the general public. However, it did come to the attention of a writer, Frank Rooney, who wrote a story about it. This wound up as a screenplay by John Paxton, entitled *The Cyclists' Raid*. The screenplay, in turn, was picked up by the Stanley Kramer Company and produced as a film starring Marlon Brando. The producers changed the name to something a little more romantic. When it hit the movie theatres in December, 1953, with a brooding picture of Brando sitting astride a motorcycle, the marquees read, *The Wild One*.

As in real life, the story was about a gang, this one named the Blind Rebels Motorcycle Club, who enter a town, raise hell with another gang, and get into a confrontation with local citizens before being run out by the police. In the film, a resident is killed by Brando's speeding bike when he's hit by a tire iron thrown by an irate mob. The *New York Times* review described the movie as, "a picture of extraordinary candour and courage – a picture that tries to grasp an idea, even though its reach falls short." Brando himself didn't much like it afterwards, saying, "instead of finding out why young people tend to bunch into groups that seek expression in violence, all we did was show the violence."

It was too late for reflection, the damage was done. Across the United States, and much of the rest of the world, the image of motorcycling was now inextricably linked with amoral, antisocial, and illegal activities. Motorcycle riders had changed overnight into "outlaw bikers" in the public mind. As if that wasn't bad enough, Harley-Davidson's image was specifically smeared, even though Brando rode a Triumph Thunderbird in the movie and posed on a Matchless in the studio still shot. This was because the public already knew that motorcyclists who travelled in large groups on club runs and Gypsy Tours were almost always Harley and Indian riders. What the movie said was that these formerly wholesome activities were now a threat to law and order. The people most impressed with the film were bikers in California, who began to imitate art by joining outlaw gangs and wearing large club badges, or "colours," on their jackets; and the state police, who started hassling any group of passing motorcyclists as potential troublemakers.

One victim in the tarring and feathering of the industry was a popular headpiece of the day called a riding hat. This device looked something like the cap worn by a telegraph delivery boy or a ship's captain, with a peak, a short visor and often a pin affixed to the front. Harley-Davidson used it in their advertising, most reputable club members owned one, and Deeley's had sold them for years. In fact they were still selling them when the movie came out for $4.75 in black or green with a white peak. Because Brando wore one in the film, the look was doomed. Not even Elvis Presley, wearing one in 1956, could save it from oblivion.

The reaction in Canada to *The Wild One* was not as severe as it was in the United States. For one thing, the motorcycle gangs were seen as an American phenomenon, like Chicago gangsters during prohibition, and thus not part of the real world. For another, the bad press didn't stick to English bikes because their riders tended to be more individualistic, and less attracted to clubs of any kind. Thirdly, the flat track racing that attracted outlaw bikers, was now giving way to road racing that did not favour their machines or attract them as spectators. The result was that the outlaw biker stigma largely failed to stick on the Canadian motorcycle population, though it found a home in the minds of many parents of young boys, especially their mothers.

Daytona was at the beginning of the year, *The Wild One* at the end. Trev meanwhile had returned to Vancouver, hung up his racing number and resumed managing a motorcycle division that continued to make a handsome profit, unlike the automotive department under his dad. A ten-week strike at the Austin plant had cut into sales by delaying deliveries and a buyers' market for cars made competition on West Broadway tougher than ever.

The poor image of motorcycling had an effect on Trev, who within months tried to do something about it. His initiative was to launch a series of trials-type events at the GVMC. This very English form of motorcycle sport involves a series of observed sections where obstacles make riding a motorcycle extremely difficult. It is done at slow speed, sometimes very slow speed, and points are deducted if a rider touches a foot to the ground to steady his machine. Lightweight bikes are an asset, particularly reliable single-cylinder thumpers that can keep turning a wheel increasingly bogged down in mud. Across the lower mainland and on Vancouver Island there was an ample supply of rain, mud and Englishmen, so the events got off to a successful start. It was also a clever public relations ploy. If anything looked less like a bunch of outlaw bikers, it was a group of Barbour-clad Englishmen in tweed caps negotiating Ariel Red Hunters over three-foot logs.

The Indian motorcycle saga, meanwhile, was still playing itself out. Ablitt had finally sold all the remainder of his parts inventory to Trev for $20,000, ten times the original amount he had offered. The haul had been enormous, motors, frames, spare parts, a Triumph 500 cc GP; all the accumulation of Ablitt's twenty years in the business. Some of the accessories were put on display, and the small high-usage parts were kept in inventory to repair the Indians that still came into the shop for fix-up. The frames were another matter. Just as his father had in the 1930s, Trev assigned mechanics to take Indian frames out into the laneway and cut them up in their spare time. Passing would-be Indian owners would occasionally offer to take a frame or pay for its scrap value. They would always be refused.

"We've got our orders," the mechanics would reply.

Finally, a day came when the motorcycle department needed more storage and the only space left was the area on the second floor where the bulk of the remaining Indian spares was being kept. The demand for Indian parts was down to a trickle, the need for more room was urgent, so Trevor ordered that the whole lot be scrapped. A hole was cut in the floor, a truck driven into the shop underneath, and the entire pile – frames, motors, tinware and spares – was tossed into the vehicle and driven away. The Indian customers in future would be told one thing; buy a Harley.

Bad press, fewer car sales and dead Indians weren't the only problems though: the Deeleys found themselves facing an internal family dispute in 1954.

Ray Deeley had never been happy with the division of power that saw him stuck with the much smaller bicycle business compared with Fred Jr.'s control over cars, and Trevor's over motorcycles. He was also unhappy with the lack of recognition the bicycle business received from his brother. It always ran at a profit, even during the war when there weren't any cars or motorcycles to be sold, but there had been no thanks from Fred Jr. for holding the fort through hard times. It rankled so much, he and his wife avoided Fred Jr. and Islay at family occasions, visiting Fred Sr. and Elizabeth separately if at all possible. When Fred Sr. decided to retire and hand the main responsibility for the company over to Fred Jr., the decision was too much for Ray. He wanted nothing to do with Fred Deeley Ltd. if Fred Jr. was going to be the man in charge.

"I want to run the bicycle business without any interference from Fred," he told his father.

"Right, the bicycle shop's yours," Fred Sr. replied. "Don't phone me; you're on your own."

The name on the store stayed the same, it was still Fred Deeley Cycles, but it was actually an entirely separate company, Fred Deeley Cycles Ltd., not a division of Fred Deeley Ltd. Just about the only person this mattered to was Ray's son. He had been working in the family business since he left high school in 1948 and was in car sales when the split occurred. Ray Jr. now decided his best interests lay with his father rather than his uncle and he quit to work in bicycles. The hard feelings that followed him out the door were to get worse. At no time in the discussion between Fred Sr. and Ray had there been any consideration given to avoiding competition between the two companies with virtually the same name. When that happened ten years later, Fred Jr. was the one who was outraged.

The year 1955 wasn't much better for the automotive division than the previous two years. A British railway strike shut off the supply of cars and set Deeley deliveries back two months. Fred Jr. kept overheads low, increased his servicing, and tried every way he could to eke out a profit from the Austin lineup. His command centre was a small office on the top storey of what had been the old motorcycle building. Staff and visitors reached it by climbing a flight of stairs to a small hallway bounded by the receptionist, a waiting area and his office door. Once ushered in, they discovered a simple, carpeted room with a large, high desk across one corner facing a dark brown leather couch on the near wall. Behind the desk to one side was a credenza, to the other a window in which sat a loud air conditioning unit. To the left of the door was a second window that looked east on West Broadway. There were also two leatherette and pipe chairs in the room and a small arborite table. On the edge of the glass covered desk was a chrome water jug. Nowhere in this spartan environment was there a hint of the financial powerhouse that was grinding away just down the hall, controlling five divisions, managing three dealer networks and looking after more than a dozen pieces of property. Nor was there any indication of Fred Jr.'s increasingly lavish lifestyle at home, with a yacht, society friends and regular vacations to the Hawaiian Islands. A potted plant, one imagines, would have given his employees the wrong impression when they asked for a raise.

At the motorcycle shop, things were different. Trev, unlike his father, had an easy feel for human relations, and established a relaxed management style in which anyone could walk into his office and speak up if they had a problem. He was a stickler for quality workmanship and housekeeping, honesty and punctuality, but somehow it was easier to take coming from him than the old man. One reason was that Trev hobnobbed with the boys. Every Friday, the staff would get together when they got off work at 5:30, buy a couple of cases of beer, and sit around and chew the fat. Trevor usually joined them, buying the beer when it was his turn. Just like the others, he regularly complained about Fred Jr. being so tight.

If you take a close look at a picture of the Deeley staff that used to gather on Fridays, you'll see a familiar, and unexpected, face — Billy Mathews. This most successful Canadian to ever race at Daytona, with two wins and two second place finishes, was now working for Trev Deeley. Mathews was a heavy drinker who managed to make as many enemies as friends in his steelworking home town. One day he called Trev and said he needed a job. Nobody in Hamilton would hire him, would Trevor? Trev immediately said yes, and wired Mathews $500 to come out west with his wife. Nothing happened. Weeks went by and Trev figured he'd seen the last of Mathews and the money. Then unexpectedly, the racer rolled up in his car. He hadn't left Ontario immediately and had taken his time to come out, but he was now reporting for work. Mathews turned out to be a good, if occasionally temperamental, employee — he once threw a hammer at Trevor and missed — who stayed with the company for a long time, before switching to the provincial government where the hours were shorter, the pay higher and a pension was provided at the end of the road. Years later Trevor would tell his friends he had got even with Mathews for the snub at Daytona by having him work for him.

The truth, as usual, was more complex. Trevor, the successful motorcycle racer, had developed a deep respect for others in the sport, and was emotionally inclined to help them out if he could. He also had his grandfather's appreciation, gained in bicycles, that his shop should have a close connection to the racing world in order to help sales and keep abreast of technical innovations. Another example of this occurred in 1955 when Ian McGuffie drove up to the motorcycle shop looking for work. McGuffie, a short Scot with a nimble turn of phrase, had raced at the Isle of Man in 1950 in a junior event and come in second. Leaving his wife Elizabeth outside in his car, he walked into the shop and asked Bobby Dawe if he needed another mechanic. As he did so, he saw a B.S.A. TT poster up on the wall and remarked he'd run in the famous race himself. Dawe, also a racer, took him straight in to see Trevor. The upshot was that when McGuffie emerged from 606 to talk to Elizabeth waiting patiently in the car, he was already a Deeley employee.

The next year, B.S.A. came out with a special version of their Gold Star 500 cc single to race at Daytona. This had the latest DBD34 motor, Amal 1½" GP carb, five gallon tank and a T2 gearbox with needle roller bearing internals. It also came with a solid rear suspension and two sets of handlebars; a wide one for the corners and clip-ons for the straights. Trevor imported six of these Daytona Specials and sold three of them, but the remaining three looked as if they weren't going to go out the door. Dawe turned to Trevor one day and said, "Why don't you give one of them to McGuffie?" He agreed, on condition McGuffie go out and race it at Abbotsford airport, then the site of roadraces sponsored by the CMA. It was a good combination. The little Scot on the forty HP machine was invincible and by the end of the year was Canadian National Champion.

"To put it bluntly," McGuffie recalls, "it went like stink. It only weighed 290 pounds and quite honestly I could just blow past people. I won races so easily, it was unbelievable."

McGuffie soon felt quite at home in the chummy atmosphere of the Deeley shop, and in the regular visits to the local pubs. As a result, he inadvertently played a part in an evening that caused red faces for practically everyone. On this occasion, as a surprise, Trev hired a good looking stripper, Vicki Bleu, to put on an act for the boys in an upstairs room at the Admiral Hotel on East Hastings. This went over well with the slightly intoxicated all-male staff, particularly Ian McGuffie, who brought along his camera to capture the exotic Miss Bleu on film. Afterwards, some of the staff wound up shooting craps with her when she got back into her clothes. At the end of the evening, Trev, by now quite smashed, drove Vicki home. When they got there, she invited him up for a drink. Who should he find there but a member of the Vancouver motorcycle squad. Just about the only other thing he can remember is that she had a row of telephones along one wall, each with a cord long enough for the user to walk practically anywhere in the apartment. The next morning, Trev badly hung over, told the staff he wasn't to be interrupted and disappeared into his office, hoping the worst effects would soon be over.

They weren't. First, Vicki, in an expansive mood after a successful event, phoned to say thank you for the good time she'd had. Unfortunately, she mistakenly phoned the car dealership, and wound up thanking the "Mr. Deeley" at 901 West Broadway who knew nothing about it. Next, the indefatigable Ms. Bleu discovered Trev's wallet, which had somehow fallen out of his pants during the visit. An hour or so later, dressed to the nines, she walked into the motorcycle shop and asked for Trevor. Doug Herbert, who was at the counter at the time, and who like everyone else had orders not to disturb the boss, said he wasn't there.

"Well," said Vicki, "give him this."

She pulled the wallet out of her purse, laid it on the counter and walked out of the shop. Whatever had happened at the apartment the night before, it was soon to be the cause of much speculation among the staff at 606. Even that wasn't the end of it, though. McGuffie, naturally enough, developed the pictures he had taken. In due course, these were discovered by Elizabeth McGuffie, who was, as Queen Victoria put it, not amused. She got on the telephone pronto and phoned the wives of all the Deeley employees who had been at the stag and gave them a full description of the snaps. As might be expected, there was hell to pay all round.

Trevor was now an increasingly busy and successful businessman in his own right. Although he still didn't sign the cheques, his store with fifteen employees was more profitable than the automotive division under his dad with 150. One reason was that Triumph motorcycles were on a roll, following the setting of a world speed record by Johnny Allen of 214.4 mph on the Bonneville salt flats with a streamlined 640 cc Thunderbird in 1956. The company quickly developed a 650 cc twin with dual carbs and a hot cam and called it the Triumph Bonneville. It was immensely popular, producing a growing following that looked down their noses at Trev's other main brand, Harley-Davidson.

This may have been one reason Trev decided to get his race bike out of storage and show his staff, his customers and his old racing buddies what the rear end of a Harley-Davidson looked like. The track he selected for his final appearance was the three-quarter-mile oval at Bremerton, Washington, a venue he had triumphed at many times before. There to meet him were some of his old racing competitors, and in particular, Gene Theisen, whom he'd raced against all over the Northwest, in Canada, and twice at Daytona, beating him in 1950, losing to him in 1953. Theisen, for his part was a good friend, but this last chance to run Trev's H-D into the ground with his B.S.A. was too good to pass up.

"I wanted to beat him so bad, but by golly, he just flat beat me,"

Theisen recalled later. "And I think that's the last race that Trevor ever rode."

It hadn't been easy, either. Trev got off to a bad start and was the final rider into the first corner. His old skills returned as he roared up the backstretch and he began to pass the back markers. It still took him most of the race to work his way up to second place. Through the dust, Trev could see Theisen was one full straightaway length ahead. He held the throttle open and reeled him in, caught him and finally passed to win.

For Trev it felt good personally and professionally to have Theisen and the others pat him on the back afterwards. He had shown everyone he was still the champ and Harley-Davidson was still the winning make. Unfortunately, he was only one rider amid a sea of British bikes on America's racetracks.

The Milwaukee factory meanwhile, very aware of the inroads being made by British bikes, moved to do something to meet the competition head on. It introduced a smaller sports model in 1957, called the Sportster, which took on the challenge with a 55 cu. in. (900 cc) OHV engine. The next year, Harley threw in larger valves and increased horsepower by twelve percent to make certain it could still win where it counted, at stop light drag racing across America.

Trev's personal life was racing ahead as well. He had borrowed from his grandfather to buy his first home at 3025 East 4th Avenue in the late 1940s, and a few years later moved to a larger home on Clinton St. in Burnaby where he had a pool built in the back yard. A unique feature of the pool was that it had a rock in one corner that Trevor left when the contractor suggested removing it with dynamite. Instead of blowing it up, Trev had steps built to cover it, turning a problem into an asset. It was a constant reminder that in life as in business, problems were just as likely to be opportunities. Trev was also moving up in the car world, taking advantage of his father's dealership to obtain demonstrators to use as his personal transportation.

The event that changed his life came in the mail.

Trevor, being the manager, got the mail when it came into the shop in the morning. This would consist of the usual assortment of bills, orders, payments, and advertising materials, and often a motorcycle magazine, because Trev subscribed to them all; *Cycle*, *Motorcycle*, and *Motorcyclist* from the United States as well as publications from England. When there was time, he would lean back in his chair and leaf through the latest issues to see what was new.

Something caught his eye. It was a small article about a U.S. soldier who had been in Japan and had brought back a 250 cc motorcycle. A picture went with the story which said the bike was "made by Honda Motor Company in Tokyo." Something clicked in his mind. In twenty-two years in the business, this was the first Japanese motorcycle he had ever seen. He put the magazine down on his desk and turned to his typewriter. Taking a piece of paper with the Fred Deeley Ltd. letterhead, he wrote a short note to the president of the Honda Motor Company in Tokyo, Japan. In it he said he had heard about their motorcycles — "read" would have been more accurate — and they seemed very interesting. The second sentence said that British Columbia was very much like Japan and so Honda motorcycles could be very suitable for this market. He concluded by asking for further information. That was it. There was no description of Fred Deeley Ltd., no mention the company was the largest motorcycle importer on the Canadian west coast, no references to Trev's two decades in the industry. The only hint was in the letterhead which said Deeley's was the distributor for B.S.A. and Triumph motorcycles. Trev put the letter in his outgoing mail basket and thought nothing more about it.

Of far more concern to him at the time were his Triumph, B.S.A., Ariel and Norton dealers across the province and, for B.S.A. and Ariel, in neighbouring Alberta. These were the days before manufacturer "floor plans," and Fred Deeley Ltd. was supporting the weaker dealers by giving them bikes on consignment. When they sold them, they were supposed to remit the money promptly to Vancouver. Some did, but some did not, and it was up to Trevor to go and winkle the cash out of them. To do this, he was increasingly on the road. Road trips had always been part of the Fred Deeley Ltd. philosophy. Fred Sr. had travelled around the country to see his dealers in the 1920s, and Fred Jr. had done so in the 1930s. But with Trev, they became a kind of religion. He began going on sales trips before the motorcycle shop moved to 606 East Broadway, and continued to do so throughout the 1950s. It was obvious if he could motivate the dealers to move the product and then keep the money flowing back to the coast, his department would have far more success than it could ever achieve on its own.

Sometimes it was hard going. Trev would go into a shop and find the consigned bike was not there and he hadn't been paid for it. He would confront the dealer who would say he'd pay for it at the end of the month. What was really galling was that there were sometimes other bikes, from other distributors, sitting on the floor that had been paid for. On occasion Trev had to become a detective, interviewing the customer to find out if he had paid, or his bank manager, before having it out with the dealer. It was a tricky balancing act. You had to push hard to get the money, but you couldn't push too hard or you might lose the dealer, and never get the money. Whatever happened, Trev had one final crisis at the end of each trip; he had to meet his father and the accountant, Lloyd Perry, and account for all the consigned inventory, paid for and otherwise. As he lay awake at night in hard hotel beds far from home, he vowed to himself he would some day separate the schmoozing aspect of his trips from the bill collecting function. It was damned hard to motivate dealers and dun them for unpaid bills at the same time.

If there is anything odd about this aspect of Trev's business career, it is how divorced he was from the actual motorcycles he was selling. Looking back today, many riders who were kids at the time can reel off motorcycle statistics, rank models inside various brands and even describe the colour schemes of their favourite bikes from year to year. Trev can't remember any of it; what brands were popular, what were good value or which ones turned out to be dogs. Looking back he remembers exchanging bikes for dealers, taking away models that didn't sell and replacing them with others, but he has no idea now which were which. You can get a sense of where his priorities lay, by his comment on bike exchanges:

"We had to do it," he says, "to get the volume."

Vera announced she was pregnant again. Despite the wishes of her doctor, and the tragedy surrounding her first child, she was determined to produce a son for her husband to carry on the Deeley name. He, while honestly concerned, secretly hoped she would. He was thirty-eight years old, soon to be into his forties; there shouldn't be too big a gap between him and the next generation.

The first reply was back from Honda in Japan. It gave the prices of a couple of models – the 50 cc Cub and a 250 cc model – and suggested he order one. Trev probably would have, too, but in the meantime he'd spoken to his father about the story and Fred Jr. had flatly rejected the idea of buying a Japanese bike. "We fought those bastards during the war, why should we help them now?" he added by way of explanation. Trev wrote back anyway and said he didn't want to order one because he hadn't seen one and didn't know how good they were. The Honda company replied that they would be opening a distributorship in Los Angeles in 1959, and suggested he could see them then. Trev replied in a letter that was an awfully long time to wait and that since, "I feel I can do a job on this, I'd like to get started right away."

Persistence must have worn Honda down, because in their next letter they said, "We're sending you a 250 cc Honda Dream free of charge."

The bike arrived in late November, 1957, a brand new, blue 250 cc Honda Dream. The Japanese factory had paid the freight; all Trevor had to do was get it out of customs. It was a typical November day in Vancouver, dark, cold and raining, but Trev couldn't wait to take it for its first spin around the block. He came back impressed beyond belief. The amazing little bike had an electric start, turn signals and was as quiet as a sewing machine, but it went like blazes. The second person on it was Bobby Dawe. Next up was Billy Mathews. Mathews shot off down Broadway and came back a few minutes later with the bike scraped all down one side. Someone had driven up to a stop sign who looked to Mathews as if he wasn't going to stop. Mathews had clamped on the brakes and the slippery new tires had instantly lost traction.

"What the hell were you trying to do," Trev yelled at him, "see how fast it would go?"

Everyone thought Trevor was joking, but he was actually pretty annoyed. The moment he'd seen the bike he knew he wanted to make another pitch to his father, and a smashed turn signal wouldn't help his case any.

Before his father saw it however, Fred Sr. showed up. The family patriarch, then seventy-six, walked all around the bike a couple of times, obviously very intrigued. He had reason to be. The Dream was beautifully put together, with excellent paint, sophisticated castings and besides its electric start, it had a twin cylinder overhead cam engine, enclosed chain and lots of chrome. Trevor watched him inspect it and thought to himself, *if it's half as good as it looks, it's going to be twice as good as anything we've got.* There was no point in comparing it to a single cylinder 250 cc B.S.A. C10 or C11, there was no comparison. For one thing, the Honda had a much higher top speed. In any contest, it would just walk away from the B.S.A. In some ways it was better even than a 500 cc Triumph. Fred Sr. motioned Trev to follow him out into the laneway.

"Look," he said, "I don't think that's going to sell. We're not going to handle it. You're not to bring in another one. That's it." And then he left.

Trev went home to Vera, who was expecting the baby in January, and told her his father and grandfather were crazy. They were missing the opportunity of a lifetime. It was as clear as crystal the Japanese were putting more value into their product than either the Europeans or the British, and Deeley's would be foolish not to handle them. There was some question in his mind how the Hondas would stand up to the abuse they'd be given by North American riders, but he was optimistic on this too. The damn thing was just so good looking on the outside, it had to be well engineered internally. Most of all, Trev was flabbergasted by the electric start. That feature alone would open the bike market up to women riders who objected to kicking motorcycles to fire their ignition and get them started.

"I'm going to quit and import them myself," Trev announced finally.

Telling a pregnant wife you are going to resign from a very successful family company takes some nerve. However, the next day, Trevor was still determined when he drove over to 901 West Broadway for a meeting with his father and grandfather. He knew Fred Sr. would be in his office, he was retired but showed up first thing anyway; and he knew Fred Jr. would arrive around 10:30, so he timed his visit for a few minutes later. Getting the two of them together, he told them the Honda franchise was the opportunity of a lifetime. If they weren't interested in it, he was going to leave the company. They weren't.

"I'm just going to leave," he said. "This is not right. We're missing out on a good thing."

Trevor might have thought about leaving in the past, but this was the first time he had actually verbalized the feeling to his father and grandfather. This time the issue wasn't about hurt emotions, it was over a significant business decision. And this time, it wasn't a threat; it was a fact. Fred Jr., the active head of the company, could have said a lot of things in reply. He could have criticized Trevor, knocked the Japanese, or escalated the confrontation with his son. In fact, what he did was conciliatory.

"Just take it easy and I'll talk to you later," he said.

Trevor drove back to his shop on East Broadway wondering what would happen next. For years he had avoided confrontations with his father, but now he had done so openly, formally and in front of Fred Sr., who as far as he knew, supported Fred Jr. The cat was truly among the pigeons.

Later that afternoon, Fred Jr. arrived at the motorcycle shop and went into Trev's office with a strange look on his face.

"Your granddad and I think you're wrong, this will never go. But if you want to give it a try, go ahead."

Vera had been admitted to hospital early because her doctors were worried about both her and the baby. When Trev went to the hospital to see Vera, he was jubilant. He had made his point, even if he had to go to the wall to do so. The future, with a new sense of respect from his father, a whole new world of importing ahead of him and a new child on the way, looked as bright as it had ever done. After further corresponding with Honda, Trev obtained the distributorship for Western Canada, and put in his first order, mostly for 50 cc Honda Cubs. Three weeks later, Vera went into an early labour.

If Trev had not been an atheist before, he was about to become one.

CHAPTER SEVEN

THE BIRTH OF Trev and Vera's little girl was traumatic in all three senses of the word: a physical wound, a physical shock following a wound, and an emotional shock following a stressful event. While Trevor waited, five days before Christmas, outside the operating theatre of St. Paul's hospital in Vancouver, the delivery was going from bad to worse. Vera's heart, damaged by rheumatic fever as a child, failed under the stress of labour and the premature baby had to be rescued by Caesarean section. The gynecologist emerged to say it was touch and go if either the mother or daughter would live. Trevor went home, opened the fridge, and lined up three pounds of butter, end to end on the kitchen table. They were the same size as his new daughter.

The next eleven days are a total blank, wiped clean of memory, feeling and emotion like a sheet of virgin snow on a northern lake in January.

Vera died of heart failure. Trevor held her in his arms until her body got cold. The funeral, delayed by the holiday, was on New Year's Eve at the Forest Lawn Memorial Park and Mortuary. It was a typical Vancouver winter day; cold, rainy and miserable. A large police escort led the funeral cortege from the funeral home at 8th and Kingsway. Trevor had to be practically carried to the open grave, one man on each side. Maria Wasilieff broke down and cried hysterically at the death of her daughter. She had lost a husband to Trev's motorcycle, now she was losing a daughter to his child. Those attending were touched by an overpowering sense of grief; Trev silent, almost comatose; Maria wailing and screaming. They were also surprised that no church service was held beforehand to help act as a catharsis for the living. Vera had been married without one, and now she was being buried without one. Tragically, the plot in the cemetery's Summit Section was less than a hundred feet from Trev and Vera's son's grave in Babyland. When it was installed, the plaque on the ground read: *Loved and Remembered – Always.*

After the burial, the guests were invited to a wake. Fred Jr., who often drank heavily in the evenings, and who had too much on this occasion, wandered around showing everyone a ring he had bought for Vera and wept emotionally. Despite this being the most private of all family affairs, one of those who attended was the new Harley-Davidson company representative for the area.

Coping with grief takes many forms. For Trev, who had genuinely been in love for nineteen years, coping with Vera's death meant getting rid of each and every object that reminded him of what he had lost. As soon as he could, he put his house at Clinton Street on the market, and began giving away, selling or discarding Vera's effects and mementoes of their life together. Even his tools, in a basement shop he had built, went out the door. The most profound reminder of Vera, of course, was their daughter, who eventually was discharged from hospital, a small baby, but a healthy one, named as Vera had wished, Dawne, and as Trevor wished, Elizabeth, after his grandmother Lizzy.

Trev moved back to his parents' home and the baby was taken in by his mother. Islay could see Trevor was in no mood to look after a new baby, so at fifty-six years of age, she offered to raise her granddaughter as her own. Trev in his anger and sorrow, agreed. He was sick with grief and he wanted nothing to do with it. What he wanted was to get away; away from the house, the city, even the country. He drove down to Bellingham, Washington, and dropped in on his old friend, Fred Pazaski, who was at work.

"Fred," Trev said, "I need your company. I want you to go to Seattle with me."

Pazaski's partner in the Harley shop said go ahead, so he climbed into Trev's car and the two buddies went off to Seattle. For three days they stayed at the City Center Motel, went to the local motorcycle dealerships, went shopping for clothes, drank VO whiskey and talked. Trev had an obsession about buying shoes, and picked up about $300 worth, quite a lot at the time. Pazaski asked him what he was going to do. Trevor said he didn't know. He was living for the moment, not the past, or the future.

Two other people he visited for several weeks in this period were Freddy Chamberlain and his wife Joan, old friends who had a house and farm near Kelowna in the Okanagan Valley. While there, to cheer himself up, he bought a brand new 1958 Chevrolet Impala convertible from Victory Motors on Pendozi St. for $4,175.87. It was all white with a red leather interior and Trev had it loaded with all the extras: a high performance V-8, a Turboglide transmission, power brakes, electric windows, GM custom radio, rear seat speaker and whitewall tires. On the dash, Trev installed a small gold plaque which read *This car especially built for Trev Deeley*. It wasn't, of course, but the plaque helped lift his spirits.

The second thing he decided to do was to take up flying. He had always been interested in aviation, had gone up as a child and had flown often as an adult on commercial aircraft. The idea of flying combined some of the elements that had attracted him originally to motorcycling – the need for judgement, the physical thrill and the importance of a good motor. It was also an excellent form of rebellion, because Fred Jr. had a pathological fear of flying and would sooner take a train all the way across Canada than step into an aircraft. But there was also another factor, a desire to do something that so concentrated the mind it wouldn't have time to reminisce on the recent past. Being suspended four miles in the air over some of the roughest terrain in the country with one's life at the whim of a carburetor would certainly provide the necessary focus. The apparent reason for starting was some persistent prodding from a long-time friend, Bill McGibbon, who worked for Auto Electric on Seymour Street, the Lucas distributor. He had a Piper TriPacer and knew Trevor needed a diversion. But there was also a subliminal impetus as well, right in his shop. Affixed to both sides of the Honda's tank was the company logo, a right wing on the right side, a left wing on the left. He had stared at the bike long enough for the message to get through: wings equal flying.

The lessons started immediately after Bill first took him up in his TriPacer, at the Aero Club of British Columbia under the tutelage of one of the club's instructors, John Backum. After two lessons in a Fleet Canuck, Backum decided to move to Whitehorse, and Trev was handed over to another instructor, Jim McGinnis.

Trev introduced himself with his usual charm and a big smile, but there was an underlying edge to the discussion that showed he didn't want to be kept waiting. He said he would be at the airport at five minutes to ten, precisely, every day and he asked McGinnis to make sure he was too.

"I've got a business to run, so I can't wait around," Trev added for emphasis.

McGinnis, who was altogether a more relaxed individual, had always had a more flexible approach, allowing two hours for a student to arrive at the airport, go up for the lesson and get back down again. It was clear, in Trev's case, he would have to pull up his socks and fill the entire lesson with work. The Aero Club at the time was run out of an old building in a grassy area just north of where Okanagan Helicopters is now located at the Vancouver International Airport. It was a relatively large semi-official organization registered under the Societies Act and affiliated with the Royal Canadian Flying Club. It had five instructors, trainer aircraft, and as with most such organizations, a bar and an active social program.

Trevor made short work of flying school, swotting the theory of flight, weather, map reading and regulations, and taking less than seven hours of instruction to master the fundamentals of aircraft control. His first solo in Fleet Canuck CF-END was on April 6, 1958. "He went solo pretty quickly," McGinnis recalls. "Trevor being a motorcycle man, nothing scares him you know. He did very well." In fact, he enjoyed it thoroughly. He had a deft touch in the air, not overcontrolling and not overconfident, and progressed rapidly towards his private pilot's licence. On occasion he would jump on a Harley-Davidson from the shop and run down to the airport for a flight and then ride back to work for an afternoon in the office.

After staying briefly at his parents' home, Trev moved into a cottage he and Vera had bought in Deep Cove while they were living in Burnaby. It looked out on Indian Arm, not far from his grandfather's place where he and Vera had stayed a little over a decade earlier. Since he had not lived there permanently, there were fewer memories to haunt him when he returned home at night or sat on the dock looking east across the water to the tree-lined shore opposite. One evening as he sat there nursing a drink, a passing motorboat conked out, just opposite the dock. As it turned out, the boat was powered by an American-made Scott Atwater, a make Trev himself had been selling at 606 East Broadway.

Trev waved the boat owner, Stuart Whitehouse, to come alongside, joshing him as he did so about not buying the unreliable motor from his store. That meeting led to others, because the two men liked each other's company and found they had a lot in common.

Trev might have had a cottage, a car, a boat and been taking flying lessons, but he was still running very close to the line financially and so made do with entertainment near to home. The most interesting spot nearby was the Wigwam Inn, at the head of the inlet. This venerable establishment had originally been built as a cottage for the Kaiser before the First World War and was now a kind of roadhouse you could reach by water. Trev and Stuart Whitehouse would run their little outboards up the inlet on a Saturday evening, have a few drinks, and roar back down to their respective homes on either side. One evening Trev, who insisted on lots of ice in his drinks, decided to take some ice back with him so he could have another drink on his way home. The only thing that could be found to put the ice into was a floppy chocolate bar box. Trev negotiated the gangway, but when he went to step on the swimgrid at the back of his boat, slipped and fell in. He sank like a stone, which wasn't surprising. What did amaze Whitehouse was that when he surfaced, Trev was still holding the tray and the ice cubes were still in it!

"Well, what the hell are you looking at," Trev sputtered. "Take the goddamn ice cubes."

It was on another evening with Stuart and his wife Mary, cruising up the inlet in their little boat, that Trev revealed one of his innermost thoughts.

"If I ever get fortunate one day and make any real money," he said, "I'm going to take you somewhere nice and sit on the back of a big yacht and be waited on and not have any money problems at all."

The Whitehouses smiled at being included in his dream, but didn't take him very seriously. For Trevor, however, it was more than a fantasy; it had become a beacon. From the period after the war when he almost quit the family company, through the current year of 1958 to the distant future in the 1980s, he would hold onto it through thick and thin. His father, who had made his life so miserable, would eventually die, and the Deeley empire would be his.

One day when he returned from his flying lesson he noticed Bobby Dawe talking with an attractive little blonde who looked very much like Vera. Dawe had discovered her working at Tesslers Dry Cleaning next door to the motorcycle store at 606 East Broadway and the two occasionally took their sandwiches to a field to have lunch together.

"Who was that?" Trev asked.

"Joy Seiba" Dawe replied. "Want to meet her?"

"Yeah, I sure would."

"Fine. I'll set you up."

Dawe was as good as his word and the relationship clicked right from the start. For one thing Trev and Joy found they had a common friend, Mary Ellen Friesen. For another, their feelings were mutually complimentary. Joy was impressed with Trev's warm personality, his status and his obvious need for affection. Trev found a woman to hold onto and a shoulder to lean on that was remarkably similar to the one he had lost. In retrospect, it was a classic rebound relationship, but that hardly mattered at the time, nor did the fact that Joy was married. It wasn't long before they were dating regularly and Trev introduced her to his other new love, flying.

Trev was spending so much time at the Aero Club, he talked Joy into taking flying lessons as well. His argument was, "Since we're going to be flying around together, we might as well both learn how to fly." Joy, obviously starting to fall for the guy, agreed and began taking lessons from instructor Tony Cosgrove. Trev, meanwhile, upgraded his licence with a tough-looking woman instructor, Helen Harrison, and got a float endorsement June 22, 1958. He could now fly a Cessna 170 he had purchased, CF-EIU, which he nicknamed "The Witch Doctor" because of the sound of the registration letters.

It wasn't all up in the clouds though; some of the action was on the ground. When the sun descended into the Pacific and the runway lights glowed in the distance under the mantle of stars overhead, Trev and Joy would go to club dances and enjoy an increasingly active social life. As they sat chatting with a group of his new friends, Trev couldn't help noticing one of the other women on the dance floor, a tall redhead married to fellow club member Bill Christopher.

Trevor had ordered about fifty Hondas; a combination of 50 cc Cubs, 125 cc Benlys, and 250 cc and 305 cc Dreams. The Benly was a particularly delightful little bike, with a huge front drum brake, silver tank, forward-inclined OHC twin-cylinder engine, electric start, five speed gearbox, flat bars and even a little plastic racing-type windscreen. But the star of the shipment was the

C100 Honda Super Cub. This little machine more closely resembled a woman's bicycle than a motorcycle, because it had a large opening in the frame between the handlebars and the seat, which gave it the nickname "stepthrough," because you could step through it to get on. It was powered by a horizontal 50 cc OHV engine that would rev to 9,500 rpm and put out four-and-a-half horsepower, enough to propel it up to forty-two mph. It also had an electric start, an enclosed drive chain, plastic leg shields and seating for two passengers. Amazingly for a motorcycle, then or now, it also had an automatic transmission.

Trev thought about the trouble he'd had convincing his dad to let him import Hondas and realized they were going to be a hard sell to his dealers as well. As a result he decided to take the bikes with him and let the dealers see for themselves how well built they were. This was quite a change from the usual routine, in which he would make the rounds with a catalogue of next year's models and an order book. It was impossible to ship the bikes to each city, so he decided to launch Honda by calling a meeting of all his Alberta dealers at the Palliser Hotel in Calgary.

To make it a more complete event, Trevor shipped his new B.S.A.s, Ariels, an NSU and a French scooter called the Manura as well as the Hondas. In Calgary the day before the meeting, he spent most of the evening bringing the bikes up in the freight elevator to the second floor, pushing them down a long hallway and setting them up in two adjoining rooms. The B.S.A.s went in the main room with the Ariels, the NSU and the Manura; the Hondas were all kept hidden next door. The next morning the eight dealers showed up and Trev treated them to a traditional western breakfast in the hotel restaurant. Those attending included Ed and Norm Green from Alberta Cycle in Edmonton, Glen Turple from Red Deer and Bob Kane from Calgary. Then it was back to the suite where Trev expounded on the features of the new Beezers and the little French scooter. And then he said he had a surprise for them. Moving to the side of the room, he threw open the adjoining door and revealed the brand new Hondas.

The reaction, was one of complete, utter disbelief.

None of them had seen a Japanese motorcycle before and they examined the machines with a sense of scorn and incredulity. Norm Green remembers his first reaction was that they were junk; he assumed the little things would probably break down going around the block. Trev talked up the Hondas, described their sophisticated technical specifications and told the dealers what they were like to ride. He could just as easily have been talking to the Rocky Mountains, sixty-odd miles away. Not one of the dealers agreed to buy a single Honda. Green, in fact, was more interested in the Manura and ordered two of them.

"I think my reaction was pretty well general," Green says. "Most of the dealers who were there, dealers from Calgary, Lethbridge, and ourselves, felt that this Japanese stuff was unknown. It was a Japanese product and therefore it was no good. Boy, were we fooled."

Trevor was now in a bind. He had fought hard to get a chance to distribute Hondas, and now his dealers had turned him down flat. "Well, look," he said to them finally. "Take a crate of three. You don't have to pay for them, I'll give them to you on consignment. What have you got to lose?" A number of the dealers more or less took pity on him and agreed to take them as long as they didn't have to pay. Trev Deeley was obviously wrong about Japanese bikes, but they owed him a few favours, so why not.

When the bikes were all rolled out the door and into the dealers' trucks, and he had shaken everyone's hand, and wished them well, and laughed at their jokes, smiling the whole time, Trevor felt intensely depressed. Just about everyone he respected in the business had now told him he was dead wrong to import the Hondas, from his grandfather, to his father, to his mechanics and now his Alberta dealers. *Well maybe they're right*, he thought disconsolately. *Maybe I am wrong.* What was worse, he would shortly have to admit this to Fred Sr. and Jr. With a heavy heart, Trev got in his car and decided to take a few extra days getting back to Vancouver, the longer the better.

As he drove west towards the mountains, Bob Kane put the wheels in motion to try and get rid of the Super Cubs he'd just been lumbered with. He put an ad in the Calgary paper that said he was selling Hondas for $235. He didn't expect much of a reaction. The next morning people were lined up at the door of his shop! He couldn't believe it. He had never seen anything like it before. For years he had been trying to whip up interest in motorcycles and now they were crowding into his store to buy these little stepthroughs from Japan. Unknown to him or to Trevor, now dawdling his way through the Kootenays, much the same thing was happening with the other dealers who had been at the meeting. Ed Green, for example, no sooner put a Super Cub on the showroom floor, than someone walked in and bought it. Hondas were hot!

Trevor rolled up to 606 East Broadway five days after leaving Calgary, with as the saying goes, his belly lower to the ground than a snake. Bobby Dawe had a surprise for him. The Hondas were already back-ordered.

It was as if the floodgates had suddenly opened. People who had never considered motorcycles before, who had never been to a motorcycle shop in their lives, people who had to find where the shops were by looking up their addresses in the Yellow Pages, suddenly took the Honda Super Cub to their heart. It was neat, it was clean, it carried two, and it was half the price of everything else on the market, particularly NSU Prinz and Lambretta scooters. The orders flooded in, the waiting lists mounted and Trev found himself besieged by businessmen who suddenly wanted to become Honda dealers. It was a golden opportunity, and a lot of unconventional businesses signed up, including camera shops, frozen food lockers and marinas. Signing was easy enough to do; in the beginning all Trevor asked was that new dealers buy at least three Honda Super Cubs in a crate at once.

In later years, Fred Jr. glossed over his initial opposition to Honda and took the credit for Fred Deeley Ltd. moving into Japanese motorcycles, partly because they were a huge success that he wanted associated with his name, and partly because Trevor was too sensible to refute him in public. In fact, even after sales started to take off, neither Fred Sr. or Jr. believed Honda had a future. Their silence on the subject stood out, especially in a lengthy interview they gave a reporter for the *Vancouver Province* that was published July 14, 1958. In this, Fred Sr. talked about the company's history and Fred Jr. discussed the amalgamation of the Nuffield and Austin companies to form British Motor Corporation. "A great future for small cars is predicted by Fred Deeley Jr," the article reported. "'We are increasing our sales every year and have doubled them since 1955,' he said." Quite apart from this somewhat rosy view of events in the car field, the story has one glaring omission: there is absolutely no mention of Honda motorcycles, by then selling like the proverbial hot cakes.

There were, naturally, a few problems with the first shipments.

Honda decided it had a better idea for gear shift patterns than the rest of the industry. Instead of four down with neutral between first and second, it made the pattern for its manual transmission bikes four down, neutral and then first. It made sense and saved the trouble of shifting back up, but it was too complicated for the Canadian public. Riders regularly shifted right through neutral on the fly and found themselves in low gear at high speed. The results were always objectionable and occasionally dramatic. More seriously, the little Honda motors broke down or blew up in alarming numbers. The main problem was metallurgy, compounded by the higher octane gasoline available in Canada. Pistons burnt out and crankshafts kept breaking. Honda, unlike English manufacturers who reacted with glacial slowness to manufacturing defects, was onto each issue like a snow leopard on a rabbit. The company changed the crankshaft production process nine times in six months until they got it right.

Honda applied the same Kaizen philosophy to the development of its first racing bike, the RC160. This machine, built to compete in the All Japan Championships of 1959, was a double overhead camshaft (DOHC) in-line four-cylinder 250 capable of thirty-five bhp at 14,000 rpm and a top speed of 125 mph. Its successor, the RC162, under the able hand of Mike Hailwood, would go on to win the world championship for Honda in 1961. Compared to the throbbing beat of its competition, the first Honda fours screamed by spectators like the sound of God ripping his bed sheets. Loud? Ear piercing? Unbelievable? They were more than that. They were the start of a revolution.

By coincidence, and apparently almost against his will, Fred Jr. found himself supporting racing in Vancouver just as Honda began its march to the world championship.

The initiative for this came from the B.C. Sports Car Club whose members decided to build a paved roadrace course to replace the airport circuit they had been using at Abbotsford. To do this, they formed a new organization, the Westwood Sports Car Club (named after the then provincial minister responsible for Lands), located a 600-acre piece of Crown property in Coquitlam, and began selling fifty-dollar debentures to finance the construction. Club members naturally approached people in the industry to support the project, and Plimleys and another large car dealership agreed to buy 100 debentures each. This put the pressure on Fred Jr., who after all was the importer of M.G. and Jaguar sports cars, so he anted up $5,000 as well. Fred Jr. hated to spend the money, but the businessman inside him beat out the miser. Racing, he knew, would be good for business.

Bulldozers were rented from a construction company, Portuguese labourers were hired to log out the track and club members pitched in to build it. When completed it was a 1.8 mile multi-turn course, with elevation changes, a hairpin, and a hump named "deer's leap" that, later on, would send faster cars and motorcycles into the air for thirty or forty yards. On the big day, a motorcade of club members and civic officials drove from tidewater to the track and cut a ribbon inaugurating the first purpose-built road racing facility on the Canadian west coast.

It didn't take long for the area's motorcyclists to realize Westwood would be perfect for motorcycle racing, and these events began shortly after sports car racing commenced. Nor did it take long for Trev to use the track for commercial advantage by encouraging his own employees to race the bikes he was importing.

As the Honda orders flooded in and the staff at 606 started to get swamped by work, the contrast with the relatively quiet, library-like atmosphere at 901 became apparent to everyone. The potential of Honda motorcycles was obvious, especially to Trevor, who could see the results in the accounts of the motorcycle department he scrutinized every day. The problem was that Fred Deeley Ltd., while the first distributor in the English-speaking world, was still not getting any financial help from the factory. Honda insisted on receiving American funds in advance before shipping anything, while the practice among other manufacturers was to provide distributors with a period of grace before they had to pay up. Trevor began to pester his father to let him go to Japan and get a better deal. Fred Jr. was against the idea. He didn't like the Japanese, didn't want to spend the money for the trip and was afraid the plane would crash. However, he finally agreed to let Trev go in October 1959, not because he expected something to come out of it, but because he felt it would do Trevor good to get away from Vancouver with its constant reminders of Vera.

A few days later, Trev was chatting with Jim McGinnis who said he felt like taking a holiday.

"What do you think about going to Japan?" Trevor asked.

"Why not?" he replied.

The plane they travelled on was quite a contrast to either the Fleet Canuck or the Cessna they had been flying up till then. It was a Bristol Britannia, popularly nicknamed the Whispering Giant by its fans, one of the largest commercial turboprop aircraft ever built. The Britannia was used on a regularly scheduled flight out of Vancouver International Airport operated by Canadian Pacific Airlines which usually took the great circle route over the north Pacific and down to Japan in one long jump. On this occasion, because of winter winds, the flight had to land in Cold Bay, in the Aleutian Islands, to refuel, and eventually took seventeen hours and thirty-five minutes. Because it was such a long trip, and because Trev and Jim were both pilots, they asked if they could go up to the flight deck to meet the crew. Indeed they could. When they got there, Jim discovered he knew the first officer, Mac McAskill, from the Air Force Reserve and Trev realized he knew the pilot, Ralph Lesley, from the Burrard Yacht Club where he was a close friend of Fred Jr. The four aviators shook hands and agreed to meet for dinner when they got to Tokyo.

Arriving in Tokyo is, for most westerners, like landing on Mars. The signs are incomprehensible, the traffic suicidal, the crowds tidal, the language unfathomable and the sense of being unhinged by culture shock and jet lag almost overpowering. Trev and Jim went directly to the then-tiny Tsukiji Hotel, in the heart of the Ginza, and hit the sack. The next day, a gentleman from Honda arrived in a big limousine and took Trevor to the company's Tokyo headquarters. It was immediately apparent Trev was being given the red carpet treatment. Officials were waiting for him, an interpreter was provided, toasts were drunk and a major effort was made to make him feel welcome. The Japanese, it turned out, already knew a lot about the thirty-eight-year-old Canadian, including the fact he had ridden their bikes, was a Harley-Davidson dealer, and was responsible for the Vancouver police demonstration team. They said Trev should get to know their company, and the country, better before any serious discussions were held.

Jim and Trevor were given the same limousine treatment the next day for more talks at Honda, a detailed review of their products, and a meeting with the company's founder, Soichiro Honda. When all the headbowing and formalities were over for the day, the two Canadians went out to sample the local nightlife, especially the ambience of a bar around the corner that had caught their attention because of its name.

This was the Checker Club, the doorway of which was illuminated by a large black and white checkerboard sign, coincidentally the same kind of checkered flag design Trev had so often seen while winning flat track races ten years earlier. Inside, in the garish and exotic atmosphere, were some of the most beautiful women Trevor had ever seen. One in particular caught his eye. She was Ayumi Wasanabi, a pretty bar girl who was charming, intelligent, and perfectly fluent in English. She also possessed the exquisite combination of deference, attentiveness and correctness that Japanese women are famous for, along with a unique spark and vitality all her own. In short, she was a stunner. The evening took on a party atmosphere, and Trev, like many a visiting sailor before him, decided to keep the party going for the rest of his stay in Japan.

On the following days, Jim and Trev were taken out to local Honda assembly plants and given a guided tour of each factory. When they returned, there was Ayumi, smiling and happy, ready to hit the bars or kick off her heels with her new companion, depending on what he preferred.

One day, between appointments, Trev and Jim slipped away from Honda to meet a friend of Fred Sr.'s, Dick Child, the Harley-Davidson and BMW distributor in Japan. He took them to a secret test track where he was busy race tuning a pair of BMW R69/Ss with U.S. model telescopic forks, Dell'Orto carburetors, and Rennsport-type tapered megaphone exhaust pipes, each bike complete with a full aluminum fairing. A local employee took one of the Beemers out on the long, banked cement circuit and flashed past the technicians in the pits. Stopwatches were clicked, results examined and eventually the racer, Fumio Ito, came in and stopped the bike in front of Child and his two visitors. He turned and asked Trev if he'd like to take a spin. Well, yes, he sure would. Trevor, who was wearing a sports coat and slacks, took off his jacket and put on the racer's leather jacket and his helmet. Fortunately, he was largely built for a Japanese and both fit. What about the pants? the employees asked, pointing to Trev's trousers. Trev said it didn't matter and he was off.

Goodness knows what Child was expecting. What he got was a lesson in technique as Trevor wound out the German motor and used his racing skills to pick the best lines into and out of the corners. The stopwatches were out again as he went by, and a second time, and a third. When he finally pulled in, the Japanese workers were literally hissing with excitement; Trevor had broken the lap record for the bike! Immediately, it was picture time, and the employees crowded round for snapshots with Trev, the company racer and the hot BMW. Ito walked over to Trev, put his arms around him, and said, "Marlon Brando," with a big grin on his face.

It was an epiphany. The test rider had evoked the only American god he could think of to compliment Trevor and the one he picked was *The Wild One*. If ever additional proof were needed of the impact of that movie, this was it, still evoked as a motorcycle icon four years later and half a world away. More important to Trev's negotiations, the high speed tour of the test track filled him with renewed confidence as well as blowing the Japanese cigarette smoke out of his lungs.

In the meetings that followed at the Honda headquarters, the sticking point was the one Trev had gone to Japan to resolve, the signing with Honda of a long-term contract with some factory credit. The Honda people would ask Trev a series of questions, then talk extensively among themselves, then ask him another bunch of questions. Trevor kept on saying separate orders were no good, he wanted to be able to get additional units as he needed them under a master credit agreement. Finally, when things appeared to be at an impasse, Trev reached into his jacket and pulled out a piece of paper and put it on the table.

Pointing to it, he asked, "How many motorcycles will this buy?"

That was the end of the negotiations. It was party time after that. Amid the sake and Kirin beer, Jim asked Trev what the piece of paper was.

Trev replied, "A cheque for a million dollars."

He was kidding of course; Trev had nowhere near that kind of money to flash around a Japanese boardroom, and in any event motorcycles were paid for with U.S. letters of credit, not cheques. Jim didn't realize his friend was pulling his leg and went around for the next thirty-four years very impressed at the Deeley finances.

Buoyed by this breakthrough, Trev, Jim and Ayumi decided to do some sightseeing, travelling to Nikko overnight by train to see the Buddhist shrines in the area. They also went back to the Tokyo motor show, which they had visited earlier. The show was held in a cavernous hall and, besides motorcycles, contained displays from all the Japanese car companies. Since he already had Honda in the bag, Trev decided to see if he could swing an automobile distributorship. Working through Ayumi, he began a series of negotiations with Nissan Motor Company, then called Datsun, for the rights to distribute their cars in Canada. Nissan was even more receptive than Honda, perhaps because the motorcycle company had already given Trevor their imprimatur. In any event, he succeeded in signing a deal to have Fred Deeley Ltd. as the exclusive importer for Nissan automotive products for all of Canada.

It was a heady experience, and not just because he was making his mark as a businessman. His initial reaction to Ayumi's

appearance and personality had been reinforced by an appreciation of her linguistic skills and cultural advice, and the feeling
had been reciprocated. What had begun professionally had
turned into friendship and blossomed into romance. Looking at
pictures of her now, one can see both what was, and what might
have been. With her almond eyes, high cheekbones and long
black hair gathered conservatively, she looked more like the
fashionable wife of a senior executive than a denizen of the
Checker Club. She was wearing a pink suit, black three inch
heels, and was carrying a black leather purse. On her left wrist
was a gold band and on her wedding finger, a large pearl ring.
Her lipstick and fingernail polish were exactly the same shade of
pink. As she leaned against the rail of a wooden bridge waiting
for Jim to take her picture, she looked supremely happy.

By the end of the three weeks, Jim thought of Ayumi as
Trev's girlfriend and Trev thought of her as his potential second
wife. The flight back was on Remembrance Day, November 11.
There was a lot to tell his father when he got off the plane.

CHAPTER EIGHT

FREDERICK GRANVILLE DEELEY has appeared throughout this story as a brilliant businessman who built up a fortune through good marketing, tight-fisted administration and aggressive real estate investments. He was more than that. He was an egotistical, manipulative, bigoted male chauvinist with social pretensions who intimidated, angered or insulted just about everyone who ever worked for him. In his photographs he looks rather theatrical, with curly white hair, black eyebrows, horn-rimmed glasses and a Hitler-like moustache. In real life, he was a monster. The likely cause of the problem, as is often the case with people who act recklessly, was booze. Fred Jr. never touched a drop of liquor before five o'clock in the afternoon, but after that he drank steadily, often polishing off half a bottle of Gordon's or Beefeater's gin in front of the television set before having dinner by himself around 9:30 and going to bed. The pungent odour of juniper berries was so strong around the house, that to this day Dawne Deeley hates the smell of gin. Most people never saw this side of his character, except during social events which, naturally, were usually after five o'clock. At one staff Christmas party, Bobby Dawe's wife Ruth was the object of his attention. Every time Fred Jr. went past her, he put his hand up her skirt. This happened so often, she finally turned to her husband and said, "Jesus, Bob, I can tell the girls next week I've been felt up by a millionaire!"

Fred Jr. eventually got so soused, Lizzy became furious with him and insisted he leave the party before the evening was over. A sober company employee was found and told to drive Fred Jr. home. Bystanders, who saw the whole performance, said it was an embarrassing episode for everyone involved.

As a result of his alcoholic intake, he made it a practice of not showing up at the office until 10:30 or even 11:00. When he did arrive, his demeanour was gruff and aggressive. On the phone, his way of asking for someone was to simply bark out their name, "Bobby," "Trevor," or "Bill Granath," nothing more. Staff picking up the phone on the other end soon got used to it. One commented, "I don't think I ever saw him walk into the place and be goddamn pleasant. He was a mean old bastard." Visitors, however, were not so accommodating. On one occasion, Fred Jr. was introduced to the Japanese representative of Yuasa batteries who was prepared to sign a big distribution deal. Fred Jr. told him to his face almost exactly what he had told Trevor when he wanted to import Hondas: "We beat you yellow bastards in the war, why the hell should we help you now?" That was it for the battery contract.

Despite all this, Trev was so excited when he got home, he went to see his father the very next morning, even though he knew he was likely to be in a bad mood early in the day. "He was as miserable as hell," Trev remembers. "I should have known better. I should have gone to see him about four o'clock, just as he was going home. Anyway, I went in and told him about the motor show and everything and he didn't even change his expression. He wasn't interested in listening to me. And then I got onto the cars. I opened up my briefcase and handed him all the stuff and said, 'Look, Dad, I think this is a winner. I know you can do a job on it and you've got the distributorship for Canada.' I handed him all this information – this is the God's truth – he turned around, dropped it in his wastepaper basket, and said, 'Is that all that happened over there?'"

Trev turned and walked out of the office.

If there was no reasoning with the old man, there was still a life to live and Trev decided to make the best of it. The business humiliation didn't feel so bad dancing at the Aero Club, sitting in the cockpit of the small yacht he now had moored at Wood-wards Marina at Coal Harbour, or high in the sky in his float plane heading over to the Gulf Islands. He could keep this up for a long time; longer than Fred Jr. could, that was for sure. As for Ayumi, there was no point even mentioning her. If his father could turn down Datsun, his reaction to a Japanese daughter-in-law would likely be even more negative.

One of the first things he did after getting back was to have Mac McAskill over for dinner at Deep Cove. When the two had met in Tokyo, they'd discovered they had quite a lot in common. Besides flying, they were both single and owned 1958 Chevrolet convertibles. It was by no means the first time Trev had used his cottage for entertaining, and it certainly wouldn't be the last. He would exploit it increasingly in the years ahead for this purpose, particularly for lavish parties thrown for groups whose company he enjoyed. There was the police gang, made up largely of motorcycle cops from the traffic division at one; the football gang, made up of the members of the B.C. Lions football club and their managers and owners at another; and the Aero Club members at a third. Most guests would have to drive to Deep Cove and then head down Strathcona Road, a winding and narrow lane that ended at the side of a cliff facing the water. Some Aero Club members, however, came in the easy way, skimming down Indian Arm in their float planes and tying up at a large floating dock Trev installed in front of the cottage. Either way they got there, the setting was isolated and majestic. The view out the windows, or from the deck, resembled the natural grandeur of a Norwegian fjord. There weren't any neighbours to complain of the noise from a rowdy party and none to make any either if guests stayed over and slept it off the next morning.

The parties left a tremendous impression on everyone. Literally hundreds of people across Vancouver still have fond memories of going out to Deep Cove in the late 1950s and early 1960s. The youngest Deeley was the perfect host, the setting was idyllic and the company always seemed more vibrant and beautiful than elsewhere. Especially prized was being invited to Sunday roast dinner, which became an institution for his closest friends. Trevor was having fun, but there was also a benefit to all the socializing, both in cultivating business contacts and in other ways. For one thing, he regularly got away with speeding violations that would have landed other drivers with heavy fines. Being pulled over by a policeman in Vancouver was often quite pleasant.

"Oh, hi Trev," the officer would say, "better keep it down a bit."

"Right," Trevor would smile.

Deep Cove was only part of Trev's busy social life. He also was active organizing and attending boating parties and fly-in parties in the Gulf Islands or on the west coast of Vancouver Island. Chief among these was an annual crab fest at Tofino that drew scores of people from the Aero Club who flew in from around the province. Many, such as Bill and Joyce Christopher, came in Republic Seebees, an amphibian four-place pusher plane that reputedly climbed at eighty, cruised at eighty, and landed at eighty. Sometimes, combining two of his passions, Trev would strap a small dirt bike to his pontoon, fly to a deserted island, and thrash around the countryside just for the sheer hell of it.

In 1960 he combined socializing, flying and a trip to Japan by organizing a charter group from the Aero Club. He hit on this idea when so many members became interested in going to Japan after seeing his slides and listening to him tell of his adventures. The trip allowed him, as the organizer, to travel free of charge, a nice bonus for any vacation.

Twice his flying came close to fulfilling his father's dire warnings. In December 1958, Trev decided to put his float plane, EIU, on wheels. This necessitated doing another flight check with Jim McGinnis. As the power came on during the takeoff roll, the back of his seat broke and he wound up in a horizontal position. Had this happened at any other time, Trevor would have been in trouble within seconds. However, because McGinnis was sitting right there beside him, he was able to smoothly take over control and complete the takeoff. They laughed about it afterwards, but it was actually a pretty close call. A second near thing happened taking off from Lake Garabaldi. The motor on his Cessna 180 CF-IDL broke a piston as it accelerated in the thin mountain air and began to lose power. Fortunately, it didn't seize up solid and Trev managed to clear the trees and limp back to the airport.

Increasingly, the woman accompanying him on these adventures was Joy Seiba, Trev's girlfriend from before his first Japanese trip. Joy was now divorced, and the relationship rapidly became very close. Trev, who'd always enjoyed the comforts of married life, decided he wanted them again. His opportunity came when Joy announced she was going on a holiday to Hawaii. Trevor and McAskill saw her off on a cruise ship with a bottle of champagne in her cabin. After they left, the two friends raced over to the airport, jumped into Trev's Cessna and flew back to give Joy an aerial sendoff. They caught up with the ship coming out from under the Lions Gate Bridge and circled it several times, taking movies as it steamed past Point Grey. The young blonde must have been quite impressed with her forty-year-old boyfriend's antics, but what she didn't expect was that this was the beginning, not the end of them. Three or four days later, Trev caught a flight to Honolulu, surprised Joy at her hotel, and proposed marriage. She accepted and they were wed. Less than eighteen months later, they were divorced. Trev won't discuss this period in his life and others who knew the couple don't or won't remember. There doesn't seem to have been anything especially wrong with the relationship, but something wasn't right with it either. In the end, Trev bought his way out of the marriage with a $20,000 alimony payment, $10,000 obtained from Fred Sr., $8,000 from his father and $2,000 from his pal Mac. Joy, who had obviously picked up something from her husband, used the windfall to buy a hairdressing salon and go into business on her own. Trev used his year-end bonus to pay everyone back.

The motorcycle business, meanwhile, was in a ferment. In addition to the explosive growth of Honda, there was a boom in scooter sales, from both England and Italy, with the most popular being Vespa and Lambretta. In Milwaukee, Harley-Davidson responded by bringing out a scooter of its own, the Topper, with a fully enclosed 165 cc motor. This had some advanced features, such as an automatic transmission, leading link front suspension, and a rubber-mounted engine. Unfortunately, it looked like a two-wheeled golf cart, and never really caught on. Undeterred, H-D management realized they had to do something to meet the Japanese menace head-on. Their solution to the problem was to purchase a half interest in the Italian firm of Aeronautica Macchi early in 1960. Aeronautica Macchi was already marketing its own line of small motorcycles for the European market, and the plan was to use the resulting company, Aermacchi Harley-Davidson, to produce part of this output for Harley-Davidson in the United States. The first fruit from the venture was a horizontal four-stroke, single-cylinder, 250 cc bike called the Sprint in 1961.

Fred Deeley Ltd. was now in an enviable position. It distributed NSU (the Fox, Max and the Supermax), B.S.A., Triumph, Sunbeam and Ariel motorcycles from Europe; Lambretta, NSU Prima and Manurin scooters, and the growing motorcycle offerings from Honda, and was a dealer for Harley-Davidson, with its Italian lightweights, Topper scooters, middleweight sports bikes (the Sportster) and heavyweight police and touring machines. It's easy to see why the company advertised itself as "Western Canada's Motorcycle Headquarters" and "Canada's Largest Motorcycle

Dealer." It had just about every make and model a customer could ask for. More important, from its own perspective, it could switch its focus to winning brands and away from failures without missing stride, or losing a sale.

It was obvious pretty quickly what was winning: Honda. The Japanese attention to detail, the readiness to fix problems and the intrinsic value-for-money in their machines, proved a surefire combination. When American sales began in 1960, another factor added to the sales momentum. Motorcycle advertising from traditional manufacturers had always been aimed at motorcyclists and had made certain assumptions about what they expected to read and see. Typical ads from B.S.A., for example, had a large full-colour illustration of one or more motorcycles, technical line drawings, a picture of a man and woman having a picnic and space for a list of technical specifications. They assumed if you were looking at a motorcycle ad, you wanted to know something about the machine. The Honda ads, in contrast, virtually ignored the bike and began dealing with the real stumbling block to bike sales, the poor image of motorcycling. In a brilliant series of ads, middle-class Americans were pictured riding Honda's smallest bikes with the slogan, "You meet the nicest people on a Honda." Because the U.S. media spills over into Canada, the Honda advertising blitz poured across the border as well, causing many Canadians who had never given motorcycling a thought to go out and buy one. If they were anywhere in the west, the purchase went through Trevor Deeley.

Sometimes, because of the influx of new dealers in the industry, Trevor had to exercise a level of price maintenance that would be frowned on, or even illegal, today. On one occasion a dealer on the Prairies was hammering the neighbouring outlets by sharply undercutting their prices. Trev called him up and said he better get his prices up or he'd cut off his supply.

"You can't cut me off," the dealer insisted.

"Well no, maybe I can't legally cut you off," Trev replied, "but my warehouse will be empty every time you place an order!"

The years 1960 and '61 were intensely busy for Trev. He was responsible for setting up the entire Honda dealer network, in addition to servicing all his regular dealers and managing the motorcycle shop at 606. This caused him to be away from Vancouver for extended periods, travelling, usually by car, to hundreds of businesses in the four western provinces. When he got back to Vancouver, he realized the Honda operation had become too big for his existing premises and he would have to find more space and hire more staff. Fred Jr. was opposed to this, as he was to most innovations, but the tidal wave of business activity forced his hand, and he agreed to let Trev move the Honda operation into a new building at 854 West 6th Avenue.

Before that happened, though, there was a telling incident involving B.S.A., their oldest supplier. One morning, Bobby Dawe got a telephone call from the factory representative, Wilf Perry, who was in Los Angeles. Perry told him he was flying up to Vancouver and would be in town around one o'clock. Dawe immediately sensed trouble: although Trev had told B.S.A.'s export manager, Bill Rawson, that he had taken on Honda, he hadn't mentioned the Japanese machines had largely taken over the shop. The motorcycle showroom was divided down the centre with all the B.S.A.s, Triumphs, Harleys and whatnot on one side and all the Hondas on the other.

"What are we going to do?" Dawe asked.

"We're just going to have to play it by ear," Trev replied. "We'll just have to see what he says."

Trevor went to the airport to pick Perry up and brought him back to the shop. The two came through the front door and Perry suddenly stopped. Dawe, who was standing in the middle of the room, said you could hear a pin drop. Finally, Perry spoke:

"Ours will be here when they are but a memory," he announced.

Time would prove that prediction exactly backward, but the incident passed otherwise without repercussions. B.S.A. kept shipping their Gold Stars, Super Rockets, Golden Flashes, Shooting Stars, Stars and Bantams to Deeley's, even though Honda had taken over half the floorspace.

Across town, the increasing number of buzzing little Hondas in Vancouver had not gone unnoticed by another member of the Deeley family, Fred Jr.'s brother Ray. Long frustrated by the success of the motorcycle division, he decided to find another Japanese motorcycle company and go into competition with Trev, and of course, by extension, with Fred Jr. The one that seemed the most likely target was Suzuki, and he began preliminary discussions aimed at becoming a dealer, or better yet, a distributor.

Trev's success also had a big impact back in Tokyo, but not the one he, or anyone else, expected. Honda sales in western Canada had reached 8,000 motorcycles annually, but to the Japanese, they weren't high enough. Trevor was again applying his standard practice of vetting potential dealers closely, eliminating candidates who looked as if they weren't in it for the long haul. Once he approved a dealer, he tried to provide him with enough territory to make a profit. This meant that in the sparsely populated parts of the country, dealerships were often many miles apart. To the marketing people in Japan, whose experience of population density was coloured by their daily trips on the Tokyo subway system, these big gaps in the map were a constant source of worry. As a result, they dispatched officials to Vancouver to meet Trev and discuss his dealer network. The representative always showed up unexpectedly and almost always said the same thing. Opening up a big map of the province, he would point to one small town after another.

"Why haven't you got a dealer here?"

"Why haven't you got a dealer here?"

"Why haven't you got a dealer here?"

Trevor remembers on one occasion the first place pointed to was Hope, B.C. Then it was Boston Bar, at the time more a cross road than a town, and on it went. Finally, after several of these surprise visits, Trev lost his temper.

"Well, I'll tell you what we're going to do," he said. "We're going to fly up and look at all these places and see what you think about it. But, before we do that, we're going to go out in the car and I'm going to ask you to stop in a town and set up a dealer for me, 'cause I haven't been able to do it."

At that, he bundled the representative into his car and drove up the Trans Canada highway to Hope, a small town nestled at the foot of an imposing wall of mountains, and the kick-off point for the scenic Hope-Princeton Highway Trev knew so well. He stopped the car on the main street and turned to his companion, a big, tall, good looking Japanese who spoke fairly good English.

"Now look," he said, "the town's not very big, but you insist we have a dealer here, so you've got two hours to find one. If you're not back here in two hours, catch the bus or some goddamn thing, 'cause I'm not waiting for you."

The Honda rep was back in about twenty minutes.

"Impossible, you can't have a dealer here," he admitted.

"Well," Trev said, "I told you that on the telephone, I told you that in a letter. What did you come all the way over here for?"

That wasn't the end of his demonstration. The next day he took the Honda official to the airport and had him get into his Cessna. Not saying a word to him, he took off and headed northeast, straight over the Lions Gate Bridge. The terrain north of Vancouver is extremely rugged with almost no sign of human habitation for hundreds of miles. Bumping along in the turbulence caused by the mountains, Trev pointed down to the limitless expanse of rock and forest.

"Where the hell do you want me to put a dealer in here?" he shouted. "If I had a parachute on you, I'd push you out the goddamned window and you could phone me when you'd set up your first dealer."

The Cessna 182 returned to home base with the representative still on board and Trev fairly certain he had made his point about dealer distribution abundantly clear. Apparently, he had not. A short time later, another Honda rep was on his doorstep, asking many of the same questions as the others. In addition, the letters from Honda's head office were beginning to have an edge to them, as if the company was unsatisfied with the performance of Fred Deeley Ltd. despite ever-increasing sales. _Well,_ Trev thought, _if we're going to stay in the Japanese motorcycle business where the big volume is, we'd better find ourselves another partner._ Just like his uncle Ray, he looked for potential candidates, but unlike Ray, he decided to start courting Yamaha. The Yamaha line was already being imported, but in very small numbers. British Motorcycles in Vancouver had brought in five and Prairie Motorcycle Works in Regina had imported six. Trev figured his track record with Honda would be sufficient to get the franchise signed over. The only problem was that he had an exclusive contract with Honda, so the negotiations, and the deal, would all have to be kept secret.

The method he used to keep things under cover was to set up a dummy company called Pacific Seaboard BC Ltd., and hire an old friend, Don Solem, as general manager. Solem was another one of the youngsters, like Dawe and Pazaski, who hung around Fred Deeley Ltd. in the 1940s and became close friends with Trevor and Vera. At one time his nickname was "Harley-Davidson," because he used to go around wearing nothing but shirts with the company name on them. In the early '50s he went off on his own, eventually winding up in the record business with Quality Records, but never completely losing touch with the Deeleys. One reason was that Fred Jr. had developed a passion for Hawaiian music on his vacation trips to Maui and he used to call Solem for the latest Hawaiian records because Don would sell them to him wholesale. Fred Jr. also bought Electrohome high fidelity sets from him and would call him out to his house every six months or so to vacuum them out because he liked the insides of his radios as clean as the outsides.

"Trevor called me one night, I was living in Richmond at the time, and he said he wanted to have a talk with me," Solem remembers. "I went over and he laid out that they were thinking of taking on Yamaha and that they had to do it secretly because they had Honda already and it would be a conflict and would I be interested in fronting it for them."

Solem, who needed a job at the time, said yes he would. This resulted in him meeting Harvey Sedgwick, now the Deeley lawyer, in order to set up the dummy company, and Fred Jr. for another, unexpected reason. Fred wanted Don to take a psychological aptitude test. This request at first might sound odd coming from someone who resisted innovations, but Fred Jr. had embraced psychological testing for employees because it revealed things about them and gave him yet another way to control his workers. Don was called back later and Fred Jr. announced he had failed part of the test. Whether he had or whether this was just part of a game of intimidation isn't known, but Don protested. He asked how could a person have an aptitude for motorcycle sales if it's something he'd never done before.

"Let me try it and see if I can do it," he asked.

Fred relented and Don was hired. In terms of Trev's relationship with his father, this is a revealing moment. Trev was the one who realized there was a problem with Honda and who came up with the idea of approaching Yamaha. He was the one who picked Don Solem and talked him into becoming the general manager of Pacific Seaboard. However, even before the company was set up, Fred Jr. had already moved to exercise a form of control by putting Don through an intimidating screening process. In the months and years ahead Fred Jr. would do this time and again, muscle in on his son, shove him aside, and take the credit for himself.

Trev had already negotiated an agreement in principle for Pacific Seaboard to become the distributor for British Columbia and Alberta. He now told Don to arrange a meeting with Burt Smith from Yamaha International to tie up the deal. Although Solem had a fake company, he had a very real bank account, and a small office in the 1900 block of West Fourth Avenue, so he was eager to get going. At the first meeting in 1962, the two men hit it off extremely well.

"Why are you just doing part of Canada?" Smith asked Don.

"Why don't you do it all?"

"I will if you're ready to give it to us," the startled Solem replied.

Don went back to Trevor and announced he was now the secret importer of all Yamaha's recreational products, from boats to skis, for all of Canada. Trev was delighted. This meant Yamaha had more potential than Honda ever had, because he could pump goods into the country's two largest metropolitan areas, Toronto and Montreal. He congratulated Don because of it, and for another unstated reason. It would irritate his father, who didn't like handling anything farther east than Alberta, but there was nothing Fred Jr. could do about it.

Yamaha wasn't the only secret on Trevor's mind, however. He was also secretly starting to go out with Joyce Christopher.

Joyce was born Joyce Lorraine Ogilvie in Victoria in 1931, the daughter of a Piggly Wiggly store manager. She got her first job when she was sixteen, and was working as a secretary with the James Lovick & Company Ltd. advertising firm when Trev was introduced to her by her husband, Bill. They kept running across each other through the late '50s and early '60s, because although Joyce wasn't that keen on flying, Bill was, and kept dragging her off to events that Trev also attended. At five foot, nine inches tall, she was a tall, good looking woman with a full mane of red hair, who was a standout in any crowd. She was also, it turned out, in an unhappy marriage that was rapidly falling apart. Trev's problem, aside from the fact Bill was one of his best friends, was that Bill was insanely jealous and a very large man. Any meetings would have to be extremely circumspect and well away from the Aero Club to which they both belonged.

Trev decided to confide in his general manager, Bobby Dawe.

"I've got a real problem," he said. "I'm in love with my best friend's wife."

"Oh," replied Bobby. "That is a problem."

The glory days for Fred Deeley Ltd. automotive had begun to fade somewhat as the company entered 1963. It was still one of North America's largest Austin dealers, with a large service department and over $100,000 worth of parts in inventory, but the products from BMC seemed to be losing their influence on the motoring public. Perhaps spurred on by the widening scope of the motorcycle division, Fred Jr. decided to take on a domestic car manufacturer for the first time. The one he chose was Studebaker, then struggling for market share itself, with three new models:

the compact Lark, the Hawk and the custom-built Avanti luxury sports car. The announcement, in deference to the family patriarch, was made by Fred Sr. He told the media that Austin customers had continued to stay remarkably loyal to his company, "because we have been honest in our business and believe in satisfied customers and first-rate service. We'll follow the same policy with Studebaker." It was one of the last public statements he was to make.

Trev wasn't quoted in the report, most likely because he was too busy to come over to the automotive showroom. The booming Honda business was reason enough, but he was also meeting Don secretly at night to help him with Yamaha. The first thing to do was to get some product into the country, so they immediately ordered thirty motorcycles. Trev told Don how he was expanding Honda, suggested people and locations, and got him out on the road setting up dealers. This proved pretty easy to do for several reasons. One was that a lot of suitable individuals had applied to become Honda dealers, more than Trev could accept, and so Don knew he had a hot prospect when he called on them for Yamaha. The second reason was that Solem had talked Burt Smith into adding the line "distributed by Pacific Seaboard of Canada" on every ad run by Yamaha in the Canadian and U.S. motorcycle magazines, a move which gave prospective dealers the idea his company was a lot bigger than it actually was. In fact, for a while, Pacific Seaboard was just Don. This caused an interesting problem when new dealers phoned its number and no one was there because he was out on the road. Some, who had sent deposit cheques in the mail, started wondering if this was a fly-by-night outfit that was going to disappear with their money. They were relieved when Don hired Wendy Smith as a secretary and calls started getting answered. The issue arose because neither Don nor Trev was approving Pacific Seaboard's expenses. The de facto treasurer was Fred Jr., who, in the interest of saving money, would frequently slip over to 4th Avenue at night and go through Don's office to see if he was wasting it. If Fred Jr. found an uncancelled stamp in the wastebasket, Don would hear about it the next day.

"Why," Fred Jr. demanded, "didn't you steam it off?"

On other occasions, Don would be called into Fred Jr.'s office and asked to explain an expense account that listed two hamburgers for lunch. There was nothing personal in the inquisition, Fred Jr. did this to all his managers, except Trev, all the time.

Fred Sr. had gone over the accounts with Ray and Fred Jr. the same way, and Fred Jr. was just carrying on the family tradition, albeit a little more in the manner of Scrooge in Dickens's *A Christmas Carol*, than his father. The first Yamahas arrived in Vancouver in late 1963 and Don dispatched them to his new dealers, some paid for in advance, others on consignment. Both Don and Trev looked forward to the new year with every expectation of selling a lot of Japanese motorcycles.

What they did not expect was that Ray Deeley would successfully conclude a deal with Suzuki to become their national distributor for Canada, operating under a new company name, Radco Sales Ltd. Ray Sr. had seen how successful Trev's Honda operation was becoming and wanted a piece of the action himself. The deal with Suzuki was a very slick piece of work because the Fred Deeley Ltd. name was already well known in western Canada and just about everyone thought Fred Deeley Cycles Ltd. was the same thing. In effect, Ray Sr. would get a free ride on Trev's pillion, as the Honda network expanded, without having to pay any royalties for the use of the family name. Fred Jr., who had long been estranged from his brother anyway, was fit to be tied. We can get a sense of the family squabble from an incident later in the year involving Reg Shanks, the Harley-Davidson dealer in Victoria who had accompanied Trev to Daytona in 1948.

Reg was in his shop when he noticed a pickup truck pull up outside with two shiny motorcycles strapped down in the cargo bed. Naturally curious, he went out for a better look. The driver, a young man, got out of the truck and came over to say hello.

"You remember me, Reg," he said, "I'm Ray Junior."

"Oh, of course," Reg replied. "How are you?"

Actually, he had never met him before, but he knew who he was through Fred Sr. who was good friends with his own father.

"What have you got here, Ray?" he asked.

"Well, these are Suzukis. Look at the beautiful finish on them."

"Magnificent."

"Yes, and they run just as nicely as they look."

"Well, I never," Reg said, examining the two machines.

"Are you interested in them at all?"

"Gosh, we've got so much money tied up, we just can't take on any more."

"Well," Ray suggested, "at least have a ride on one."

Recounting the meeting many years later, Reg laughed, and said: "Wise man. Typical Deeley."

Ray unloaded one of the bikes from the truck, checked to see there was gas in it and handed it over to Reg. The first surprise came starting it up. Reg had a lot of experience with English two-strokes made by Villiers. This was nothing like them; it was completely effortless and almost inaudible. He got on it and rode up Fort Street, east to Cook, down Cook for several blocks and then turned and came back to his shop.

"That's a delightful thing," he exclaimed when he got back. "Charming."

They certainly were, and Reg bought them both. A couple of weeks later he got a phone call from Fred Jr., not an uncommon occurrence considering he was Reg's Harley-Davidson distributor.

"Here, what's this Reg, I hear about you taking on the Suzuki line?" he asked in his usual belligerent way.

"I didn't take them on," Reg replied evenly, "I bought a couple of Suzukis from young Ray."

Fred Jr. seemed to sputter over the phone.

"Well," he said, "Trev's not gonna like this."

This was news to Reg. Until that moment he had thought the Suzuki distributorship was part of the Fred Deeley empire. But now his dander was up.

"Well, Fred," he said tartly, "you should understand that Brooklands is a sovereign firm. We make up our own lines. If Trevor is vexed or unhappy, I'm sorry, but the thing still holds."

"Trevor won't be happy," Fred Jr. muttered and then hung up. In fact, Trev, who got on well with Ray Sr., Ray Jr. and Reg, was never told about the exchange.

If this kind of confusion was taking place with someone who knew the Deeley family intimately, you can rest assured it was certainly the case with businessmen in Winnipeg, Toronto and elsewhere who only knew the name. Nor was Reg Shanks' confusion entirely without basis. Despite the very public split between the two parts of the family, Fred Deeley Cycles Ltd. continued using the services of Fred Sr.'s accountant Lloyd Perry right up till the formation of Radco Sales Ltd. Even then, when he transferred the books to his office at 1107 Homer Street, Ray Sr. did all his banking through the same branch of the Canadian Imperial Bank of Commerce built at 796 West Broadway especially for Fred Deeley Ltd. The manager of this remarkable branch had already begun to see very large drafts and letters of credit cross his desk, and these grew rapidly in the following years into the millions of dollars. No wonder. The one small building at the corner of Willow was acting as the financial clearing house for Honda, Yamaha and Suzuki all at the same time.

Ray's justification for starting Radco was simple enough. In response to Fred Jr.'s charge of bad faith, he said, "Well, you know that's all very well for you to say that sort of thing, but the cycle division years and years and years back were responsible for the importation of B.S.A. motorcycles. The only difference is that now we're going along with Suzuki." The difference was quite a bit more than that, but there was nothing Fred Jr. could do about it.

Trevor, meanwhile, was having trouble with his new romance. The problem was that even though Joyce had now left Bill and was living at home with her parents, her husband still couldn't accept their marriage was over. The two lovers tried to keep a low profile in public, but Bill was determined to make life difficult for them. He even followed Joyce around in his car, a threatening practice that nowadays is described as stalking. In the end, the pair tired of being romantic nomads and decided to make their home at Deep Cove. As a precaution, Trevor tied a string on a gate behind the house, led it through a window and fastened it to a light on a nightstand beside the bed so at least they'd get some advance notice if Bill started skulking around the cottage. It was a good guess; the tripwire worked perfectly. Bill finally learned of the affair through the MacDonald Detective Agency and decided to confront the lovers at Deep Cove, accompanied by a detective named Gough. He arrived in the middle of the night, smashed in the front door with his shoulder – he was built like a linebacker – and confronted Trevor and his wife in the bedroom. Joyce leapt out of bed in the nude and Trevor and Bill grappled with each other. The fight went round the room several times with Joyce screaming at her husband to leave and at Trevor to paste him one. At one point Bill pushed Trev's shoulder through the gyprock wall, but Trev fought back aggressively, opening a cut on Bill's face that left blood stains all over the bedroom wall.

"God, I'll never forget it," Joyce remembers. "I got mad. I just got mad at him because you see the thing was he said to me: 'I don't care what you do. I don't want you. You don't want me. Fine. But, I'll never ever give you a divorce.' I always say thank God for Trudeau. He may have done nothing for this country, but he did something for the divorce laws."

Bill, thoroughly beaten, stumbled off into the night, and apart from a few bruises, a smashed door and a broken and stained wall, everything was all right. It would be years before Joyce would get her divorce, but the affair was now out in the open and they could start seeing their friends again. There were some psychological benefits from the fracas as well. Trevor had the uniquely male satisfaction of having fought for his lady, and Joyce had the uniquely female reassurance of having two men scuffle for her heart. It may have been frightening at the time, but the couple later grew to view it as the pivotal point in their relationship, a bedroom farce yes, but a touching, heartfelt moment as well. Shortly afterwards, Joyce quit her job and moved in with Trevor as his common-law wife.

Honda started to put on the pressure, cutting Fred Deeley Ltd.'s territory down to the three western provinces, and then just B.C. and Alberta. Trev's response, initially, was to raise the stakes by taking on Honda automobiles as well as motorcycles. He flew to Tokyo with Jack Wilkinson, the Austin car service manager, and successfully negotiated the deal, in part making up for Fred Jr.'s decision not to take on Nissan. Unfortunately, Honda botched its product launch by coming out with a car that had a poor heater and a chain drive transmission, just like its bikes, that Canadian drivers couldn't get used to and wound up trashing. He imported 256 cars and virtually all of them came back in the shop for major repairs. Honda sent over a team of experts for the repair program, but the hassle was incredible and left everyone involved with a bad taste in their mouth.

The close working relationship meant Honda eventually found out about Yamaha. The message they gave Trevor was clear and to the point: get rid of Yamaha. Trev's response was equally clear; he decided to get rid of Honda instead. His reasoning was that Yamaha had more potential because he had the national franchise, whereas the territory for Honda was down to two provinces. If he played it right, he could also unload his problems with Honda's cars. At the time, everyone thought Trevor was nuts.

Despite the reaction, Trev went to one of his father's automotive competitors, Clarke Simpkins, and asked his sales manager, Doug Firth, if Simpkins would like to buy the motorcycle business. The only stipulation was that he had to buy the car business as well.

"Sounds great," he told Trev. "I'll get back to you in a few days."

Simpkins, who was immediately interested in the idea, drove down the coast as far as San Diego visiting as many Honda dealers as he could to check out the motorcycle business at the retail level. There appeared to be a lot of potential, so when he got back he decided to accept Trev's offer.

Trevor then went and told his dad what he'd done. His father, as usual, was anything but supportive.

"Don't bother with him," he said, "he hasn't got any goddamn money. He's no good and he'll never buy it. You're just wasting your time."

Trev knew his father was a crony of Simpkins so he put a lot of weight on his negative comments and went looking for another suitable buyer. He suspected Honda wanted to take over the franchise anyway, so better to sell it than lose it. A couple of days later, Simpkins — who actually was very well capitalized — called and said he wanted to go ahead with the deal. In a meeting with Fred Jr. he struck a pretty good bargain, buying the inventory for $750,000 and getting the distributorship and good will for free. Trev was pleased because he had got out of Honda cleanly. Simpkins was pleased because he picked up a thriving motorcycle distributorship and a new car line at the same time.

As the sale was going through, Trev heard via the grapevine Simpkins was planning to set his son Chris up as the Honda manager. Trev had never met him, so he called Chris up.

"You've never been in the motorcycle business before," Trev began. "I'd certainly like to spend some time with you, have lunch or whatever, and answer any questions you might have and give you some suggestions as to how you might carry on."

The young Simpkins was anything but receptive.

"Look," he said, "I don't need any advice from you. I know all there is to know about business."

That was the end of that.

The sale meant Trevor could stop his clandestine meetings with Don Solem and take over effective control and management of the company. He would be able, among other things, to start hiring the people he wanted first hand, instead of by remote control. Among his first decisions was to move Yamaha out of its building to 1101 West 8th and to separate the wholesale and retail functions of the motorcycle division. Retail continued at 606 East Broadway, the wholesale function was moved to 7th and Ash and Yamaha went to 854 West 6th, the former Honda location. The wholesale division was given the responsibility of maintaining an accessories warehouse and developing new products that looked promising. The most important of these were motorcycle helmets, then being made compulsory across Canada, which Trev began manufacturing.

If Trev was happy, Don Solem was not. Even though he had known Trevor was a hands-on kind of person, it still felt unfair to have Yamaha yanked out from underneath him when it was doing so well. He had established a national dealer network and was selling a lot of motorcycles. His methods were different as well, supporting Yamaha dealers with more direct advertising and loading up their showrooms with more units than Honda dealers were receiving.

Less tangible, but just as real, was the matter of the firm's esprit de corps. Solem and his small staff had been fighting Honda for new business with some success, having muscled into second place in Canada ahead of Suzuki, who were second to Honda elsewhere in the world. Their little 100 cc twin was outselling the Honda 90, and the Yamaha 250 was also doing well. In addition, Yamaha skis were a growing business that Honda hadn't matched. Now the head of the competition was taking charge. Trev made the announcement at the national Yamaha dealer meeting for 1967 at the Skyline Hotel in Toronto. He told them he was the secret backer of Pacific Seaboard, that he had sold the Honda franchise to Clarke Simpkins and was assuming command of Yamaha. Solem, who felt the worst of the group, was deeply upset and his depression seemed to carry over to the others, who began talking about quitting. The unhappy group clambered on board a Canadian Pacific flight to the coast and proceeded to get totally drunk. It was practically an empty flight, so the four stewardesses joined in and made it into a wake for Pacific Seaboard that carried on right across Canada. Jim Elligott, outdoing the others, wound up locked in a washroom with one of the stewardesses, and had to be rescued by a maintenance man after the plane landed. The completely bummed out employees were met by Slim Magnussen, the company controller, who picked them up at the airport and got everyone to come back to their senses. As an exercise in helping a transition go smoothly, it was not one of Solem's better efforts.

Actually very little that Trevor could have done would have satisfied Solem, short of leaving him alone, and that was impossible.

CHAPTER NINE

THE YAMAHA ERA should have been one of the best chapters in Trev Deeley's career. The explosive growth and expansion of Fred Deeley Yamaha Ltd. was in many ways a model marketing exercise that combined considerable skill in dealer relations, financial planning and product knowledge to pull off successfully. In fact, it was the most difficult period in his professional life. The problem was that Trevor personally, and the key employees at Pacific Seaboard as a group, had totally different agendas, despite the fact they were all in the same business trying to do the same thing. The different perspectives, like so much in life, came from their different beginnings.

Forming a company and building it up from scratch comes close to rivalling sex for pure unadulterated enjoyment. A company's first employees put in masochistic hours, travel Columbusian distances and act in selfless ways reminiscent of revolutionaries overthrowing a tyrant. The payoff is that, in the process, they get a tremendous amount of job satisfaction. That reward, plus the shared discomfort, intrigue and excitement, form the participants into a band of brothers whose spirit of fellowship remains long after the battle is won or lost.

This is the way it was with Pacific Seaboard – a core group composed of general manager Don Solem, secretary Wendy Smith, Paul Abrams in parts, Jim Elligott doing sales, and Bob Work responsible for service, racing and warranty. They, and a handful of others, fought their way into the second place position among motorcycle importers in Canada, and frankly, were proud of it.

When Trev Deeley arrived, his mind was still fixed on the remarkable feat he had pulled off of switching horses in mid stream without getting wet, or to put it more plainly, of switching Japanese suppliers without getting sued or losing his shirt. As a result, he failed to fully understand the emotional dynamics of the staff members he was inheriting and left most of them feeling distinctly under-appreciated. This insensitivity in part stemmed from the kind of treatment he got from his father – Don Rickles in reverse is the way one employee described Fred Jr. – and in part from the fact that for many years he had considered himself one of the boys and still did so, even though for Don Solem and some of the others, he no longer was. When the roles changed, and he stopped drinking with the gang every Friday night after work, he didn't change his operating methods along with them. What his employees wanted was financial recognition for their achievements and the freedom to continue making them. What they got was the same paycheque and more control from the top.

The disaffected mood at Fred Deeley Yamaha Ltd. began with the emotional take-over announcement, simmered quietly during the company's nine-year lifetime, had one last flare-up at the end and still remains to this day. Most of the senior employees felt bruised at what happened, even though they have long since come to terms with events. They like Trevor personally and enjoy his company, but they shake their heads at his management style during the exciting days when little Yamaha screamers were nipping at the heels of the Honda success story.

At its heart, the issue was about relating to Fred Jr.

There is a telling story that on at least one occasion when Fred Jr. telephoned Trev at Deep Cove, Trevor insisted on putting on his clothes before answering the phone. It is apparently apocryphal, besides being difficult to imagine. But the fact that anyone would even dream it up speaks volumes about how intimidated Trevor appeared to be of his father. There is ample evidence to back up this contention, from the way Trev accepted his parents' arrangements for his first wedding and his response to Fred Jr.'s repudiation of the Nissan contract, to the loss of his Japanese sweetheart. People close to him couldn't help noticing that Trevor seemed to be locked into an abusive, co-dependent relationship with his dad. One year at a Christmas cocktail party thrown by Islay, Joyce noticed Trev and Fred Jr. talking in the hall, eye to eye. She couldn't hear what they were discussing so intently, but she noticed the effect on Trevor; he was so hurt at what his father was saying, there were tears in his eyes. Another instance involved B.S.A., Fred Sr.'s old company in Birmingham. Trev had been trying hard to get a long-term contract out of B.S.A., working through export manager Bill Rawson. Finally, B.S.A. agreed and sent out one of their senior people, Sir Leonard Joffrey, to sign the contract. Before he arrived, the English company rented a big suite at the Bayshore Inn, and Trev set up a couple of motorcycles in the lobby and invited the press to attend. He then told his father about the ceremony and said where it was and when it would start. When Fred Jr. got there, he did more than attend, he took over the event.

"He wouldn't let me in one picture, not one discussion," Trev remembers. "I never made a speech, never shook hands with anybody from B.S.A., including Joffrey. I was really devastated that night. As a matter of fact, I think I left and went home before it was over. Much as I love the guy in other respects — and this is a terrible way to have to think about him — he was a bugger, he really was, with me anyway."

To deal with his father, Trevor resorted to passing information through intermediaries, especially his pilot friend Mac McAskill. Mac would meet Fred Jr. for lunch and quietly suggest that something Trev wanted to do was maybe a good idea. As a method of communication between father and son, the system was haphazard at best; as a way of managing a company, it was ripe for disaster. As the years went on, and Fred Jr. could see how successful his son had become, the situation improved and Fred Jr. began backing Trev's business decisions, increased his pay and fattened his bonuses. But initially and well into the Pacific Seaboard period, things were still strained between the two.

"Fred was a pretty tough guy," Mac says now. "He was pretty hard on Trevor. Trevor could never really satisfy the old man."

In fact, Trev stood up to his father more than outsiders realized — among other things, he often discussed Solem's requests with his father in private before his dad approved or rejected them — but he publicly deferred to Fred Jr. as well, a recognition of family authority that grated on some employees who didn't like to admit they were working in a family busines. Solem, in particular, couldn't get over his loss of power and took every opportunity to belittle Trev in the eyes of the others.

Given this background, it's not surprising there was tension in the office between Don and Trev after Trevor showed up and took over the day-to-day running of the company. This was made worse by several other factors. One was that with Joyce back at Deep Cove, Trevor started to act less like a man obsessed with business success and more like an average person. Unusual for him, he actually started to go home at the end of the day, instead of working late at the office. In a less driven company, this wouldn't have been noticed, but in the hothouse atmosphere of Fred Deeley Yamaha, it stood out like a sore thumb.

A second problem was that Trev couldn't always deliver on promises he made to the staff. Because he wasn't in charge of the company's finances and because communications were poor with his father, promised pay raises sometimes didn't materialize in an employee's pay packet at the end of the week.

The final irritant was a company-wide feeling that Trev played favourites with the staff, and specifically with a new staff member, Don James. This kind of reaction happens in any organization when someone is put on the fast track to promotion. The reason it rankled at Fred Deeley Yamaha was that the track seemed so personal, rather than professional.

Don James was a university student at Simon Fraser taking economics and commerce in 1966 and teaching skiing at Whistler on the weekends. When he heard Pacific Seaboard was importing Yamaha skis, he walked in and asked if he could have a demonstration pair to show to his students. Solem said yes; it was, after all, a way of getting the Yamaha name in front of skiers at the area's biggest ski resort.

In April, after using the skis all winter, James came back to see Solem, who stunned him by asking him if he'd like to manage the company's ski business. James wasn't expecting the offer, but immediately thought to himself, Wow, what an opportunity! and accepted. Solem then took James in to meet Trev, who had just taken over the company. The chemistry between the forty-seven-year-old Deeley and the charming young commerce student worked perfectly and within minutes they were talking like old friends. The result was that almost before he realized it, Don James was off to Seattle for some training at a trade show and shortly after that, driving east in a new car with an eight-track stereo and an expense account calling on potential ski accounts.

All this seems reasonable enough, a skier with a background

in commerce is just the kind of person you'd want setting up a sports equipment distribution network. However, to the hard-bitten types at Fred Deeley Yamaha, who had dedicated their careers to the motorcycle business, the impression Don left was of a young man on a permanent vacation at company expense. They figured the only explanation for this was that Trevor had adopted Don as the son he had always wanted.

Partly they were right, but there was very little Trevor could do intellectually to counter a gut feeling as strong as this was. It is a truism we always treat our children the way we wish our parents had treated us. In Trevor's case, the impulse to be a father was so powerful he couldn't resist transferring it to the family business. The result was that while he quite properly brought Don along as a sales representative, paying him the same as the others, he did so in a way that looked as if he was providing him with special favours, as a father would a son. Behind his back, the staff referred to James as a brown noser, to his face they were grudgingly cordial. Trevor appeared oblivious to this mood, which subsequently worsened when he gave James responsibilities in the motorcycle area, sacred ground to the rest of the staff.

Although no one said so, another reason for the black looks directed at James had to do with class. Motorcycling had always been a working class sport and skiing an activity of the upper classes and idle rich. Add to that the fact James had gone to university and the other employees had not, and you had a situation where educational envy was added to class consciousness and fear of favouritism. Whether Trevor could have done anything about this, even if he had wanted to, is problematical. It was going to happen again and again as more educated and more upwardly mobile employees joined the staff, and as the company put more effort into non-traditional, non-motorcycle areas.

Despite a dysfunctional family and some unhappy employees, Fred Deeley Yamaha did very well indeed. The foundation built by Trevor through Pacific Seaboard was solid and sales were skyrocketing. The Canadian Imperial Bank of Commerce said it was the fastest corporate growth they had ever experienced. The first year Pacific Seaboard imported thirty motorcycles. The second year, it brought in thirty-four. By the third year, after Don travelled the country in his car with a trailer of Yamahas drumming up new dealers, Pacific Seaboard imported 3,000 bikes. The next year it was more and it just kept growing. Partly Yamaha was selling well because of the phenomenal rise of Honda in the public consciousness. Partly it was because Yamaha had good bikes to offer, particularly solid, reliable two-strokes, such as the YDS3C Big Bear, a 250 cc twin that produced twenty-one horsepower at 7,500 rpm and had a top speed of eighty-eight mph. But mostly, it was that Yamaha was winning on the racetracks of the world. The company won the 250 cc World Championship in 1964, the year after Pacific Seaboard was formed, and won it again in 1965. In 1967 it won the 125 cc title and the next year it captured both championships.

To Trevor, the born racer, the temptation to take a TR series Yamaha race bike out on the track when he assumed control of Pacific Seaboard was almost irresistible. He did the next best thing, he formed a racing team and started campaigning with Yamaha just as vigorously as he had ever done with Harley-Davidson or B.S.A.

Winning teams need racers with both the skill and courage to rise above the pack in the heat of balls-to-the-wall professional motorcycle competition. In looking over the field of promising Canadian amateurs, Trev's eyes fell on Yvon DuHamel, an aggressive young rider from Quebec who had campaigned at Daytona from 1964 on B.S.A.s and Triumphs. He had been very competitive when his equipment worked, but each year his machine died before it got to the chequered flag. DuHamel was also recommended by one of his Quebec dealers. Early in 1967, Trevor wrote him a short letter offering a ride on a Deeley Yamaha in the 250 cc class at Daytona. DuHamel, who had never met Trev, accepted. After all, a ride was a ride. Because his English wasn't good, he had his sister write his reply. In a few days, he got another letter from the west coast telling him to look for Bob Work when he got to the track.

When DuHamel arrived in Daytona he was given a one-year-old bike with which he qualified in the middle of the field. In the race, his talent overcame the limitations of the machine, and he managed to finish in eighth position. Work was so enthusiastic, he telephoned Trevor from the phone booth at the track gates.

"Look," he said, "Yvon finished 8th. He's really, really going fast, but he didn't have the speed and didn't have the right equipment. We've got to do something better for him."

A couple of months later, Yvon received two brand new bikes, a 100 cc racer and a 250 cc twin to campaign at Harewood Acres, Mossport and in Quebec. At the first race at Harewood, a short flat course built on a disused airport, Yvon had his first meeting with his new sponsor.

"Hello, Mr. Deeley," he said, shaking his hand.

"Look," Trev replied. "If you want to talk to me, you've got to call me Trevor or Trev. You're not to call me Mr. Deeley."

It was an interesting moment. People who met him assumed Trevor wanted to get on personal terms almost immediately. That was true, but Trevor was also trying to distance himself from the person who most denied his own existence, *the* Mr. Deeley, his father, Fred Jr. Then, and for years to come, the name Deeley was not something Trevor felt comfortable with. It was the name on his driver's licence, but it was not the name in his heart.

Trevor's choice of DuHamel was a good one. The bearded French Canadian began winning races at home and in the United States and continuing the next year when he became Canadian Champion, won the 250 cc class at Daytona and came second in the Daytona 200. Seeing the sparkling blue and white Fred Deeley Yamaha colours in the winner's circle gave Trev a lot of satisfaction. He was following his grandfather's marketing maxim, *racing sells bikes*, and he was a success at picking the right team to wrench and to race the bikes he was selling.

Picking the right team back in Canada was also going well, but inspiring them was not so easy. The problem wasn't with the dealers, whom he seemed to have a deft touch at selecting and nurturing, it was with his immediate staff. In contrast to the easy-going ways he had always had before, his relations with his new Yamaha employees were anything but rosy. Trev could be funny and charming, but at times he turned into an absolute tyrant, dressing people down at the top of his voice in front of all the staff and any customers who happened to be standing around. The effect on the selected victim of this verbal abuse was to make the employee feel publicly humiliated. Don Solem, for one, decided to quit. Another senior employee went to a doctor for tranquilizers to cope with the stress. Trevor was obviously passing along the feelings he got from dealing with his father, but the outbursts left a lot of bruised egos and hurt feelings among the staff who felt, probably rightly, they were mean spirited and excessive.

It was just as well Trevor had Joyce to go home to at the end of the day. Even though he kept his business problems to himself, her acceptance and affection were a blessing. The peace and solitude of Deep Cove, now greatly enlarged from the little cottage it was originally, provided a respite from the pressure of work and the continued meddling, manipulation and mental games played on him by Fred Jr. It was with both happiness and relief, therefore, that the couple was informed that Joyce's divorce was finalized February 19, 1969. They married almost immediately, on February 26, and went south for a quick honeymoon in Acapulco. The reason for the haste wasn't just that Trev wanted to make Big Red an honest woman; he wanted to get the celebration over in time to fly to Daytona and see if DuHamel could win the 200 miler.

Joyce remembers it with a smile. "He put me in this bloody little awful motel stuck out by the track and said, 'Well, good-bye dear. I'm gone.'"

Trevor's anticipation was justified. Yvon DuHamel, who had again knocked off the 250 cc championship, won the pole position with the first ever 150+ mph lap in Daytona's history. And then, the rains came down. Daytona in March can be as miserable as Vancouver in December, worse even, because the Florida rains when they come, are driven by massive storm fronts of cool air that whip the palm leaves and throw sheets of water on the pavement so that they hiss like a thousand snakes. The racers practised in the morning, but became increasingly concerned about the rain and asked for a postponement. After a heated discussion, the event, which had been billed to run "rain or shine," was put off till the following Sunday. This annoyed thousands of race fans, many of whom had to return home, and wasn't greeted with much enthusiasm in the motel room where Joyce was spending the second half of her honeymoon watching television by herself.

When the event finally got going a week later, DuHamel was one of the leaders right from the start, along with Rod Gould from England and Ron Pierce from the United States. By the twelfth lap, Pierce had built up a slight lead over DuHamel and the leaders were starting to come up on the back markers. Just as they did, Dave Scott fell exiting the infield portion of the track. His motorcycle threw gasoline as it skidded along and the leader, Pierce, hit the patch of fuel and crashed. DuHamel had just enough time to see what was happening and avoid the problem. Unfortunately, his little Yamaha began to have problems of its own, and he found himself out of the race on the twenty-second lap. Trev and Joyce still had a lot to cheer about though, because another member of the team, and another Canadian, Mike Duff, brought his Fred Deeley Yamaha across the finish line in third place. It was, by any measure, an impressive performance. The team had won the 250 cc race, fought hard for first place in the 200 mile feature, and finished a very respectable third. Added to the 250 cc win and second place finish the previous year, it showed Trev was even more successful as a race manager than he had been as a racer himself.

Afterwards, he invited DuHamel to come out to Vancouver and race at Westwood, an invitation DuHamel accepted with pleasure. It was his first trip on an airplane – he had always driven to Daytona – and his first visit to the west coast. Trev gave him the red carpet treatment, taking him to a fancy restaurant, up into the mountains and out fishing on his boat. DuHamel proceeded to catch a salmon, something that surprised his host, who said there weren't any as far as he knew in Deep Cove.

"We ate that fish on the boat cooked over charcoal," DuHamel recalls. "He was a nice man. I used to say he was my second father, Trevor."

The feelings were reciprocated. Yvon was everything Trevor could ask for in a son, talented, personable and absolutely fearless on the track. Unfortunately for this apparently fundamental need in his life, what Trev actually had wasn't a son, but a daughter, Dawne Elizabeth.

At first when Dawne was born, he had kept his distance, emotionally if not always physically. Gradually, though, he began to warm to his offspring, holding her in his arms, and taking the toddler on short trips as she got older. Islay, who is referred to by everyone who knew her as a saint, was a loving and attentive guardian. Fred Jr., for his part, made sure the little girl was bundled off to a private girls' school as soon as possible. A company employee would be dispatched to drive her to York House School at Granville and King Edward, dressed smartly in her Black Watch kilt, white blouse and green sweater and wearing the school tie of green and gold. Another employee, or Trevor, would pick her up after school for the short trip back home. God forbid any granddaughter of Fred Jr. should take the bus. On the weekends or holidays, Trev would collect Dawne and expose her to a completely different environment, the noise and excitement of motorcycle racing. She remembers when still very young meeting the racers, touching their motorcycles and especially smelling the pungent odour of Castrol R racing oil that seemed to hang in the air at Hannigan speedway and Westwood racetrack. Other trips were to the Pacific National Exhibition and to Deep Cove for holidays on Trevor's boat. The rest of the time, which was most of the time, she went to school and lived with her grandparents.

They were, she says diplomatically, "quite strict" and "very protective," giving her little chance to make friends and almost no chance to meet boys. If Dawne stepped out of line, Fred Jr. would clip her across the head or spank her until she couldn't sit down. The school she went to for twelve years kept her similarly isolated. You might expect, looking back, that Dawne would harbour some feelings of loss, or perhaps anger, at the way she was treated during her childhood, by her father or her grandparents. In fact, speaking of how they raised her, she is very positive. "They instilled a lot of good old-fashioned values," she says of Fred Jr. and Islay, "values you just don't see these days, that I'm very grateful for."

Curiously, in light of the strictness involved, none of those values appeared to come from any form of organized religion. Fred and Islay never took the little girl to church, nor did her great grandparents or Trevor instill or suggest a belief in, or a view against, a Divine presence. In fact the lack of religion, as such, is one of the mysteries in the Deeley family history. If you go back to the first decade of the century, and look at how people described themselves, in addition to their ethnic background, class and language, they almost always held firm to a religious belief. Even those who eschewed traditional churches, made a point of doing so, declaring they were atheists, agnostics or even for the avant garde, pagans. It was not something people at the time had any confusion about. Yet, despite this, there is not a hint of any of the usual religious trappings, from a Jewish menorah, to a high Anglican feast, to a Catholic christening in any family story about any of the Deeleys. Christmas was celebrated as a secular day for gift giving and Easter hardly rated a mention. Dawne says her grandmother was United, presumably Methodist, and her grandfather Church of England. There is no record of either of them attending services at a church of either denomination. When they died there was no religious ceremony and afterwards no cross was placed on their plaque. All that can be said unequivocally about their innermost beliefs is that Islay believed in Fred Jr., and he believed in making money.

Dawne, whose only contact with religion was at school or with friends, uses a uniquely religious verb in describing how Fred Jr. treated her father. "He had my dad crucified," she says. "He bucked all my dad's business decisions. He was confrontational. He was argumentative. He was just . . ." words fail her and she sighs. When she resumes, her description of Fred Jr.

would do credit to a diplomat at the United Nations. "My grandfather was unable to see a lot of things, except in a two dimensional way and a lot of times that wasn't in colour, that was in black and white. So he really set a lot of limitations for people around him that sometimes I feel were completely unreasonable."

After a long struggle with Alzheimer's disease, Alfred Deeley died in 1970, age eighty-nine. Trevor's sadness at the passing of his grandfather was mixed with quiet astonishment at the outcome. Fred Sr. left all his money to his sons and their wives and not a penny to Trevor. He said in his will, "To Trevor, I leave nothing. He has proven he can do well enough on his own." Although he had been well paid as the head of the motorcycle division, it would only have been human to expect something from his grandfather, in effect a bonus for years of sacrificing his personality for his father and the family business. It was not to be; instead of a bank draft he got a compliment. It didn't matter, of course, Trevor was still in line of succession.

One limitation Fred Jr. couldn't force on the new, self confident Trevor was regarding travel to the Orient. Because of his growing Yamaha business, Trev had to visit Japan regularly to buy new products, meet company managers and exchange business development information. Eventually he made fourteen trans-Pacific crossings. On one visit, he shipped over a Bombardier Skidoo he bought retail, then growing in popularity as a recreational vehicle. Since it was powered by a two-stroke motor, and since Yamaha was a world leader in this technology, Trev suggested Yamaha start making snowmobiles. The first efforts were a perfect copy, but the Japanese company decided to improve on it. This wasn't very successful. The next models weighed more than a Skidoo, had five-speed transmissions and experienced a lot of mechanical problems, the carbs caused misfiring, the intake manifolds fell off, the mufflers went and many frames were defective. But, just as Honda had done before with motorcycles and cars, so the Yamaha product managers did with snowmobiles, attacking each weakness until they eliminated it. The chassis was lightened, an automatic transmission was added, reliability was improved. In four years, Fred Deeley Yamaha was selling thousands of snowmobiles as well as motorcycles across Canada.

We get a snapshot of the company in 1971 through a lengthy interview Trevor gave Bill Fletcher, a financial writer for the *Vancouver Sun* newspaper.

Trev had just come back from Japan where he had signed for 15,000 Yamaha motorcycles, bringing his grand total of imports to 90,000 machines since 1958 — 40,000 Hondas and 50,000 Yamahas. He said he had had a twenty-six percent market share and anticipated selling 16,000 motorcycles at an average net of $500 each, 6 to 7,000 snowmobiles at an average net of $700 each, plus $1 million in parts. Sales of Yamaha outboard motors and skis would be on top of these figures. His distribution network, he said, included warehouses in Vancouver and Toronto, 400 motorcycle dealers and 500 Yamaha snowmobile dealers. To service these outlets, he had a staff of sixty, compared with 165 in his father's car division.

After noting he was working with fewer people than his dad, Trev made a point of saying he was going to make more money. The motorcycle division of the company, Fletcher reported, "is expected to rack up more than $15 million in sales, outdistancing the Austin dealership section run by his father Fred G. Deeley on West Broadway."

If ever a son could be seen sticking his finger in his father's eye, this was it. Anyone who knew Fred Jr. and Trevor would have read the interview for exactly what it was, a victory speech in the competition they had carried on since the day Trevor was born fifty-one years earlier. Trevor had beaten his father at his own game; it was time to tell the world who was really making Fred Deeley Ltd. a successful company. For Trev, victory was sweet.

Victory was also short lived.

The problem was the snowmobile business. Unlike the motorcycle industry, which could sell bikes no matter what the weather, with snowmobiles, when it didn't snow, they didn't sell. This is just what happened in the winter of 1971. Fred Deeley Yamaha imported about 13,000 snowmobiles and because of a warm winter in the east and a saturated market, wound up with 4,500 left over in the spring of 1972. At this point, Trevor was working on six-month letters of credit, enough for one season, but not long enough to carry the inventory over to the next. He realized if he didn't cut a deal with the factory, he might be hung out to dry for the old machines and still have to finance the new ones for next year. With that in mind, he and Don James went to Japan in November 1972 for a meeting with the top people at Yamaha. When they got there, Yamaha had a surprise for them; they wanted Deeley's to take 13,000 more snowmobiles!

"I just thought, *That's it. That's it.*" Trev recalls. "I didn't like the snowmobile business anyway. I said I was a motorcycle distributor, and that's what I wanted to be. But they wouldn't divide the business."

Trevor had the financing arranged to make a deal. The CIBC had said they would carry the unsold inventory and provide a letter of credit for the following year's stock. However, he had also been asked by Fred Jr. to reduce the company's exposure, not increase it. The debt load was so huge it had been keeping Fred Jr. awake nights worrying about it. With that on his mind, Trev was prepared to accept a smaller order than the previous year, but he was certainly not about to increase it. As a counter proposal, he suggested Yamaha split the business and take over the snowmobile end for themselves. This would leave Fred Deeley Ltd. carrying the motorcycles they knew they could sell and lumber the Japanese with the snowmobiles that Trev knew they couldn't. The big Yamaha team sitting opposite them refused. It was all or nothing.

At this point, he turned to the Yamaha managing director, Mr. Eguchi, and said, "It can't be done. Maybe it's time you bought us out." Sitting beside him, Don, then Trev's executive assistant, was shocked. In all their discussions, the sell option had never come up. He waited expectantly to hear the Japanese reaction.

The factory, which probably was waiting for just this kind of opportunity, agreed immediately. The tentative deal, when they finished drawing it up, was that Yamaha would pay fair market value for everything in stock, every nut, bolt and screw; hire all the staff, lease the buildings, including the large new warehouse being built at 13500 Verdun Place, and pay Fred Deeley Ltd. a million dollars for good will. They would also pay the racers Trev had under contract for the 1973/74 season, both snowmobile and motorcycle racers, and they would cover the cost of the snowmobile show for the 1974 model year which was scheduled for Toronto in the spring. There was one condition from the Yamaha side; Trevor had to stay on as a senior advisor for three years. Yamaha's plan was to keep him from competing against them by putting him on the payroll for thirty-six months. Reluctantly, because of the feelings of his father, and the need to get the company off the hook for the unsold snowmobiles, Trevor agreed. What was a $3.6 million debt that could have become a $13.2 million liability on snowmobiles alone had been turned into a $1 million profit.

The two Canadians went back to their hotel in Hamamatsu,

walked into the bar and ordered some drinks, rye and 7-Up for Trev, rye on the rocks for Don.

"What are you going to do? Trev asked.

Yamaha had alluded to Don staying on as vice-president and then moving up to president once Trevor finished his contract. It was a pretty nice opportunity, but Don didn't feel good about it.

"You know, Trev," he said, "the value I have in this whole thing is from you. I don't really want to work for a big corporation, I never have. I really like what we're doing and the relationship we have. The way we operate the business is the way I like to do it, so I think I'm going to look for something else."

"Why don't we buy the warehouse operation from my dad?" Trev asked. "You could run it until I finish this Yamaha deal."

"Okay," Don replied. "Sounds good to me."

What he was wondering was how would he buy anything. He had been married in 1969 and was only making $600 a month. Buying a car was a big purchase, much less buying a business.

"Don't worry about it," Trev said when he asked. "We'll get together when we get back."

The two had planned to stay in Japan for three weeks, so the sudden decision to sell Yamaha left them with time on their hands. They decided the best way to kill it was to stop over in Hawaii which was on the way back anyway. They flew to the Islands, stayed at the Westin Hotel in Honolulu and went sailing with two of Trevor's friends, Bill McGibbon and his wife, Jean. Trev had come to enjoy the Hawaiian Islands as much as his father and he relished the sunshine, the ocean and the feeling of relief from the overhanging debt caused by Yamaha's snowmobiles. Now, in a declining snowmobile market, Yamaha could carry 17,500 of the little critters themselves. Somehow, sitting in the sailboat cockpit, with a cold drink in their hands and the tropical breezes blowing over their bodies, the prospect of the manufacturing-mad Japanese stuck with their own inventory made everyone very happy.

There remained a lot of problems, the first of which was to sell the proposed deal to Fred Jr. This proved easy to do because while the Yamaha business had been good for the company, the margins had been low and the pressure from the Japanese to take more and more product had been intense. The snowmobile carry-over was the last straw for Fred Jr. as well. He was so pleased to be rid of it, he agreed to Trev's request to buy out Fred Deeley Ltd.'s wholesale business, and even helped with the financing. Trev put up $6,000, Don put in $3,000 and Fred Jr. took the rest of the

Vera bakes Trev a cake and throws a party prior to a big race at Riverside, California. The perfect loving couple.

A blur of speed as Trev heads north up the beach in 1950.

Trev's second attempt at Daytona. Beside him is Gene Thiessen.

Deeley's Dope

Fred Deeley Ltd.

606 East Broadway **FAirmont 9673**

Canada's Largest Motorcycle Dealer

"ESTABLISHED A THIRD OF A CENTURY"

December, 1950	*New Shop*	Vancouver, B.C.

EDITORIAL

July 2nd was a proud day for the Deeley clan. It commemorated the opening of a new Motorcycle Store at 606 East Broadway. On January 19th, 1914 we started business at 1075 Granville Street — a store 12½' x 50' of 650 sq. feet. Today we have grown to the point where we now have half a million square feet to do business. From bicycles to motorcycles, from motorcycles to motor cars, and we have endeavoured to serve our customers in Western Canada with all these commodities to the best of our ability.

Deeley's Dope announces the new motorcycle store on East Broadway.

The Vancouver Police Motorcycle Drill Team. Trev is on the left.

In charge at last. Trev in his element at 606 East Broadway in 1953.

Trev's last race in the United States. Thiessen is in the lead, but Trev eventually powered by to win.

Trev at the BMW distributor's test track in Japan.

Trev and Ayumi Wasanabi in a Honda powerboat in Tokyo. Note the large pearl ring on her wedding finger.

Talk about gall! Fred Sr. and Jr. mount the little Hondas that sold like hot cakes.

Trev and his Yamaha racing team at Daytona. Yvon DuHamel on the right, Bob Work between them.

The first cross-Canada expedition stops at Elk Lake outside Victoria. Trev and Joyce are on the left, Don James and his wife, Ruth, are on the solo machine at right.

Dawne Deeley on her custom-built Harley-Davidson.

The famous eagle in the lobby of the Harley-Davidson head office.

Trev is presented with a plaque at the "Field of Dreams" baseball complex at the Victoria Airport.

Trev and Joyce with their personal Harley-Davidson motorcycle.

Jay Leno poses with Trev and two friends, Oliver Fhokouh and Ed Tauber. Note the insignia on Fhokouh's belt buckle.

183

The Nova Project bike. It looked like a traditional Harley, but in fact it had a four-cylinder, water-cooled motor. Cooling air entred through the fairing and was ducted to a radiator under the seat. Trev opposed it and it was never put into production.

The Cove Lady *in port.*

Trev Deeley at the helm.

From dirt tracks to ivory carpets, Trev relaxing today at his home in Sidney.

value back in a promissory note. What they got in return was a 4,000-square-foot rented warehouse at 595 West 7th Street, a $400,000 parts inventory and eight mostly long-time Fred Deeley Ltd. employees. Fred Jr.'s only provisos were that the inventory be paid for at book value and the deal not go through until the end of the Triumph model year. In light of what happened subsequently, it was a very sharp deal for both father and son.

The next step was to inform the employees the take-over was coming. The announcement in January tried to put the change in a good light by guaranteeing job security, promising higher pay rates and predicting more opportunities for promotion. The reaction, however, was anything but positive. There was a sense of betrayal among senior staff members who had built the company up from the start when unpaid overtime and personal sacrifice had been the norm. Far from being pleased about having job guarantees, they were bitter they had been sold to the Japanese along with the furniture, waste baskets and boxes of paper clips without the choice of being paid off for their years of dedication to Fred Deeley Yamaha. Some of the anger was aimed at Fred Jr. who owned the company, but most was directed towards Trevor who had been its active manager and still was the company vice president.

In truth, the upset probably couldn't have been avoided, no matter who was at the helm. What Fred Deeley Ltd. employees were familiar with was an autocratic, family-run firm with the personal relationships and authoritarian management style that kind of company represents. Yamaha Motor Canada Ltd. would be a modern, impersonal corporation where promotion and salaries would be based on merit and meeting corporate objectives rather than on friendships and loyalties. The two cultures were light years apart and, instinctively, everyone knew it and feared it.

Before anyone got too worked up, Trev put them to work with a system-wide inventory of Fred Deeley Yamaha. The check-off of parts and assets was especially thorough because the more that was found, the higher the payment would be from Japan. James remembers every last desk, every nut, bolt, screw, pencil and typewriter was counted and the totals put into a book. The book went to Yamaha and they bought the lot, just as they'd promised. Before that was even finished, however, Trev moved Don to the warehouse department and made him the manager. When the Japanese arrived, he would no longer be anywhere near Fred Deeley Yamaha.

The transfer of ownership took place May 31, 1973. Fred Jr.

signed the sale agreement with Yamaha and Trevor signed his personal contract to act as an advisor. Officials from Yamaha, in turn, signed a cheque. The actual ceremony took place at five minutes to six on a Friday night. Because the cheque was so large, Trev phoned ahead and the bank stayed open past closing time waiting for Fred Jr. to rumble down Broadway with the multi-million dollar deposit.

The deal had earlier been announced to the dealers in two letters signed by Fred Jr. and Satoshi Moriya from Yamaha. Fred's letter read:

Dear Sirs:

It gives me great pleasure to announce that I have completed arrangements to sell the Yamaha Division of Fred Deeley Limited to the Yamaha Motor Company of Japan. Many reasons prompted the decision to sell our Yamaha Division to the Yamaha Motor Company. The fantastic growth of Yamaha in Canada necessitates a team of young dynamic people and Trev and I are not getting any younger as time goes by. The name of the new company will be Yamaha Motor Canada Limited and the changeover date is effective June 1, 1973. I am most happy to announce that Yamaha Motor Canada have appointed my son, Trevor, as Vice President of the Canadian company, and I know this will be most enthusiastically accepted by all Yamaha dealers in Canada. I wish to thank you all at this time for your supreme efforts on our behalf, and I sincerely hope that somewhere along the line I will have been instrumental in bringing you products that have helped make your business profitable and successful.

Wishing you and yours the very best of health and success in the business in the future, I remain,

Yours very truly,

Fred G. Deeley
President

The letter from Mr. Moriya was even more cordial than Fred Jr.'s. His read:

Dear Sirs,

This letter is to introduce you to our new company, Yamaha Motor Canada Limited, which officially commences June 1, 1973.

We, at Yamaha, feel very pleased that we have been able to take over the Yamaha business of Fred Deeley Limited, who have been one of our finest distributors over the past ten years. The business successes and acceptance of Yamaha products has without doubt been made possible by the fine efforts of Fred Deeley Limited and all of you Yamaha dealers. We have many plans for advertising, promotion and expansion, and we feel that you, as a Yamaha dealer, will benefit from the new products and plans for increase [sic] market penetration that we have to bring you. Many more details will be following in the near future. It gives me great pleasure to announce that Mr. Trevor Deeley has been appointed Vice President of Yamaha Motor Canada, and I am sure he will greatly contribute to you and the new company through his long experience with Yamaha.

Sincerely yours,

Satoshi Moriya
Executive Vice President

Mr. Moriya's hopes were not to be fulfilled.

CHAPTER TEN

ON THE MONDAY after the transfer Trevor got a telephone call from John Davidson, then president of Harley-Davidson.

"You son of a bitch," Davidson shouted. "I hear you sold Yamaha."

"How'd you hear that?" Trev replied.

"Never mind how I heard it. Did you or didn't you?"

"Yeah, I did."

"Great," said Davidson, "we want you to be the Harley distributor for Canada."

Trevor just about swallowed the telephone. The ink was barely dry on his new contract over at Yamaha Motor Canada Ltd.

"Jesus John, I can't do it. I just signed a contract three days ago."

Davidson hit the roof. In the entire world, Harley-Davidson had never had a distributor before, they had handled all their distribution themselves. However, complaints from Canadian dealers about slow parts deliveries, difficulties in creating more dealerships and problems selling snowmobiles had convinced the factory it should break its tradition, for Canada at least, and follow the practice pioneered by the Japanese. They had selected Trev to take on the job because he was the logical person and because they liked him as an individual. Fred Deeley Ltd. was their oldest dealer in Canada and Trevor had successfully run both the Honda and Yamaha distribution networks. On top of that, John had met Trev during the war when he was stationed in Washington state, had entertained him at his home in Milwaukee, and had vacationed with Trev and Joyce more recently on Nitnat Lake on Vancouver Island. To the Davidsons, the Deeleys were almost family.

"When can we get together?" Davidson said finally. "I want to talk to you."

"I'm going back to Toronto for Yamaha snowmobiles next week." Trev replied.

"Okay, I'll send Charlie up to see you."

Trev kept the good news to himself. He was afraid if he told Fred Jr., his father would insist on taking over the franchise, just as he'd muscled into the Yamaha deal and the Honda franchise before that. Trevor could even imagine what his father would say if he told him John Davidson had offered the Harley-Davidson distributorship: "Well, you wouldn't have got it if it wasn't for me. So it's ours." *Bullshit,* Trevor thought, *it's not ours, it's mine.* Not talking about it eliminated the problem.

The following week Trev flew to Toronto for the Yamaha show and met Charlie Thompson, the Harley-Davidson vice president at the time, and explained his situation. He said he very much wanted to be the distributor for H-D in Canada, and was setting up a mechanism to do it through his own company, Fred Deeley Imports Ltd. The only problem was that he wouldn't get the company nailed down until the summer at the earliest and he still had a three-year commitment with Yamaha. Thompson said he would wait a year to appoint Fred Deeley Imports as the Canadian distributor if Trev would find a way to break his contract at that time. Then he unloaded his zinger; to become the Canadian Harley-Davidson distributor Trev would have to take on Harley-Davidson's ageing line of snowmobiles. Trev winced, knowing those snowmobiles would have to go up against a huge surplus of Yamahas in a declining market, the same Yamahas he was officially trying to sell out on the floor of the show. He thought quickly. If he could delay his entry into the big eastern Canadian market of Ontario and Quebec for a year, Harley would take such a shellacking from the Japanese it might quit the snowmobile business before he had to get into it. He accepted the deal. Then he suggested, to make the introduction easier, that they split the distributorship package into two, with Trevor taking western Canada where he was well known in the first year, and picking up the rest of the country in year two. The two men shook on the deal and went happily on their way. *With any luck*, Trev thought, *the Harley snowmobile effort will go through the ice this winter.* It must also have passed through his mind that every Yamaha snowmobile sold made that outcome more, rather than less, likely.

It's worth pausing for a moment to review what Trevor was doing and how he was doing it because he had two secret deals in progress simultaneously, either one of which could have collapsed the entire plan. The creation of Fred Deeley Imports was being done without the knowledge of Yamaha Motor Canada, who, had they known, might have launched a lawsuit alleging breach of contract. At the same time, his deal with Harley-Davidson to become the Canadian distributor was being kept from his father who, had he known, almost certainly would have put the sale of the wholesale department on hold while he folded the H-D distributorship into Fred Deeley Ltd. Secrecy, therefore, was crucial to the plan's success. Fred Jr.'s overbearing attitude had forced Trev to act secretly years before when he wanted to save motorcycles from the scrap heap and he had used the same skills to launch Honda under the noses of B.S.A. and to get Yamaha going while he was still importing from Honda. Now, he was up to his old tricks, only this time he was working for himself.

Trev had a year to get his ducks in a row. The first order of business was finalizing the deal to take over the wholesale department. This had been held up because Ray Deeley at first was reluctant to let Trev and Don use the name Fred Deeley Imports, ostensibly because his own company was called Fred Deeley Cycles Ltd. The real reason, of course, was that Ray didn't want to do anything to help Fred Jr. It was only when Trevor convinced him that the new company would be a completely separate entity from Fred Deeley Ltd. that he agreed to let Trev use the family name. The sale of the wholesale department and the creation of Fred Deeley Imports Ltd. took place September 25, 1973, and the new company started operations officially November 1 with Don James as vice president. Don, who had one-third of the shares, had one-third control of the company and Trev had the remainder. The understanding, in a buy-sell agreement, was that Don would be able to increase his share to forty-nine percent over time, and that eventually Trev would sell him controlling interest. The deal also stipulated that if Don left the company, he would have to sell his shares back to Trev.

No sooner had the company been set up, however, than its

main source of motorcycles dried up. The wholesale department had imported 915 Triumphs for 1973 and hoped to do even better in 1974. Unfortunately, management ineptitude and a bitter labour dispute brought production to a standstill in England, and the next year Triumph shipments were virtually nil. The manufacturer, Norton-Villiers-Triumph, was still building Nortons so Trevor and Don tried to switch over to them. Norton was being handled by British Motorcycles, but they convinced NVT to let Fred Deeley Imports act as a second distribution network, providing they stayed out of the British Motorcycles territory. That lasted for about four months before Don sold to a dealer he wasn't supposed to and the arrangement fell apart.

The employees, who faced the winter of 1973/74 with Moto Guzzi as their only supplier, no doubt wondered why Don James was still so confident everything would work out in the end.

There was no such good will over at the new Yamaha headquarters at Verdun Place. In the first two months, Trevor and Moriya locked horns practically every day, with Moriya, the new boss, winning one round after another. The issues were both cultural and corporate. The Japanese management style involved weeks of group discussions, endless talk in smoke-filled rooms and after-hours drinking with the same bunch of people. Trev's style had always been quick and to the point, he preferred drinking in mixed company and he didn't smoke. Style aside, he was no longer the boss. In his own world, away from his father, Trev was used to being a leader whose opinions got translated into action without much argument. In the new Yamaha set-up, he was just one sports coat and trousers in a sea of penguin-like black suits and white shirts.

Transcending both style and leadership, there was the bigger issue of dealing with the dealers. This is the basic activity of any distribution organization and it was the area in which Trevor had the most knowledge from his years of experience and his unique position as both a distributor and a dealer. He respected his dealers, knew them all personally, and tried to ensure they had the financing, territory and support necessary to make their businesses a success. His new Japanese masters had other ideas. They wanted motorcycles and snowmobiles rolled out the door and they didn't care how they did it, or who got hurt, in the drive to achieve higher sales quotas. Trev could see it coming almost immediately; some of the dealers Don Solem and he had worked so hard to set up were going to be squeezed out of business by Yamaha's preoccupation with sales at all costs. Another cause for the dispute between the two men was that Moriya was under orders to move the head office to Toronto, the centre of the Canadian business world, as soon as possible. Trev was not about to move east and away from his new business, his new home on the North Shore, his new boat at the RVYC or his new aircraft at the Aero Club of B.C. The more Moriya pushed, the more Trevor resisted.

All in all there was a lot to disagree about and Trev remembers the disputes became very personal.

"The guy they sent over to run Yamaha, Steve Moriya, didn't treat me very well. The worse he treated me for the first two months, the worse I treated him for the last ten months. It just became a point of honour." From the outside, Don could see Trev was having a very hard time at Yamaha. "It was a terrible time for him, with a lot of anxiety because he was watching them mess up stuff that he'd built. It was an impossible situation."

There are various versions of how Trevor left Yamaha. Trev, himself, says it was a "parting of the ways." The rumour among company staff in the east was that he was fired because he'd been seen quietly pushing Harley-Davidson snowmobiles at Yamaha snowmobile dealer meetings. Another story was that he was caught negotiating with Harley-Davidson while still a Yamaha employee. In fact, what happened was that Trevor, exactly according to plan, lit the bomb under the Yamaha job himself by announcing on May 15, 1974, that Fred Deeley Imports had been appointed Canadian distributor of Harley-Davidson motorcycles and snowmobiles. It took Yamaha over a month to figure out that with Fred Deeley Jr. aged seventy, the Deeley in charge of the new company had to be their high-priced advisor. He was called into Moriya's office on Friday, June 21, and was told he was finished with Yamaha. In one slash of the pen, Moriya paid out his contract for the full three years and Trev left the building. Halfway down the block, he remembered he was driving a company car, so he turned around and went back and bought it from them with a cheque of his own.

Then he got back in his new car and headed straight to his bank. He walked in, asked for the manager and said he wanted to cash the Yamaha cheque. The manager gulped, he didn't have $200,000 in cash on the premises. Instead, he asked if he could give him a bank draft for it. That was fine with Trev. What he'd been afraid of was that as soon as the news of what Moriya had done got back to Tokyo, head office would put a stop order on the cheque.

It was, of course, a business coup of major proportions. Trevor had managed to get out of his contract two years early with a substantial golden handshake at precisely the moment he needed to launch his career with Harley-Davidson. If there were champagne glasses filled in the Deeley household that weekend, it would have been understandable. Not only did he have his own business free of any interference from his father, he had the national distributorship of one of the oldest and most respected names in motorcycling, he had his trusted lieutenant Don James, he had Joyce at his side and to top it off he had two years' salary in his pocket for spending money. In all his life, through all his motorcycle triumphs, personal tragedies, parental humiliations, and business shenanigans, this moment was the pinnacle that made everything worthwhile. Behind him, everything was history; before him, everything breathed promise and potential.

For Moriya, the buyout was a disaster. He was recalled to Japan in disgrace and was eventually fired.

Trevor walked into the little Harley-Davidson warehouse on River Road in Richmond, B.C., on the morning of June 24, 1974, and said, "Hi, I'm here! We're going to be working together." He was greeted by Don James and the small staff who welcomed him to his new office with its old furniture. Trev looked around with a big smile, "This," he said, "is where I want to be." He was fifty-four and for the first time in his life he was working for himself.

Later in the day, news of the big split reached *Cycle Canada* and Trev got a call from a reporter. What had happened, he asked? "Whether I was dismissed or fired or whether I quit doesn't matter," Trev replied. "The point was that I could carry on no longer." He said he and Steve Moriya had "many differences of opinion about operational methods. After twelve years of hard work building Yamaha in Canada, I felt very upset about leaving," he said, "but today I feel very happy. In fact, I'm absolutely ecstatic about my future with Harley-Davidson. It's like a new breath of life, I feel at least ten years younger." Actually he felt a lot younger than that. Being named the H-D distributor reminded Trev of how he felt as a boy. "In 1935 when I was fifteen, I got my first bike, a Francis Barnett, which I rode to school every day. On the way home, I'd always stop at the shop and just sit and look at the Harleys. Harley-Davidson has always been my true love. Even when I was at races with Yamaha, I'd find myself rooting silently for the guys on the Harleys."

For someone who loved Harleys, Trevor's sudden appearance on the scene as Canada's first national distributor wasn't welcomed with open arms by all the Harley-Davidson dealers.

There were so few dealers across the country, many of them had actually become distributors in a small way themselves, getting machines from the factory and passing them along to non-authorized shops in smaller communities. They were afraid that the creation of an official distribution network would eliminate this lucrative re-selling operation, and cut into their profits. Worse, from their point of view, was the possibility that Fred Deeley Imports was planning to open more Harley-Davidson dealerships. The fear was entirely justified. In his talks with John Davidson, Trevor had been told H-D wanted a hundred H-D dealerships for Canada, eighty-seven more than the thirteen that were then in place. Harley got the number by applying the old ten percent rule to Canadian distribution. They were trying to expand to 1,000 dealers in the United States, so Canada with a tenth of the population should have 100.

Grant Budd, of Prairie Motorcycles in Regina, was one of these long-time Harley-Davidson dealers who wasn't happy when Fred Deeley Imports was placed between him and the factory in Milwaukee. "Not at first, I wasn't," he recalls. "I could see the probable writing on the wall where I was going to lose out on an agency. However, I understand the factory had given him emphatic notice that he was not to disenfranchise these elderly dealers. But, after the clouds cleared, and Trev and I got together in a businesslike way, it worked out fine. As a matter of fact, I've made more money while dealing through Trevor than I ever did dealing directly with Harley."

Budd was partly right. Trev had been asked not to cancel any old dealers *immediately*, but he was otherwise given a free hand. In the event, he didn't cancel anyone anyway.

Working for Trevor, and quelling some of the disquiet, was his reputation and that of the Deeley organization. Dealers who knew his grandfather, his father and himself, knew they would get product, in quantity, on time, at a price they could make money on selling. This was one factor that eased Budd through the transition because he had been signed up by Trevor as a Honda dealer in the early '60s and respected his way of doing business.

Another dealer with a long history of working with the Deeleys was Bob Kane in Calgary. He was at the famous meeting at the Palliser Hotel and so became one of the very first Honda dealers in Canada. When Trev sold the company, he switched to Yamaha and when he sold Yamaha, Kane decided to concentrate exclusively on his original franchise, Harley-Davidson. At one point during the Honda boom in the early '70s, Harley-Davidson only represented three percent of his sales, and most of these were to the police department. "My problem in '71-'72 was that I was selling a lot of motorcycles, but not making any money. We'd have people come in and assemble ten to fourteen bikes a night so we could sell them the next day and at the end of the year, why my profit only showed ten dollars or so. I said, well there's something wrong here." Trevor, still working for Yamaha at the time, tried to argue him out of becoming an exclusive dealership, but Kane was adamant. "I decided that I was going to go to one make of motorcycle and just have one line of parts and one line of mechanics. I don't think Trevor agreed with me on this because he thought that one dealer couldn't make it on one make of machine, but I decided I would try it anyway." When Trev showed up in 1974, now promoting Harley, Kane felt his earlier decision was vindicated. He also felt pleased to be associated again with Deeley's because over the years they had extended him almost unlimited credit, allowing him to become a large volume dealership.

The fact that he and other dealers thought they were dealing with "the Deeleys" or the "Deeley organization" shows how right Trevor was to insist on naming his new company after that of his grandfather. They assumed Fred Deeley Imports was part of the Deeley empire, with near limitless financial resources, when in fact Trevor was operating with a much more limited cash flow than anyone knew. Even now, looking back, Kane felt he was part of the family. "When we went to the Harley shows, and the shows Trev put on, there was almost always like a family feeling in that you felt you were part of the Deeley organization. That always gave you a good feeling when you had tough times you know."

As the western dealers came on side, and new ones were set up, Trev and Don discovered they had a problem they hadn't anticipated. Harley-Davidson quality had slipped to its lowest level ever. "The stuff they were building was so much junk," Trev says. "We had more damn trouble with warranty, trying to fix the stuff and keep things running, than we did selling them. But we just stuck with it, and stuck with it."

The source of the quality problem went back to 1965 when Harley-Davidson went public in order to raise additional funds to pay off debts and finance expansion. The company's stock was well spread out among the officers and the public when, late in the decade, it became the target of a hostile take-over from another company intent on making sweeping changes. To fend off the raid, H-D negotiated a merger with an eastern conglomerate called American Machine and Foundry, which bought the historic motorcycle maker in 1969 for $14 million. The take-over was like being swallowed by a whale. Even though the AMF chairman, Rodney Gott, had been a Harley-Davidson rider in the 1930s, and was pictured riding a Sportster on a visit to the factory, the company almost immediately began to lose its focus, and quality suffered.

This wasn't immediately apparent to potential customers, because of Harley racing successes. Cal Rayborn won the Daytona 200 in 1969 and in 1970 he led an American team in a series of six Anglo-American match races in England that stunned the European motorcycle world. Rayborn ran away with three firsts and got three second place finishes riding the "iron XR," Harley's new XR-750 racer. Quality, however, or the lack of it, was noticed by the dealers and eventually by the riding public. Harleys, always the most reliable bike on the road, started to break down for unexpected reasons, parts that had previously been trustworthy would crack, and oil too often dripped from blown seals and gaskets. The company continued to honour its warranties and supply the necessary replacements, but the inconvenience factor for owners, dealers and the Canadian distributor was considerable. Trev didn't know this at the time, but as the decade wore on, the problems were to get worse.

His big problem as he began 1975 was to digest eastern Canada, the part of the country with the largest population and the part in which he was least well known. Even though Pacific Seaboard had been national, and Trev had made the presence of Fred Deeley Yamaha known, he was not the unmistakable figure in the east he was in the Pacific Northwest. He was especially not known to the Harley-Davidson fraternity who, as a group, loathed the Honda and Yamaha invasion with a passion.

Trev's solution was obvious to anyone who liked motorcycling as much as he did; he'd ride across the country on a Harley and introduce himself to the company's dealers along the way. To make it more of an event, he enlisted his vice president, his boatbuilder and a friend who owned a photofinishing business to come along with him. The eventual coast-to-coast expedition was made up of Trev and Joyce, Ruth and Don James, Mary and Don Matheson (the boatbuilder) and Milt and Marge Goodman (whose father owned Crystal Photo Finishing on West Broadway). Trev and Joyce in a sidecar, accompanied by Don and Ruth on a solo machine, were to start off from St. John, New Brunswick, and be joined in Toronto by the other two couples, both of whom would have sidecars on their Harley FLHs. All three outfits were emblazoned with the slogan "Atlantic to Pacific by Harley-Davidson." Ruth James, writing in *The Enthusiast*, had the typical amazement a car passenger displays when encountering long distance motorcycling for the first time. "9:00 AM June 20th, 1975 – Trevor (or Number One) led the caravan out. Between chattering teeth and shrieks of 'slow down' I barely managed to notice the rolling green hills and the charming old homes with their stark, simple lines. Many of them had lovely big porches with decorative carvings and roof lines. Maybe this motorcycle business wasn't all bad; but wait – rain. Out came all the rain gear and we all began to feel quite comfortable and complacent. The Gods hadn't finished though – hail! Yow! Stinging little pellets right in the face accompanied by a gag to keep me from shouting 'my body for a car ride,' to all the passing automobiles."

Trev at fifty-five years of age was more than Number One, he was a regular Rommel leading his troops across the desert. Every day they would roll out of their hotel and set off on a run that could be anywhere from 275 to 400 miles. The stopping points would be H-D dealerships, where Trevor, who had met them at his first Harley-Davidson dealer show, would say he was looking forward to working with them and then be on his way to the next location. There was no time for stopping and smelling the roses because Trev had also arranged for the local news media to record their arrival in each town in which a dealership was located. The highlight of the day became the packed lunch, the responsibility for which was rotated among the couples, with each trying to outdo the repast of the previous day. Then it was back on the bikes, with pit stops timed to the minute, riding west until it got dark and they arrived at their next scheduled hotel. It was fun, but it was also hard work, because in addition to keeping the machines clean, there was also a fair amount of maintenance, caused in part by the problems Harley-Davidson was having in quality control.

Disaster struck on one of the prettiest stretches of the Trans Canada highway along the north shore of Lake Superior near

Wawa. The group had been having trouble with their wire wheels along the way, and at this inconvenient point, the wheel on one of the sidecars collapsed completely. The dealer in Sault Ste. Marie was called and asked to take a wheel off the Super Glide he had on the floor as a replacement. He drove up to the marooned tour party, but instead of bringing the 16" rear wheel, he brought the 19" front wheel. He apologized and drove back, dispatching one of his employees to return with the correct unit. This unfortunate individual got to within ten miles of the now black-fly-infested executives, decided they must have miraculously fixed the sidecar themselves, and turned back. Don James, the only one with a solo machine, was dispatched after the retreating employee and finally caught up with him almost all the way back down to the Sault. By the time he got back, it was dark and cold, and the exhausted party limped into Wawa many hours behind schedule. The trip wasn't helped any when another of the machines developed a short and lost its headlight, forcing it to ride right on the tail of the combination in front. The only consolation was that no media had been waiting for them in Wawa and so there was no national story on the Harley importer being stranded by a broken wheel.

That just about happened in Winnipeg a few days later, when one of the wheels on Don's bike collapsed while they were heading towards the Manitoba capital. By then they were getting used to respoking their wheels, so they headed off to the nearest garage to get it done. The problem was that neither they nor the kid on duty at the Shell station they found could budge the tire from the rim. Finally, they wound up using a Land Rover on a hoist to slam down on the tire to break the bead free. At this point, the garage owner showed up, really upset at the kid, at Trevor for using his tools, and at everybody. Trevor, as he had done on his trip to the 1948 race at Daytona, turned on his charm and smoothed things over. As a result, there was no hint when they were interviewed by the TV crew in Winnipeg that things were falling apart.

There was also no hint then or later that none of the sidecars had been set up properly by the mechanics who serviced them originally. Harley-Davidson had an adjustable steering head that allowed riders to change the rake to make steering a sidecar unit easier. Trev only discovered none of them had been changed to sidecar specifications when they got into the Rockies. Another thing missed was a necessary change in the countershaft sprocket to make the gearing lower. Fortunately this was discovered in Regina, mostly because no one could get the loaded combinations to go faster than 40 mph in the stiff westerly winds. Grant Budd had the satisfaction of showing his new boss he had all the necessary parts in stock.

The temperature through the Rockies was well over 100° F, but Trevor, keeping up the pace to the end, insisted on pressing on to the next destination. This eventually was too much for his volunteer crew, so they began to lag behind. Finally, when he and Joyce were out of sight, they stopped altogether, leaped off their machines and ran into the Smilkameen River fully clothed to cool off.

The 4,000-mile journey could easily have been a public relations disaster. Instead, it was a great success, earning a mention in newspapers and on television stations along the way that was priceless publicity for both Harley-Davidson and Fred Deeley Imports. More important, it touched ninety percent of the dealers in the country, allowing Trev to introduce himself, his wife and vice president in a way that promoted local dealerships and in a manner no one could complain about. It was literally a case of hand holding the existing dealers, because only days later Trev and Don were planning to sign up more dealers and push their quotas of lightweight Harley-Davidson imports from Italy and snowmobiles."

After thanking their wives and friends, and firing off a heated complaint to H-D about shoddy wheel building, Trev and Don flew back east, leased a warehouse at 55 Penn Drive that had been used by Yamaha, and hit the road.

It was the worst kind of central Canadian summer — 90° in the shade with the humidity at 100 percent. The pair had to leave their rental car running with the air conditioner on to make it at all bearable. This would have been bad enough by itself, but because of their arrangement with H-D they were also selling snowmobiles! The deal they offered prospective dealers was simple; if they wanted to sell H-D big twins, they had to order snowmobiles as well, and of course, the Italian-made Harley-Davidson lightweights.

This wasn't a problem for most of those they approached, as Harley-Davidson dealerships had always been prized and had rarely been granted. Trev was offering them a chance of a lifetime and they knew it. Things were more difficult with the old dealers, especially the biggest dealer, Percy Poole in Hamilton. He had the province's second-largest city to himself as well as the Niagara Peninsula and all of southwestern Ontario, including Windsor. Because he was doing so well, he asked how Trevor thought he could help him do any better. Trev's answer was that he would be able to draw on parts from Toronto, just thirty miles away, rather than wait for them to be shipped from Wisconsin and clear customs at the border. In addition, he promised Poole more motorcycles than he'd been getting on his own.

To emphasize the point he'd be getting better service with Deeley's, Trev and Don flew east and loaded Poole's next order of Harley-Davidsons on a Hertz rental truck and delivered them personally to his shop in Hamilton.

Don remembers it was a tough go. The established dealers viewed him and Trevor as trespassers on their territory, which was a hard argument to counter because it was absolutely true. The wiser ones realized more dealers and an active distributor meant more advertising, more public awareness and, if truth be known, more opportunities for them to make money. They took the attitude that if they couldn't sell a bike to a customer, they would send him over to a competing dealer, so at least he would get something they could peddle accessories for or take in trade later.

They also realized that in Trevor they had someone who would listen to them about the quality problems that were filling up their service bays. Trev did more than just listen. When he attended his first Harley-Davidson Dealer Advisory Council that year, he laid it on the line – quality *had* to get better! Unlike other representatives on the twelve-member council, who were elected by dealers from regions around the United States, Trevor had what amounted to a permanent seat at the table as the Canadian distributor, and he used it aggressively. Problem after problem, item after item, he said this wouldn't do, that wasn't acceptable, this would have to be changed. John Davidson, who had seen his company taken over by coin counters and pencil pushers, was secretly elated. His plan to light a fire under the AMF people was taking shape very nicely.

When Trevor got back to home base there was some interesting news from the other branch of the family, insofar as Ray Sr. had sold Suzuki back to Suzuki. One by one, the Japanese factories were taking over from their original Canadian distributors, three of whom had been Deeleys. The announcement from Suzuki made Trevor smile because it confirmed the wisdom of his decision to sell Yamaha.

The next year it was more of the same, vetting more dealers, setting up his parts operation, getting staff on the road. The first salesman to start visiting dealers was Harold Lenfesty. He had joined Fred Deeley Ltd. as a warehouse clerk in 1972 at the age of eighteen and was both bright and eager to get hustling. There was a lot for him to do, because in addition to looking after warranty work, he was put out on the road selling parts and accessories. If he didn't know it then, he would eventually realize this was an almost certain indication he was being groomed for greater things. Trev himself had been sent out on the road by his father, and he had sent Don out to service a dealer network. Now Don was giving the shove out the door to Harold.

Fred Jr. now decided it was time to close down the flagship of the Deeley empire, his own long-running automotive enterprise on West Broadway.

The reasons were both personal and professional. Much as he hated to admit it, at seventy-one he was starting to lose his ability to concentrate, was tired of going to work every day, and, frankly, was fed up with Vancouver's often abominable weather. In addition, it was clear, looking over the books, the automotive division was starting to lose money. The basic problem was his product line which appeared to be getting worse, not better. Studebaker had stopped production in 1965 and been swallowed up by American Motors Corporation, and Austin had been folded into British Leyland. Neither company was doing well and neither had a new model for the mass market that could appeal to Fred Jr.'s traditional working class client base. On top of this, he had just watched B.S.A. and Triumph fail in the motorcycle business for exactly the same reasons. If he was ever going to get out of automobiles, this was the time to do it, before the value of the business totally evaporated. Quietly, he put the word out he was ready to make a deal.

The key player in the drama that followed was Fred Jr.'s sales manager, Jack Levy. He approached John McLoughlin of Bowell McLean, another car dealer down the street, and the two of them put together an offer to buy Fred Jr.'s automotive business for just over $14 million, with the bulk of the money coming from a loan secured by Fred Deeley Ltd.'s inventory and property holdings on West Broadway. In effect, they were offering to take on Fred Jr.'s debt, for his assets, or to put it another way, Fred Jr. was prepared to sell off his land to pay off his loan. At this point, Fred Jr. decided he'd had it with bargaining and left everything in Trevor's hands to clean up, while he went on a two-month vacation to Hawaii. The final negotiations, therefore, were conducted between Trevor and Levy, someone with whom Trevor had never had much success. As the proposals were made, Trev would get on the phone to his dad in Hawaii and seek his approval for one clause after another. His other task was to take a complete inventory of the company's assets. The only thing he missed was the gas in the underground holding tanks of the company service station. When he went to McLoughlin and explained he had forgotten the fuel, McLoughlin refused to pay for it. That wasn't enough to hold up the deal, so it went ahead anyway, becoming effective January 6, 1976. What the new owners got were the new, used and leased car businesses, the parts and service operations, and most important, the land they all sat on. What they did not get were the properties of the other businesses or the name Fred Deeley Ltd. What Fred Jr. got was the discharge of his $7 million debenture at the CIBC, and almost the same amount again to put in his personal bank account.

It was all very neatly done, especially considering what came afterwards. McLoughlin and Levy, despite their many years in the car business, went bankrupt almost immediately, and the company that bought them out did the same. Fred Jr. had been worried about his automotive business with good reason. He had stepped from a sinking ship into a lifeboat in good time and in good order. The finesse with which he carried it off, and the secrecy under which it was subsequently buried, imply that Fred Jr., the consummate businessman, was pretty sharp right to the end. It was almost a foregone conclusion that the last Austin imported into Canada – a lacklustre econobox called the Marina – would be sold just five years later, in 1981.

Were Fred Jr.'s mental failings a smoke screen then? Probably not. He was tired, he was disinclined to pursue a hectic work schedule and he didn't have the stamina to conclude the final negotiations himself. On the other hand, he knew when to act, what to do, and who best to assign the task to; the person who knew his business methods most intimately, his son Trevor. One gets a picture of a relay runner passing the baton to a fresher team member, just in the nick of time. It is a surprisingly loving gesture, given the poor fit between their two personalities. Fred Jr. was giving Trevor the responsibility of saving the family's assets, equity he would eventually inherit himself.

When he came back from Hawaii, Fred Jr. asked to be taken to his old office at 901 West Broadway. Trev, who had built his father a new office with a commanding view over the water in Park Royal, West Vancouver, replied, "Dad, you can't go there anymore. It's not yours." They went anyway and he had one last look around, before Trev drove him to the new office on the north shore. There, in the matching teak panelled room, he found his old desk, his old leather couch and a roomful of friends and acquaintances to congratulate him. There were tears in most eyes. It was a poignant moment.

That his son was still at his side and that there were any friends to find for the occasion was a miracle in itself.

There remained one last public event that, like the sale of the business, was better in print than in fact. At a festive retirement luncheon at the Bayshore Inn, Fred Jr. was given an aluminum bird on a block of stone and a $22,323 Jaguar XJ-S sports coupe by the successor company to Austin, British Leyland. Don Pocock of Toronto, president of British Leyland Canada, said Fred Jr. was their leading dealer in Canada in 1975, a record year for the company and the entire auto industry. Sales of British cars, he said, had increased twenty-one percent in numbers of units. Part of the reason was Fred Deeley Ltd., which had, over the years, sold an estimated 30,000 cars. It was an effusive send-off designed to cover the obvious fact that Fred Jr., who knew what the real story was, was kissing British Leyland goodbye. The effect was considerably diminished two weeks later when British Leyland sent him an invoice for the car. He paid it and promptly turned around and resold the "gift" to cover the debt. After forty-five years in the car business in Canada, and even longer in the U.K., Fred Jr. wound up getting the bird instead of an automobile by way of thanks.

The Jag presentation had been the headline in one report of the luncheon, but when another reporter commented on it later, Fred Jr. set him straight.

"Present, hell," he exclaimed. "They gave me an Austin thirty years ago. I bought this!"

The important point about the retirement announcement was that it marked the official handing over of the Fred Deeley name from the second to the third generation and the end of Fred Jr.'s public and business life. He would continue to conduct his affairs privately, assisted for a time by Lloyd Perry, but he was now off the stage and indeed, often out of the country. Fred Jr. had left the neon neighbourhood, the automotive business, the motorcycle business and the bicycle business.

Despite this, he could reflect, with a sense of satisfaction he never showed, that part of him was still very much a player in one of those fields.

CHAPTER ELEVEN

IT SAID "HARLEY-DAVIDSON" on the door, but it was the ski business all over again inside Fred Deeley Imports Ltd. on River Road. For one thing Trev and Don had practically no dealers, and for another they were on very thin ice financially. The problem was that the traditional British parts business was down to a trickle, and the Harley-Davidson business was costing more money to get up and running than it was making.

This didn't worry the two executives. They relished the challenge, devouring each problem as it came up like a red hot at a county fair. For Trev, it was what he had been doing since before he turned twenty, spotting and servicing motorcycle dealers across the west. It was as much second nature to him as riding a bike. For Don, it was just like setting up dealers for Yamaha skis — check out their credentials, check out their financing, get a commitment for inventory, service and display systems, sign the deal, and hit the road to the next place. The product might be different, the traditions might be older, the costs might be more, but the basic idea was the same as always; sell the most units that can be moved at a profit.

As a result, 1976 was a period of furious growth, dealmaking, advertising and expansion. Fred Deeley Imports Ltd. was setting up a much larger Harley-Davidson dealer network than had ever been seen in Canada before. The number of dealers doubled, then tripled. It was a total revolution in H-D marketing.

The biggest problem was getting sufficient motorcycles for the new dealer network. Canada had always been treated as a kind of distant cousin by Milwaukee, and it was hard for Trev to get his orders filled before those of individual American dealers. It was also slow because the factory was unused to volume orders and tended to fill small quantity parts orders before the much larger orders placed by the Canadian distributor. When Trevor pleaded for more bikes, the factory said it would ship him some additional large Harleys, but only if he would take the last 219 snowmobiles made. Trev quickly agreed, providing his new dealers with larger discounts and additional financing in order to get rid of the orphan machines.

The interesting thing about this exchange is that Trev correctly weighed the importance to Harley of getting the last few snowmobiles out of its warehouse versus the problem of moving them through his dealer network in a rapidly melting market. For Harley, the death of the snowmobile business was a major embarrassment; for Trevor it was a minor inconvenience. Helping out put Fred Deeley Imports in the factory's good books, just where Trev wanted to be when the negotiations began for new product shipments in 1977.

Trevor had other aces up his sleeve as well, one of them being British Columbia's magnificent scenery. Shortly after he became the national H-D distributor in 1975, he invited John Davidson, then the company president, to come out to B.C. for some fishing. Having been instrumental in having him appointed, it was perfectly natural for Davidson to come up to Canada to see how Trevor was doing. It was also natural, when he arrived, to find Trev had also invited his bankers out on his yacht for some salmon fishing, entertaining and jawing about business.

To the many people who have criticized Trev Deeley for the opulence of his lifestyle, this little cruise would have been instructive. Bankers and company presidents are, after all, only human, and all of them were impressed by Trev's immaculately equipped boat, his attractive and amusing wife Joyce, the lavish spreads set out for them to enjoy and the magnificent scenery that lay around them. In effect, Trev was using his lifestyle to project an aura of success at precisely the time when he needed his bankers to ante up for some large loans. By bringing in Harley's president, he was also reassuring them that Fred Deeley Imports had the full support and backing of the Milwaukee manufacturer.

People who look at business success stories often keep their eyes focused exclusively on the boardroom, when, in fact, much of the real action takes place over highballs at country clubs, fine restaurants and, in Trevor's case, in the cockpit of the *Cove Lady* cruising the Gulf Islands. These personal, social contacts, extending over many years and through many situations, are a kind of "back channel" of information, understanding and communication that exists at the senior level of most large North American corporations. Trev was not unusual in sending Christmas cards, organizing parties, presenting gifts and going on trips with his well-off friends. What was unique, was the panache and flair with which he pulled it off. No one who has ever been to a Trev Deeley event has ever forgotten it, and people who are in the inner circle of his friends and acquaintances feel truly blessed.

The downside of this success, of course, was that some people became overly impressed, and attributed to Trev financial resources vastly greater than those he actually had. Rumours of enormous landholdings in Vancouver, a munificent inheritance from his grandfather and a bottomless chequebook floated around Trev like morning mist rising over the black water of the Pacific. Mostly they were untrue, but while they served his business, and let's face it, his ego, he let them continue.

Instead of dealing with rumours, Trev was far more interested in re-establishing his reputation in the racing world, and at the same time, taking a jab at his old boss at Yamaha, Satoshi Moriya. By a happy coincidence there was a vehicle at hand that could do the job, the RR-250. This was a remarkable water-cooled, two-stroke racer from the Italian Aermacchi Harley-Davidson plant that was to win the world 250 championship in 1974, '75 and '76. When the model debuted in the United States in 1974, Gary Scott won the 250 cc race at Loudon, New Hampshire, bringing Harley into the lightweight winner's circle for the first time in years. Trev brought two of the bikes into the country, a 250 and a 391 cc, and got a Washington rider, Jimmy Dunn, to campaign them at Westwood, across Canada and at Daytona under the Fred Deeley Imports Ltd. name.

Dunn raced for Fred Deeley Yamaha at Daytona in 1971 and came in thirteenth. In 1972 he was tenth and in 1973 his Yamaha went out after eight laps. As a result it was with considerable satisfaction that Trev went to Daytona in 1975 and saw Dunn come home in seventeenth place on the Fred Deeley Imports RR-250. All sixteen bikes ahead of him were Yamahas, but there were a whole lot more Yamahas behind him. Just as important to Trevor, and to Harley-Davidson, Dunn's was the first H-D across the line. Despite a considerable factory effort in the United States, it had taken the Canadian importer and an Italian machine to put the orange and black shield into the top twenty.

At the same time he was sponsoring this road racing effort, Trev was also sponsoring an XR-750s, ridden by Doug Sehl, on the AMA national circuit at dirt tracks in eastern Canada and in the United States. The rider's name was just a coincidence, but *sales* were really the name of the game for both racing efforts. Trev had learned from his grandfather that racing keeps a company's name in the public eye, and that awareness builds sales. It also tended to provide Fred Deeley Imports with knowledgeable staff members. Everyone associated with racing had to keep up to date with technology, techniques and tires and this information proved invaluable in handling dealer questions and anticipating owner accessory and performance purchases.

The new dealers who began to come onstream were independent businessmen, some very knowledgeable about the motorcycle business. To Trev, however, they were more like novice fast food franchisees who needed to be taught the business from the ground up. Whatever their preconceived or ingrained ideas, he wanted them tossed out and replaced with a new motorcycle sales concept he was going to teach them, based on the success of his own store at 606 East Broadway.

By now, this unique enterprise had developed a reputation of its own. To other motorcycle dealers it was affectionately called the "Broadway Bandit" because it relieved so many passing motorcyclists of their money. There were a number of keys to its success, including superior product displays, knowledgeable staff, prompt service and pride of workmanship, but underlying these there were basic principles he hectored his dealers to emulate: selection, satisfaction and profitability.

Product and parts selection was something Trevor had learned more by accident than design. In the contest between price and availability, availability was by far the most important. He had learned this because by being a distributor, he *had* to have all the parts his dealer network required, even the most obscure and slow moving. Because he had everything, customers knew if they went to Deeley's, they'd find what they wanted, even if they had to pay the standard markup to get it. The point was that most motorcyclists were prepared to pay non-discount prices, rather than wait a month or more for a part to be shipped in from out of province or overseas. The riding season in Canada was too short to wait, and since most bikers were young men, they were too impatient to wait anyway.

They were also, by and large, not penny pinchers when it came to the parts themselves, preferring to buy "original equipment manufactured" (OEM) items or nationally branded replacements, rather than no-name knockoffs from Japan or Taiwan. Trev, as a result, preached big inventories and genuine parts for his dealer network, an investment in customer service that, for some, took their breath away it was so large.

Another big pillar of Trev's philosophy was customer satisfaction. This is such an overworked phrase these days, it's almost lost its meaning. To Trevor, however, then and now, it had a very specific purpose — to keep the customer coming back. He told his dealers motorcycle buyers weren't to be treated like marks, but as trusted friends. This meant each and every transaction should leave the customer with a sense of being well treated, and that no customer should leave the premises with a chip on his shoulder.

An example of this attitude cropped up on one occasion when Trev was still the vice president of Fred Deeley Yamaha. A customer in Ontario had an RD350 that kept fouling spark plugs, no matter what the dealer did to fix it. Tony Cox walked into Trev's office one day, explained the situation and asked what he should do. Trev told him to go into the warehouse, open up a brand new crated RD350 and take the engine out of it for shipment to the dealer. From a narrow economic standpoint, it made no sense to cannibalize a new bike, but from a customer satisfaction point of view, it made a lot of sense. Trev knew the customer would be satisfied, would tell all his friends he was satisfied and undoubtedly would be back for his next bike sometime in the future. Never lose a customer, he told his dealers, they're too hard to come by in the first place.

Never prostitute yourself or the industry by discounting, was his third point; sell the public at a profit. Trevor strongly believed in maintaining prices in order to carry inventory, hire professional service people and stay in business. He used to say to his dealers, "If a customer is looking at a bike that has $500 worth of profit at list price and you sell it to him at a $250 discount, that's not his $250 he's walking out the door with, it's your $250."

What he meant was that a bike sold at a discount wasn't product moved out the door, it was profit moved out. "You're just giving it away," he would say. "You're giving it to him, which is not the way to go at it." If a dealer wanted to give away money, he said, they should put it in the industry, supporting training, racing or other motorcycle events. Those kinds of "give aways" would eventually pay the dealers back.

Surrounding these themes, and pervading his whole approach, was the importance of the impression the store made on a customer walking in the door. Trev told his dealers to imagine, once a month, they were a customer and to go through their stores with a completely unbiased eye. Did they see an attractive display or dirty coffee cups and ashtrays overflowing with butts? Did the operation look professional? Were sales staff available and helpful? Trevor was used to service people who wore smart white coveralls, like technicians in the aerospace industry. He was not impressed with scruffy jeans and bandannas as a substitute, and he told his dealers to raise their standards.

One wonders, looking back at this era, how Trevor could have guessed these kinds of changes would be necessary to lure the new yuppie upper middle class into becoming Harley owners in the late 1980s. It was certainly not clear to most other people at the time. To some, his dedication to professionalism seemed both excessive and unnecessary; after all, they argued, the people walking in the door were "bikers" who had a black leather culture all their own. Trev just kept prodding away. Motorcycle shops, he implied, were a self-fulfilling prophesy; if they looked like a barn they'd attract animals; if they looked like an art gallery, they'd attract your friends and their wives.

While Trevor preached this upscale, profitable future, the reality back on River Road was anything but rosy. Besides the shortage of stock, the worsening quality control was giving staff the impression the rumours in the industry about Harley's financial future were probably true. Bikes were arriving from the factory in so many pieces, the mechanics used to say a new Harley was a kit of parts that came in a box partly assembled. A new FLH full dresser, for example, was shipped as a bare bones motorcycle. All the chrome goodies that made the bike look unique were in boxes inside the crate and had to be added by the dealer, a process that took the better part of a day for each machine.

Trev joined a rising chorus of complaints from the company's U.S. dealers about late deliveries, marginal quality and lack of support and eventually Harley-Davidson got the message. The precipitating cause was the defect rate on one of two new 1977 models. The factory, prodded by Willie G. Davidson, had introduced the FXS Low Rider, with a low seating position and available forward controls, and was just about to bring out the XLCR Cafe Racer, a black beauty with rear sets and a bikini faring designed to open the market to sports bike enthusiasts. A service department supervisor went to see Vaughn Beals and said pre-production models of the XLCR were coming back riddled with defects. Beals, who had just become president, was shocked and decided to make the Cafe Racer a symbol of the quality Harley should stand for. He organized a group of engineering, service and manufacturing managers and sent them down to the chassis plant with instructions to do whatever it took to make sure they came out right.

"The first hundred," he says, "cost us $100,000 to fix, but it made us concentrate on problems upstream. We later institutionalized that concept in the quality-audit program that's still an integral part of manufacturing, along with such procedures as just-in-time manufacturing and statistical process control."

All the in-house quality improvement took time and the Cafe Racer got to market nearly two years late.

It's interesting that Harley-Davidson's improved quality began with the Cafe Racer because while quality made H-D the success it is today, the XLCR was a dud in the marketplace and was dropped after the 1978 production run. The FXS Low Rider, on the other hand, was a tremendous hit, and became the forerunner of the whole "custom cruiser" motorcycle style.

Why this was so says a lot about American motorcycling in general and Harley-Davidson's traditional customers in particular. The Low Rider encouraged a laid back form of motorcycling, with the rider's feet forward of his hips, and his back tilted away from the steering head. The Cafe Racer, on the other hand, put the rider's feet below his hips and tilted the body forward to reach the handlebars. This may not sound like much of a difference to a non-motorcyclist, but it was the fundamental distinction between all subsequent Harley models and the sports bikes from Europe and Japan. Harley riders wanted to lean back on their bike, usually against a sleeping bag or packsack, the way they sat in an easy chair at home. This is the way American saddles were made, with long stirrups and bedrolls, and the tradition was carried over in the public mind from horses to motorcycles.

European bikes, on the other hand, were based on the tradition of European saddles, with short stirrups and the rider leaning forward over the horse's neck. As a result, their seat heights were higher, their handlebars farther forward and their brake and gearchanger lever farther back.

In practice, the low rider style, based on home-made H-D "choppers," was remarkably comfortable at speeds below sixty-five mph providing the rider had something to lean against and the road wasn't too bumpy. Above this speed it was another matter, with less than optimum control and severe buffeting from the wind hitting the rider's outstretched body. The Cafe Racer, on the other hand, wasn't much fun at slow speeds, especially in stop-and-go city driving, and only really started to feel comfortable above seventy mph when the wind would get under a rider's chest and provide some relief for the weight on his hands.

In Europe with higher speed limits (or no limits at all) the forward style made a lot of sense, but in the United States, with much lower limits, long periods at fifty-five mph on the inter-state highway network could be excruciating. It's not hard, based on this understanding, to realize why the FXS was a winner and the XLCR was not. In the years ahead, all the Japanese factories, and even a few European makes, would try to emulate the leaned-back styling of the FXS with varying degrees of success. Harley, for its part, would keep upping the price of admission with more radical customizing, culminating in the FXSTS Springer Softail which looked like a model from the 1940s, a step backward in styling the progressive Europeans and Japanese just couldn't follow.

Harley-Davidson would also, mostly in secret, keep trying to find a way to tackle the sports bike market again, despite the marketing failure of the XLCR.

At this point, Trev had an influence on Harley-Davidson's history he didn't expect and couldn't have predicted. The story of his trans-Canada tour in 1975 was well known to John David-son, and other members of the board, and late in 1977 Charlie Thompson suggested they do the same thing in the United States. This won the approval of Beals, who thought a mass ride of H-D executives would be just the thing to draw attention to Harley-Davidson's seventy-fifth anniversary in 1978. Accordingly, sixteen executives, ranging from managers to the chairman, departed from cities on the perimeter of the United States and followed seven routes across the country to a rendezvous at the Louisville motorcycle races in early June. Along the way they collectively travelled over 37,000 miles and visited 160 H-D dealers. It was a big success, serving as the model for future anniversary rides that became larger and more popular as the years went on. Few, if any, of the tens of thousands who would take part in them would know Trev Deeley had begun it all.

Trev wasn't finished with the idea either. While the U.S. executives motored across America's heartland, he and Don James repeated their 1975 tour, riding across Canada on Electra Glides, and visiting as many of his new dealerships as possible. His message was optimistic and upbeat, but the quality problems were continuing and his new dealers gave the two of them an earful as they rolled across the country. Most of the blame was directed at AMF, the conglomerate that had taken over H-D and put its initials on the gas tank right beside the honoured brand name Harley-Davidson. Trev saved his reaction for the Dealer Advisory Council, where he made it clear he and his dealers weren't happy with the bikes they were receiving.

"For a start," he said, "you can quit importing minibikes from Italy and concentrate on the big twins. There are problems with both models, but the large ones we know we can fix."

The writing was on the wall anyway. The Japanese had graduated minibike owners up to middleweight 750 cc machines and beyond, and small street machines were a declining commodity. In addition, the contradictions in marketing both to big bike customers and the riders of smaller machines had never been successfully resolved and, indeed, had become worse with time. It was clear to everyone H-D had to sharpen its focus on its core product. What was not clear yet at head office, was that the reputation for poor quality, gained during the AMF era, was about to deal the company a near fatal blow. Riders accustomed to refrigerator-like reliability from Japanese cars, cameras and motorcycles, were becoming increasingly disenchanted with blown seals, mismatched parts and faulty electrics on motorcycles from York, Pennsylvania. They were buying the big twins in record numbers, but they were getting a record number of problems.

Back in Canada, the growing size and complexity of Fred Deeley Imports made Trev realize it was time to hand more authority and more ownership of the company over to Don James in Vancouver and Harold Lenfesty in Toronto. As a result on February 2, 1979, he appointed James president and chief operating officer, Lenfesty vice president and eastern general manager, and made himself chairman and chief executive officer. Trev was beginning to see the point of continuing education, and the first thing he did was ask his new president to go to Harvard to take an "Owner/Presidents Management Program." For himself, he might have thought it was time to slow down and smell the roses, but in fact, the 1980s would be a period of considerable challenge for both Fred Deeley Imports and the Motor Company.

"The company was growing so rapidly, we were all in over our heads," James recalls. "Harvard was the best educational experience of my life, absolutely crucial to where we were at."

One of the biggest projects at the time was the introduction of the 80 cu. in. FLT Tour Glide, with a five-speed transmission, oil-bath enclosed rear chain and a vibration-isolated engine. This was the designated successor to the FLH "King of the Highway" and the engine isolation was essential to pamper the new breed of demanding long distance tour riders.

The second innovation was the Sturgis, named after the town in South Dakota that had become a mecca for motorcyclists in the central United States. Trev had long demanded an oil-tight primary case and reduced chain maintenance and the Sturgis met those requirements by using a belt for both the primary and secondary drives. Not only did the primary belt do away with the primary chain oil-bath, it and the secondary were maintenance free and transferred virtually no vibration through to the swing arm and the frame.

Events at Harley-Davidson now began to move very quickly. AMF looked at Harley's balance sheet and, despite revenues of $300 million, decided it was losing money and had to go. A group of H-D executives, including Vaughn Beals, president Charlie Thompson, Willie G. Davidson and others, put in an offer February 26, 1981, to purchase the company for $75 million. The return to private ownership was announced at Daytona on March 3, and completed June 16 with a ride by the new shareholders 900 miles from York to Milwaukee, proclaiming "The Eagle Flies Alone."

What they found when they got there were the makings of a disaster. Sales were tumbling, warranty claims were increasing and inventories were bulging. The quality improvement program begun by Beals was intensified under a new slogan, *I Make the Eagle Fly,* and two new models were introduced – the FXR Super Glide II with a rubber-isolated, five-speed power train, and a new welded and stamped-frame Sportster – but Harley sales continued to drop. Between 1979 and 1983, the company's share of the domestic market for motorcycles bigger than 850 cc sank from thirty-nine percent to twenty-three percent. This was largely Harley-Davidson's fault, but the big bike market was shrinking as well, down 33,000 units between 1981 and 1982, so the figures were actually worse than the percentages. As a result of the reduced sales, H-D was forced to lay off workers for the first time.

The curious thing was that despite the shrinking market, the big four Japanese manufacturers were continuing to increase their inventories in the United States. This is something Trevor had noticed before with Honda and Yamaha in Canada — an apparently insatiable desire to throw motorcycles at the marketplace — and to the new owners of H-D, it began to look more like a plot than a plan. It appeared to them the Japanese were prepared to take a big loss in order to drive America's only motorcycle manufacturer into bankruptcy. In desperation, Harley-Davidson petitioned the International Trade Commission for tariff relief from the Japanese.

In the middle of this period, with the factory desperate to move inventory, Jim Patterson flew up to Canada to unload fifty motorcycles on Fred Deeley Imports. Trev's warehouse was already full and his dealer inventory was up, so he knew it was going to be a hard sell. When the meeting started, he went into his pitch about taking more stock and Trev broke in on him.

"Listen," he said, "you made a trip up here. How many do you need us to take?"

"Well, I need fifty," Patterson replied.

"Okay," Trev replied, then turned to Don and several others in the room and added, "What do we need to do to sell them?"

Don James protested, pointing out the warehouse was chock-full and more bikes would only add to their problems.

"Yeah," Trev replied, "but Harley needs us to sell fifty bikes and you know, they're doing this all over the world. If we don't step up to bat, then Harley's not going to be around, so then you won't have to worry about how many are in the warehouse. What do we need to do to sell these motorcycles."

It was an example of altruism that Patterson, who was vice president of marketing at the time, never forgot.

Christmas rolled around with H-D still teetering on disaster, but even for the irreligious Deeleys, it was a time to get together. Islay, Trevor's mother, had been in failing health and was receiving nursing care, but she was determined she was going to invite her son, and his wife and daughter to a Christmas dinner with her husband, Fred Jr. To prepare, she had her hair done, got dressed, and was helped to the couch in her living room while the dinner was made ready in the kitchen. When Trev, Dawne and Joyce came in, she greeted them warmly as she had in the past and asked them to go on through to the dining room. Unable to eat, but unwilling to give up easily, she was aided back to her bedroom where she asked for Trev to see her privately. Trevor entered the room and Islay told him to divide her jewellery equally between Dawne and Joyce. Then she told him she had some traveller's cheques stashed away in the room he was to have for himself. When she finished, she asked Trev to go back to the family because she wanted to take a nap. After dinner, Dawne went to say good-bye to her grandmother, who looked frail, but otherwise much as she had for months. When she and the rest of the family left, they had no idea it was the last time they were to see her alive. That night Islay quietly passed away.

The classy method of her parting was in contrast to what happened later when Trevor told his father of Islay's last wishes. Fred Jr. denied there were any traveller's cheques and when Trev went and found them exactly where she had said they were, he snatched them out of his hand and said she had never told him they were for Trev. The same went for the jewels, and for the fur coat Islay had promised to Dawne. To Fred Jr., a miser to the end, even his wife's last wishes were less important than holding onto every penny he could. For Trev, the experience was deeply unnerving. His beloved Vera had died at Christmas and now his mother, who had loved him just as much as she, had gone during the holiday as well.

His father's attitude he could understand. He was acting totally in character. The actions of a malevolent God, who took his family from him at what was supposed to be the happiest time of the year, he could not.

In Milwaukee, the new owners were scrambling to find ways to keep Harley-Davidson alive. One inspired suggestion from business consusltant Mike Kami, was the formation of a factory-sponsored motorcycle club, the Harley Owners Group. It was inspired because it allowed H-D management to tailor the organization to attract the upper middle class type of rider who had the money to buy its motorcycles but wasn't attracted to the idea of joining a motorcycle gang. The club had, by a happy coincidence, the acronym H.O.G., which had long been a nickname among motorcyclists for the large Harleys.

A second idea that got moved to the front burner was even more dramatic – a four-cylinder model to deal with the Japanese head on.

This plan was initiated under AMF and contracted out to the Porsche Design Group in Europe where it was code-named the Nova project. The resulting bike was available for testing in 1982 at Harley-Davidson's racing facility at Taledega raceway in Alabama. It was as much a marketing compromise as an engineering project, because every effort had been made to keep a look that would be familiar to Harley-Davidson owners. As a result the engine was an 1100 cc, air cooled V-4 mounted across the frame rather than longitudinally. This gave the bike an appearance similar to the existing big twins, although the mass of the motor appeared much bulkier.

Trev was one of the first people to ride it and he did so for hundreds of miles, testing every aspect of its performance and handling. After these gruelling sessions in the saddle, he had one recommendation:

"Don't build it."

"It looked pretty good," he said later, "but I knew that if we okayed it, we were going to wait three years to get it and the day I was riding it, it wasn't good enough in performance. So what the hell was it going to be like three years down the road? It would have been pathetic."

Trevor recommended the factory stick to the traditional models, precisely because they weren't competing with the large displacement Japanese sports bikes capable of 150 mph. They would need a much better bike if they were going to compete with the Japanese directly.

The management group, which was already concerned about the bike, accepted his advice and the Nova project was scrapped. Sticking to the traditional engine, however, meant there would have to be a new chassis with rubber engine mounts if vibration was going to be reduced to an acceptable level. The chassis design chosen, designated the FXR, used a system that had first appeared on the 1980 FLT Tour Glide. This dramatically reduced vibration, but it also radically altered the low rider look and feel of bikes like the 1980 Sturgis and Wide Glide. Trev didn't like it one bit. It was a more functional chassis, it was easier to ride, but it lacked the sex appeal of the low rider look and Trev thought it was a mistake. As a result, he argued for changes to lower the bike that eventually produced the FXRS Low Rider in 1988.

Perhaps the most historic bike from this period is the FXRT Sport Glide. This sports touring bike has the FXR rubber-mounted engine, but it also has the front portion of the Nova fairing, the only part of the V-4 prototype to make it past the Harley-Davidson factory gate. If you've ever thought the Sports Glide fairing looked a little odd, a little larger and rounder than the FXRT needed, you were right. Take a look at the photo on page 184 to see what the fairing looks like on the bike it was designed for.

It was at the H-D announcements meeting in Hershey, Pennsylvania, in 1983 that Trev managed to goad the "suits" in the company into rediscovering motorcycling. He was sitting opposite a table of H-D financial executives and the company's bankers and they looked so uptight he challenged them to get off their duffs and get out on the road. This got the conversation at the table going and Jim Patterson and Rich Teerlink, neither of whom were riders, were bet by the bankers they wouldn't ride to Daytona the following March. After the meeting, both men enrolled in a Motorcycle Safety Foundation rider education course at the York plant and got their licences in time to roll down to the beach for Bike Week, winning the bet.

"It was one of those things," Paterson recalls. "We all knew we wanted to do it, but during those days of tight financial problems, really 'how do we stay afloat, make sure the shipments got out and so forth,' there wasn't much time to go out and ride motorcycles. But Trevor was the one, he kind of got that one going."

It was quite an achievement, because it not only brought the top people in the company out into the street, it also brought them face-to-face with the riding public. Trev knew the moment dedicated Harley owners had the chance to talk to senior management, they wouldn't hesitate to let them know what they liked and didn't like about the product. The fact was he already knew what they liked, and had been asking for these rider-requested changes at the Dealer Advisory Council meetings. Now, the riders the brass met on the road would be telling them the same thing. To some, a jocular remark at a bar might not seem like much, but it was to have remarkable and far-reaching effects. In the years that followed, Harley-Davidson developed a national reputation for listening to its customers and responding to their requests.

Some improvements that soon made it to the showroom were a new anti-dive suspension and, for the first time, electronic ignition. These helped handling and reliability, but the Shovelhead engine was by now well past its prime and needed to be replaced. This was done in 1984, with the introduction of the 1,340 cc V^2 Evolution motor which was lighter, cleaner running and – most important of all – extremely oil tight.

The new motor came in a number of models, but the biggest impact was with the FXST Softail, a design that was really shock dampened but looked like a solid rear end. The combination of a modern motor in a modern suspension that looked like a traditional motor in a traditional suspension was an instant hit. Harley-Davidson had discovered what its buyers wanted was reliability wrapped up in nostalgia, exactly what Trev had been preaching.

A parallel with this was what happened to Volkswagen. The German automaker made a tremendous impact on the North American car market with the Beetle as long as it maintained its pre-war shape and rear engine design. As soon as it switched to a more conventional econobox look, it lost the affection of its customers and its leadership position in the industry. Volkswagen made the change to reduce manufacturing costs, adopt a more efficient and powerful OHC design, and because it was hard to make the air-cooled Beetle motor quiet enough, or clean enough, for tightening North American standards – all apparently very good reasons. Air-cooled motors require relatively large piston-to-cylinder wall clearances because they go through a wide heat range from cold to full operating temperature. Inevitably, this means some oil gets past the rings and valve guides and goes out the exhaust pipes during warm up. A water-cooled motor, on the other hand, can be built to tighter tolerances because the water jacket can keep the motor within a narrower heat range. A second benefit is that the water jacket around the cylinders dampens the noise and makes water-cooled engines inherently quieter than air-cooled motors.

H-D was faced with the same facts and would come to much the same conclusion as VW with regard to its motor, but it was rightly worried about the effect of radical change on its traditional customers. Efficiency and power were one thing, but as Volkswagen found out, nostalgia was not to be tampered with lightly. (VW has since seen the error of its ways and has announced a new Beetle-lookalike with a modern motor.)

The changes H-D did make, however, were enough to produce a turnaround in the marketplace. For the first time in years, Harley-Davidson motorcycles received favourable reviews in motorcycle magazines. The combination of an oil-tight engine, rubber mounting, belt transmission and a new five-speed gear-box was the key to success. Harleys were now smooth to ride, didn't leak oil and had a maintenance-free transmission. H-D won the California Highway Patrol contract and additional po-lice orders began to flow in to Milwaukee.

Trev wasn't the only person calling for these kinds of im-provements, but he was one of the loudest and most persistent, badgering the senior executives unmercifully to boost quality. In-stead of objecting to this constant harassment from the Great White North, they did exactly the opposite in 1985 and invited him to join the board of directors, one of the first three outside directors in the company's history. At first he didn't want to ac-cept the honour. He was sixty-five years old and the board meetings in the east would involve numerous long trips. There would also, he knew, be many subjects discussed in which he had absolutely no interest. However, the chance to influence the development of the motorcycle brand he loved proved irresist-ible, and Trevor accepted.

"The board has a lot to do with finance and salaries and I didn't care what those guys were making," Trev recalls. "I didn't want to go over forty guys every six to twelve months and say they should have a raise or should not have a raise. Christ, we had enough to worry about at our own place to do that. But an expansion of production, allocating funds to buy certain things, like the $7.5 million needed to tool up for a five-speed transmis-sion for the Sportster, that stuff really interested me."

Trev had no sooner taken his place on the board than H-D found itself facing a major crisis. Members learned one of the four banks financing the purchase of the company wanted to back out of the deal. The company needed cash in a hurry and Teerlink, the new biker and now chief financial officer, was sent out to find some. By late December, he successfully negotiated an-other loan-financing package and the company was saved. The following year, Trev was also there as Teerlink and Beals took the company public with an offering of two million shares of common stock on the American Stock Exchange. The Motor Company had rolled up to the abyss, then roared away from it with the Cana-dian distributor a fully committed, and often vocal, participant.

Trev's interest in the product extended far from the board room table and into the operating departments. Because of his years on the Dealer Advisory Council he already knew a lot of the senior Harley-Davidson people, such as Jerry Wilkie who started the dealer development department, and Willie G. Davidson, in charge of design. Trev would wander through the executive offices, renewing acquaintances, shaking hands and making suggestions. When he got to the engineering area, he'd keep right on going, talking to the people responsible for this issue or that and arguing for improvements.

This process of personal contact wasn't documented, and Trev doesn't remember it as anything special. The fact is, however, many detail improvements in Harley-Davidson motorcycles came about because a smiling Trevor Deeley kept badgering the engineering and design staff in Milwaukee. The contacts happened every time the board meeting was in Milwaukee, but they also happened a lot when the board wasn't meeting. Trev would hear a new test bike was available, jump on a plane and fly down to Milwaukee or Taledega and ride it, often for hundreds of miles at a time. When he got off, he'd say exactly what he thought. Because of his family's connection to H-D, his six years as a factory-sponsored racer, his dirt track success, sales ability, dealer and customer understanding, and more, Trevor was listened to.

Perhaps the best example of this is what happened when Trev was invited down to Milwaukee in 1987 to try out the new FXSTS Springer which sported a leading link externally-sprung front end similar to the kind H-D had in the 1940s. This unit was, according to *The Big Book of Harley-Davidson* (an official publication of Harley-Davidson, Inc.), "the subject of more computer-aided design and finite elements computer analysis than any other component in Harley-Davidson history." Trev got on the bike, and as was his practice with a new machine, dropped the clutch while still holding onto the front brake. The motor stalled out of course, but the sudden shock caused an immediate problem with the fancy new front end. As a result, a change in materials had to be made in time for the model's introduction in 1988.

Not all Trev's suggestions received such prompt attention.

"A lot of my desires as to product would be done outside the boardroom," Trev says. "I had such a good rapport, there wasn't a department I couldn't go into. But some things I wanted we haven't got yet and Christ knows if we ever will. For instance, a big tank on the Sportster. I pushed that until nobody wanted to hear it anymore. We still don't have it. Of course the five-speed transmission and more horsepower in our big twins. I was pushing for a 1,500 cc twin, which they made, and I went back and rode it extensively, but surprisingly it didn't have the performance of the 1,340, and I don't know why. And then of course there was the paint facility."

Paint was the bottleneck that was throttling Harley production in the mid-1980s. Bikes were emerging from the York plant looking great, but often it was as a result of extensive rework that slowed production just when it should have increased. Jim Patterson, the vice president of marketing, brought the matter before the board. He said the company needed to spend $5 million simply to stay in business because the existing paint process was letting off too many harmful emissions.

Trev immediately piped up.

"What are you going to do that for?" he asked. "What's a new paint facility going to cost you?"

Patterson just happened to have the figure in his pocket, $20 million.

As a result of Trev's interjection, and the support of board members Mike Kami and Fred Brengel, the board gave Patterson preliminary approval for a new paint plant. If it's going to be $20 million, they said, don't be afraid of it, that's what it's going to be.

"Now you know Harley had never made an expenditure anywhere near that in its history," Patterson remembers. "Our total capital expenditures in 1981 and 1982 were about $8 or $9 million total for the whole year and here the board was talking about a paint facility in the $15 to $20 million range. Trevor just said, 'Hey, come on guys what are you doing? Are you in business here? Is this the way to run it?' That's Trevor. It's not like, 'What's blocking me, Why can't I?' it's 'What do you have to do to get it done?" It's the optimistic attitude as opposed to the pessimistic."

Patterson remembers the optimism. Trevor remembers the need.

"The paint facility was one that I pushed very hard for because Jim Patterson wanted it very badly. He knew, and I knew and a lot of other people knew that it was absolutely essential if Harley was ever going to pick up production. You couldn't be painting with a spray gun and a waterfall behind and that kind of old fashioned stuff. So when they came to ask for money for the paint facility, I was very strongly for it. And I wouldn't sit down and quit talking until finally it was voted on and voted in."

It was too bad Trev wasn't there to spread some optimism around when costs rose to $23 million and the paint plant was delayed by technical problems, causing a production bottleneck of its own. Eventually, in 1992, the issues were solved and the robotic painting system proved its worth in boosting production to an all-time high, a figure that was surpassed in 1993. Although he left the board at the mandatory retirement age of seventy in 1990, Trevor's efforts to eliminate the biggest obstacle in Harley-Davidson's growth would pay off many years into the future.

The last project he was directly involved in was the Dyna Glide chassis first seen in the 1991 FXDB Dyna Glide Sturgis.

At first glance, this looks very much like its 1980 predecessor with a black engine and orange detailing. In fact, it was the first H-D designed from the ground up on a computer and featured a totally new frame, a two-point rubber engine-isolation mounting system, an oil tank mounted under the transmission, and a more accessible rear belt. The express intention, as always with H-D, was to combine the look of an earlier era with the technology of the present.

Trev and Don James were both intimately involved in its development, along with Jerry Wilkie, vice president of sales and marketing. The two Canadians would fly in from the coast, join Jerry on the road and push the prototypes as hard as they could. The big issues at the time were chassis components, clutches, engine mounting locations and fork angles. Some days the trips were absolutely miserable, with cold and rain turning a pleasure into an ordeal. One time Trev stopped at a local department store and bought bath towels for the group to wind around inside their jackets to keep warm. It was an old racer's trick, which, of course, was why Trev was invited to punish the H-D test mules. He was the "old racer" personified.

When the development program got to the track stage, Don and Jerry flew up from Daytona to Taledega and spent a day at the track testing various parts of the Dyna Glide program.

"Within our engineering group, we have test riders that are on the motorcycle every day," said Wilkie. "They typically test specific components. But when it comes to making a product development decision — should the package be tweaked in this direction or that direction — then I'll put together my own jury." For many years, Trev was a member of that panel, invited to say his piece no matter whose ears got burned in the process.

In 1993, when Trev opened his motorcycle museum in Richmond, B.C., he was presented with an FXDB Dyna Glide Sturgis to put on display in recognition of his efforts in its development.

CHAPTER TWELVE

WHILE HE WAS helping get new investment and new models approved by the board of directors at Harley-Davidson, Trev was also involved in a relationship with a very different set of executives, the leadership of the Hells Angels.

As might be expected, there was no official connection between Trev and the Angels, who by the 1980s were the dominant outlaw motorcycle gang in British Columbia. There was simply the fact that like most "bikers," the Angels vastly preferred Harley-Davidson motorcycles to other brands and Trev Deeley was the H-D distributor for Canada. As a result, tough-looking men with tattoos and large gold rings could often be seen around Trev's dealership at 606 East Broadway, where they were some of the best customers in the store.

Trev would probably have kept dealing with them on this basis if it hadn't been for the Angels' penchant for riding without helmets and removing the mufflers on their bikes and replacing them with straight pipes. The first practice, which was shared by most other hard core bikers, was the cause of a running battle with the provincial government when it began trying to enforce a mandatory helmet law. The helmet issue affected all motorcyclists, but it especially grated on Harley-Davidson owners because the lifestyle that had evolved around the marque was one of rebellion, not social acceptability. Sports bike owners had been riding with full face helmets for years, but arguments over personal safety had never cut any ice with the crowd that liked sporting large-scale tattoos, wallets with chains and miniature pony tails tied up with elastic bands. The bikers responded by going to court, often with Jim McNeney of McNeney & McNeney, who had a reputation as a bikers' rights lawyer. He would regularly get them off the hook, but it was becoming clear to all those involved the issue had to be dealt with actively on the political level, rather than passively in court.

Accordingly, a committee of a dozen concerned bikers got together to map out a strategy in 1986. Only one member of the group was an Angel but, when the committee called on concerned bikers to become founding members of the British Columbia Coalition of Motorcyclists (BCCOM), the Angels threw their support behind the new organization and many joined up at $100 a pop. In the end, 999 bikers shelled out, by any measure a remarkable fund-raising achievement. The biggest contributor was none other than Trev Deeley, who pledged $1,000 to the new organization and was rewarded with membership #1 for himself and #22 – his old racing number – for his daughter. In the end, BCCOM won a partial victory on the helmet issue; it got the government to recognize helmets that were little larger than beanie caps in exchange for bikers at least wearing something.

The second issue, loud bikes, was also a lifestyle decision. Hard core bikers, of which the Angels were the hardest around, enjoyed the authoritative rumble they got when they ditched the standard baffles and replaced them with open mufflers or no mufflers at all. While this had never endeared them to the police, it particularly outraged officer #1176 of the Vancouver Police Department, who went on a personal rampage across the city in 1988 and slapped tickets on every Harley-Davidson he could find. Even Harleys that had stock mufflers began getting $500 fines.

The BCCOM responded by taking eighteen cases involving the one overzealous officer to the Supreme Court of British Columbia, and won. It then sued his employer, the City of Vancouver, and the officer was reassigned away from the Traffic Division. Finally, and most important, BCCOM got government officials to agree to new provincial regulations that created a system of privately-run motor vehicle testing stations and allowed mechanics with more than ten years' experience to be licensed as inspectors. One reason for BCCOM's success was Peter Jack, a former vice president of the International Brotherhood of Painters and Allied Trades, who had become its full-time organizer and lobbyist. Although he denied any special credit, BCCOM was remarkably successful at uniting the interests of outlaw bikers with those of the general motorcycling public in its campaigns.

The net effect of the changes in the inspection regulations was to strictly limit the ability of police forces across the province to harass bikers on custom Harleys by citing them for riding unsafe vehicles. In effect, BCCOM's actions protected Harley-Davidson's market position in British Columbia as well as that of the entire H-D after-market parts industry. It is not surprising, therefore, that Trev was an enthusiastic member.

While the Angels kept their relationship with BCCOM at arm's length, there was no such reticence about their friendship with its number one member. Trev Deeley's Vancouver Harley-Davidson still holds an annual "customer appreciation day" that is really more of an Angel party than a public gathering. The former president of the Vancouver Island chapter of the Hells Angels has visited Trev at his exclusive waterfront home in Sidney and others come to receptions at his motorcycle museum in Richmond. Trevor enjoys these encounters, the rough-edged talk of his visitors, and the esteem in which they hold him. Whatever their other failings, outlaw bikers have certainly been loyal customers for H-D and for Trevor since they burst onto the scene in 1947. They have also contributed greatly to the tough guy image attached to the Harley-Davidson brand name that, in sanitized form, has become all the rage with yuppie bike owners across Canada and the United States.

There is another reason for Trev's appreciation. At age seventy-four he is much frailer than he was in his prime, and with much more to protect. His relationship with the Angels is well enough known that very few crooks would consider it worth their while to make a move against him, his wife Joyce or his daughter Dawne. To the H-D racer who used to talk with his fists, it is literally a comfort in his old age to be a friend of the Angels.

It would be nice to say another comfort was Dawne, but his thirty-six-year-old daughter is as much a mystery to him now as he was to her as a child. The father-daughter relationship, which was distant from the beginning, developed some additional problems during an overprotected childhood and an uncertain entry into the business world.

The issue, basically, was that while Dawne wanted her father's praise and affection, and was prepared to go to extraordinary lengths to get it, she didn't understand until well into her thirties that he wanted her to take command of her life without his direct assistance. In fact, instead of making her life easier at Fred Deeley Imports, Trev almost went out of his way to not show favouritism towards his only daughter. She, not realizing this was more an act than an attitude, felt rejected by him when he was only following the pattern set by his father, Fred Jr., of making things tough on the next generation. This lack of understanding between father and daughter was recognized by other company officers and executives, some of whom resented another Deeley in the company and exploited it whenever possible. The result was that through much of the 1980s Trev and Dawne never really connected.

They worked together, they were friendly, but neither really understood what the other was all about.

Dawne, most of all, wanted Trevor's recognition. As a result, the first thing she did as an independent person was to accept his offer to work for him in his store. Instead of flying off to a finishing school in Switzerland, she dove into the rude, crude world of the motorcycle parts business. She has never verbalized this to Trevor, but it's obvious the reason she did so was in the hope that since Trev took motorcycle parts seriously, he might take her seriously too if she worked in the same area.

The problem with this plan was that Dawne contained genes from her great grandfather, the competitive bicycle racer, Fred Deeley Sr. These propelled her into a ten-year career as a bicycle racing athlete, a career that frequently conflicted with her job at 606 East Broadway and later at Fred Deeley Imports Ltd. Trev followed her racing career with interest, often travelling to meets, but it was clear his main interest was in business, not bicycle racing. As a result, he sent out mixed messages as well, in effect challenging his daughter to be an aggressive businesswoman, while at the same time, protecting her from the rigors of the business.

A good example of this dichotomy occurred when Dawne told her father she wanted a motorcycle of her own. Trev, although he had taught her to ride a dirt bike when she was ten, was, in her words, "dead set" against it. He refused to help her in any way and dismissed the idea out of hand. Dawne at first accepted this injunction, but after four years of working in the shop, decided to get her motorcycle licence anyway. Enlisting the help of some BCMF instructors, whom she swore to secrecy, she underwent a motorcycle training course and got her motorcycle driver's licence without Trev's knowledge. Then she waited two more years before working up the gumption to tell her father what she'd done.

The new 883 H-D Sportster had just come out in late 1985 and a black one was in a prominent position in the shop window. One day when Trev came in, Dawne pointed to it and said, "Dad, I want one just like that." His response was, "Yeah, well it'll be a cold day in hell before I ever buy it for you." Several months later, both Trev and Dawne were at the annual Harley-Davidson dealer show. At the awards banquet, an 883 was highlighted beside the podium as Trevor went up to speak. Dawne thought nothing of it; there's always a H-D on display at these events, and the new model was a logical candidate. It was only at the end of the presentations she realized what was up. Trev told the assembled dealers he wanted to make a very special presentation, he wanted to give the keys to the Sportster to his daughter. Dawne, in her words, "came unglued" as, tearful and emotional, she walked up to accept the keys. The emotions went both ways. Trev, who had lost his father-in-law to a motorcycle accident, was now giving his daughter a bike, despite his vow never to let someone close to him ride one.

If Trev was worried about his little girl, Dawne went out of her way to reassure him she could take care of herself. In one demonstration of her capabilities, she enrolled in the H-D service school in Milwaukee to become a licensed Harley-Davidson mechanic, and learned about H-D engines, transmissions and everything else. In another, she began breeding and training vicious-looking American pit bull terriers. In a third, she became a top-flight amateur lightweight body builder. These efforts to be more like the boy Trevor had wanted didn't always have the desired effect because they diverted her from the area Trev was really impressed by, the motorcycle business.

Dawne had worked at 606 from the age of eighteen until she was twenty-six and transferred over to the head office of Fred Deeley Imports in Richmond. When she arrived, instead of being challenged with new responsibilities and authority, she was allowed to pursue her other interests and given a year off in 1988 to do so. When she returned, she was asked if she would like to open a Harley-Davidson boutique. This might have appeared like a good idea because Harley-Davidson accessory boutiques were becoming popular in the Untied States. However, it would also have moved her out of the front line in decision-making at Fred

Deeley Imports, a step she naturally rejected.

"I didn't want to be a fluff budget," she said. "I wanted to be working with motorcycles."

This was proving hard to do because she also wanted to be a successful nationally-competitive bodybuilder. Taking time for that took time away from her duties as national warranty manager. The result was Dawne began to be regarded as something of a loose cannon by the management team of Don James, Harold Lenfesty and a banker, Malcolm Hunter, who had been brought in to beef up the company's financial muscle in 1976. Poor communication and hurt feelings became the order of the day. Harley-Davidson's eighty-fifth anniversary ride in 1988 was a case in point. Dawne was planning to be a road captain, one of the company officials leading a group of riders to the reunion in Milwaukee. Just before it was to take place, she was told by Hunter she would only be going on the ride from Vancouver to Seattle.

"How come?" she asked.

"Well, you're not," was the answer.

Dawne, feeling rejected, said to herself, *What the hell, I won't go,* and didn't make the trip. Afterwards, Trev "ripped a strip" off her for not attending. "You should have been there," he yelled at her.

"I wasn't asked," she replied. "I was told I wasn't going."

When Malcolm Hunter was later questioned about the incident, he said he figured Dawne was going to be busy with a bodybuilding show.

If Trev sounds unreasonable in this episode, he had an excuse that was proving to be a major problem to him personally and an irritant in his dealings with others; he had contracted rheumatoid arthritis and was, at times, in almost constant pain. He began taking heavy doses of drugs, changed his handshake from his right hand to the less affected left, and added an elevator to the new house he was building beside the old one in Sidney.

Meanwhile, for Dawne, the same kind of thing happened over the 1988 dealer show in Moncton as had at the reunion ride. Dawne had asked that the kitchen of the hotel be checked to see if it could prepare the kind of food she wanted for her training regime. This had been done and the hotel said it would accommodate her. Then when she asked for her airline tickets a week before the meeting, she was told, "I didn't know you wanted to go."

"It was selective comprehension," Dawne recalls, "little, nit-picking bullshit. I couldn't deal with it. That, plus my lack of authority in my own department, drove me up the wall."

There were other incidents — lack of recognition at company meetings as a shareholder, the failure to book her room near her father's at hotels — that Dawne took as a snub by her father's closest associates and aides. In this analysis, she was probably right. The last thing upwardly mobile women in the company needed was a woman between them and their male bosses, and the last thing the FDI executives needed was an heir getting interested in the family business. Her response was just what they might have wanted; she quit the company and went to work as a volunteer for a twenty-four-hour animal shelter.

To Trev, Dawne's failure to carve out her own territory at FDI was only a matter of passing regret. Since he had always treated Don and Harold as sons, he still had the satisfaction of being a father with the reassurance that his organization and traditions would continue under them.

It was, and is, basically a misunderstanding between father and daughter as to what each really wanted. Dawne thought Trev wanted a son and tried to act like one. What he hoped for, in fact, was a dedicated business person — sex wasn't really an issue — just like himself. Dawne has now grasped this distinction, knows her father's business methods, and understands the challenge that lies before her if she wants to follow in his footsteps. It will be interesting to see if the tough little girl with Harley-Davidson in her blood decides to take on the marketing and financial people now running the family firm.

While Trevor was trying to understand his daughter, he was also confronted with a traumatic event that befalls every son, the death of his father.

Fred Jr. spent the last years of his life in declining health, the final two of them in his bed receiving round-the-clock nursing care. He died at his home on July 31, 1988, and was buried August 5 in crypt 12, block A, Garden Mausoleum at Forest Lawn Cemetery. In a last gesture, that spoke of his lack of interest in all religion, he asked that the music at his memorial service be "That Little Grass Shack in Hawaii." While this unlikely tune played in the chapel, mourners speculated on the size of the inheritance Fred had left to his only son.

No one had the nerve to ask Trev himself, nor were they able to because he wasn't there. Shortly before the service he came down with viral pneumonia and was taken to hospital, an almost predictable response to the dramatic conclusion of his relationship with his father. One of his closest friends, John Copp, said he expected to see Trev wheeled into the funeral parlour, but it didn't happen. Joyce and Dawne attended, but they were largely invisible as well, viewing the service from behind a privacy screen at the front of the chapel. Also there to pay his respects was Ted Deeley, one of Ray Deeley's two sons. The other son, Ray Jr., did not show up. In fact, he phoned Ted to try and talk him out of attending.

"Are you going to Uncle Fred's funeral?" he asked.

"Yes, I am," Ted replied.

"Well, we'd appreciate it if you don't. We prefer you don't go."

"Ray," Ted said, "he's my uncle, that's why I'm going to go."

Ted went and hung around afterwards until everyone else had left. Then he went up to the open coffin, placed his hand on Fred Jr.'s and said, "Thanks for being my uncle," and walked out. The family spat that separated Fred Jr. and Ray in life, which none of their sons was ever privy to, continued even onto death. Whatever it was over — women, money, power — went with Fred Jr. to his grave, and with Ray to his.

Funerals, especially of those burdened with the physical problems of old age, are often a release, even a social occasion, particularly if the person involved had a major impact on many people. So it was with Fred Jr., especially at the reception that followed at the Delta Airport Inn. As had happened after Fred Sr.'s death, business associates and friends joined family members in toasting the dearly departed. Miles away in hospital, Frederick Trevor Deeley's health began to mend, his life-long goal of satisfying his father finally made impossible, and thus unnecessary.

When Trevor recovered, he went through his father's home, disposing of effects. Many, as might be expected, were inconsequential items that could be junked, given to Goodwill or sold. A few were more valuable: Islay's fur coats, her jewellery and china and some pieces of furniture. Despite Fred Jr.'s frugality, there was less than $500 in his safe when Trev opened it.

When all the accounts were reviewed, the assets evaluated and the will sent to probate, Trev wound up with between $16 and $18 million. Dawne, whose chief asset to this point was her eleven percent share of Fred Deeley Imports Ltd., received $750,000 in cash and a further $750,000 in an untouchable trust fund. Fred, who clearly did not approve of temporary domestic arrangements, stipulated the interest from the trust fund should go to Dawne's children, should she bear them while married, or to the University of British Columbia, if she had them while living common law. In the event, she did not have children under either circumstance and successfully appealed to have the provision revoked as unreasonable.

For Trev, the long wait was over. The struggle to put up with his father in business, which had dominated his life for so many years, was finally finished. Fred Jr. had not gone willingly into the night, but he had gone, the monies had been transferred and it was time to celebrate.

The party began a little less than a year later. Trev decided to make good on the dream he had revealed to Stuart and Mary Whitehouse so many years earlier in his little boat on Indian Arm. He would gather up his closest friends, fly them somewhere exotic, and live it up like a raja. Whitehouse had long since forgotten the youthful pipe dream while he concentrated on making his personal fortune in importing. The fact that Trevor had not is a testament to the emotional struggle he had endured. Month after month, year after year, decade after decade his father's malevolent influence had permeated his life like the smell of mildew in an old house. There had been few beacons to guide him through this malodorous fog, but one of them had been the dream of the big trip where he could, "go somewhere in the world and sit on the back of a big yacht and be waited on and not have any money problems at all."

Trev picked up the phone and called Whitehouse in Palm Springs. He reminded him of the dream in the boat and invited him and his wife on a "mystery trip" that spring. Other phone calls went out to Don Matheson, a yacht builder, and his wife Mary; John and Mary Copp, who had made their money in land development; and Rudy Morelli, a lawyer in Kamloops, and his wife Rae. All were asked to come to the Airport Delta Inn in Vancouver at 2:30 PM June 14 and bring their passports and resort clothing for two weeks. When the four couples arrived, they found a large number of Trev's other friends had been invited for a party, so it was impossible to know how many people were going on the mystery trip or which of those present were on the list.

Trev broke the suspense by individually handing out four sets of travel bags, containing the itinerary, to each of the four lucky couples. In addition, each received a jacket and other pieces of clothing with *Mystery Trip* embroidered on them.

Then they were off, Trev, Joyce and their eight friends first class by Air Canada to London, all expenses paid. After a night at a top hotel, the party boarded another flight to Nice, spent the night, and travelled over the Italian border to San Remo. There at the quayside was their destination, a 132-foot Feadship called the *Fiffanella*. This brand new beauty – it had just been built the previous year in the Netherlands – had a luxurious master stateroom for Trev and Joyce, four guest staterooms, two with double beds and two with queen size beds, and a crew of nine to look after their every whim.

For the next seven days, the ten of them had the time of their lives, cruising the Mediterranean with an American captain and his multi-national crew, stopping off at San Rafael, Cannes, Monte Carlo and San Tropez. It was everything Trevor had always wanted, and more than anyone else had ever dreamed. Then it was back to Nice, up to London for three days of shopping and going to shows (including *Les Miserables*), and home. Everything was first class, everything was paid for, everything was organized to the last detail.

It was, to that point, the biggest blowout Trevor had arranged, but it was only the beginning. In 1990 and again in 1992 he did the same thing all over again with most of the same people, winging them across the ocean, wining and dining them and cruising the Mediterranean like Aristotle Onassis.

One reason Trevor threw his money around with such abandon was that, in the words of George Herbert, "living well is the best revenge." A second was that three years earlier he had almost died. He, Joyce and John and Mary Copp had joined the *Royal Princess* in Vancouver and had begun a cruise down the coast. Two days out and Trevor came down with bronchitis which gradually seemed to get worse the farther south they went. The party continued their vacation trip, disembarked eighteen days later and flew to Palm Springs. When the doctors saw him there, they diagnosed full-blown pneumonia and began more intensive treatment. Trevor finally rallied, but it was a close thing and he knew it. He had almost died before his father, a possibility that would have meant all his sacrifices had been in vain.

Fate, however, had another surprise in store for Trev in '89, this time with his heart. He and Joyce had a condo at Puamana on Maui, an exclusive 28-acre tropical hideaway only the affluent can afford to join. It had not, however, been exclusive enough, and Trevor decided he wanted to remodel it to his own specifications. What he hadn't planned on was that work in paradise doesn't proceed with any sense of urgency. The Maui workers worked on Maui time, and when the surf was up, they didn't work at all. As the construction delays worsened, Trev got more and more agitated, finally sending his heart into a form of fibrillation. To all intents and purposes, he appeared to be having a heart attack, and by the time paramedics got to his unit, he had collapsed. When Joyce and Mary Copp saw him being loaded into the ambulance, neither woman thought he would come out alive.

The 25-mile trip around the periphery of the island to the hospital was a horror show. Despite its siren, the ambulance was continually blocked by traffic on the narrow road and Trevor became violently ill to his stomach on the way. On arrival, the doctors stabilized his heart rate and pronounced that the problem had not been a heart attack as such. It would, however, have to be controlled with drugs. The incident convinced Trev and Joyce to sell their remodelled Puamana house and stick to Palm Springs. Had Trevor actually been struck down by a major heart attack, he undoubtedly would have died on the arduous trip to the nearest medical facility.

Even proximity to state-of-the-art medical technology would not have saved him on his next close call without Joyce's assistance.

The second big bout with pneumonia stemmed from the fact that Trev loved designing and customizing boats and his friend Don Matheson just happened to own a yacht-building company, Canoe Cove Manufacturing, a few miles across the Saanich Peninsula from Trev's home. This had led, over the years, to the construction of a lot of fancy fibreglass.

Trev has had a variety of boats from little outboards in the 1940s and '50s to cabin cruisers in the early '60s, but he didn't really get started as a cruiser collector until November 1967 when he bought a thirty-seven-foot Challenger Sedan from Canoe Cove. This boat with two 325 horsepower Mercruiser inboards was delivered in July 1969 and very nearly proved the end of both his collection and of him. With just thirty-nine hours on the engines, Trev ran the Challenger aground in Blind Channel and was unable to drive it off. Knowing the tide was low, he and Joyce enjoyed cocktails on deck and waited for the tide to turn and lift the boat off the rocks. Unfortunately, the tide runs through Blind Channel with some force and the rising water piled up at the stern and got into the engine compartment before the boat started to move. Joyce and the family pet took to a Boston whaler and Trev dove off the bow as the nearly new vessel sank with all their personal belongings.

It was subsequently dragged off the bottom with a tugboat, rebuilt and recommissioned in the spring of 1970. Figuring this was a good chance to put a little more muscle into his motors, Trev took them to his father's shop and had high lift camshafts and other performance goodies added. The units were then reinstalled, but on the boat's first high speed run, one of the hopped-up engines blew up, souring him on the whole project. When he told Stuart Whitehouse he was thinking of selling it, Stuart bought it himself and renamed it the *Casablanca* after his name in Spanish.

Trevor's next boat was a forty-one-foot Coho tri-cabin with a pair of 325 horsepower inboard/outboards. The tri-cabin was delivered in October 1971 and lasted until boat number three, a fifty-three-footer with a pair of 370 horsepower Cummins diesels, which he launched in October 1973.

He kept this one until October 1976 when he traded it for a much smaller thirty-seven-foot sports fisherman with a pair of 225 horsepower Caterpillar diesels.

The fisherman turned out to be too small, so the following year he purchased boat number five from Canoe Cove, a forty-one-foot sport sedan with a pair of "triple nickel" 555 cu. in. Cummins diesels.

In due course, the sport sedan was sold, and Trev ordered boats number six and seven, both forty-eight-foot sedans. He sold one with a pair of 6-71N, 310 horsepower Detroit diesels in California, and kept the second which had a pair of 6-71TI, 410 horsepower diesels for himself. His friends weren't surprised he kept the more powerful motors. Should the two identical boats ever meet in the waters around Vancouver Island, Trev's would walk away from its sibling.

The combination of accommodation and power still wasn't right, so in June 1980, Trev had it stretched to fifty-three feet, resulting in a larger cockpit which he enclosed and made into a lounge. This gave him and Joyce more room, but the power seemed down, so in 1983 Trev boosted the output with fuel modifications to generate 450 horsepower.

In 1988, Trev departed from his practice of ordering his hull from Canoe Cove, and bought a forty-six-foot SeaRay instead from the factory at Palm Coast, just north of Daytona Beach. This was delivered, without engines, to Canoe Cove, which proceeded to install a pair of 6V92TA Detroit diesels and bring the interior up to Trev's very high standards. Trevor ran the boat for forty hours before selling what was the most extensively customized SeaRay in existence to a very happy buyer. The reason he sold it says a lot about friendship and explains much of what had seemed to outsiders to be an aimless turning over of expensive cruisers. Trev, as the leading customer of Canoe Cove products, had become one of the company's best salesmen. By word, deed and reputation he was pulling in business that both helped his friend and the local economy.

This now went into a nosedive. The recession that hit Canada in the late 1980s had a disastrous effect on the yacht business and Matheson told Trev he was scrambling to keep the company afloat. Well, said Trev, "I'll build a new boat if you get a new hull." Matheson proceeded to do so, and so work began on *Cove Lady* number nine, a sixty-foot sport convertible with two twelve-cylinder V92TA Detroit diesel turbocharged motors, each capable of producing 1,080 horsepower. Trev had seen blond bird's eye maple on the *Fiffanella*, and so this was specified for the interior, along with a silk headliner, taupe and pink Ultrasuede panels and deep pile ivory carpeting.

As with all his boats, the nineteen-foot-wide vessel contained a number of unique details. The dinghy, for example, is held in a custom mount that combines hydraulics and davits that Trevor designed and had fabricated locally in Sidney. The boat also doesn't have a bow pulpit for an anchor like most similar sized yachts; the anchor comes right through a trough in the hull to keep its overall length at sixty feet so Trev could get it into his boathouse.

In addition to making changes on the blueprint, Trevor also made them in wood, metal and fibreglass if he didn't like the way things were turning out, a process that extended the cost and construction time. The bird's eye maple was ripped out several times because the match between panels wasn't exact and Trev wanted it to be perfect. The attention to detail, the regular trips to the boat yard in winter, and the frustration Trev felt in conveying his desires, began to have an effect on his health.

He and Joyce, as had become their custom, travelled south to Palm Springs where they hoped the balmy climate and the absence of the boat project would prove a tonic for Trevor's condition. During the winter vacation, two of his visitors were Don and Mary Matheson. The four friends had the same food for lunch and dinner, but Trev came down with salmonella poisoning. For thirteen hours he was sick to his stomach, spending much of the time in the bathroom throwing up. Joyce phoned his doctor but got his nurse, who said it sounded like flu, and prescribed some medication over the phone. Joyce realized things were more serious than that when she went into the bathroom and found Trev curled up in a fetal position on the bathroom floor seriously dehydrated. When the ambulance came this time, Don said he didn't think he would ever see Trev alive again. His face was the same colour as the carpet.

Within minutes Trev was receiving emergency care at the Eisenhower Medical Center, with up to five different containers of I.V. fluid going into his arm at a time. Doctors there said he was in "pretty bad shape," and that had he arrived an hour or two later he would not have made it. Joyce was livid. She confronted Trev's doctor in the Emergency Department and tore a strip off him.

"Goddamn you people with your nurses who start prescribing medicine over the telephone. They really should know the difference between someone who's seriously ill and someone who isn't."

The doctor apologized and said she was right. The nurses, he said, "do it to protect us."

For Joyce the whole experience was both scary and immensely frustrating. There she sat in a million dollar house within spitting distance of the best medical care in the world and she had almost lost Trev because of poor communication with his doctor. Trevor, meanwhile, improved quickly, got back on his feet, and returned with her to Sidney, almost as if nothing had happened. He held the boat launching and launch party (*see Chapter 1*) as planned, but that was just a bit of show for the troops. The next day, the new *Cove Lady* was back in the yard getting ripped apart to resume the final fitting out process.

The strain of the delayed completion, the mixed medications for his heart and his arthritis, the poisoning episode, all proved too much. Trev came down with pneumonia and had to be taken to Victoria's Royal Jubilee hospital where he just barely pulled through his second major bout of the killer infection.

"He was almost down for the count," Joyce says candidly. "It took a lot out of him."

When Joyce is asked to discuss Trevor's health, she does so with a sense of amazement at what he's come through. She catalogues his illnesses, upbraids his doctors, and comments openly about the series of incidents that have laid him low since 1986. She is, on the whole, philosophical rather than fearful.

"We're both lucky. He has pain, but he hasn't, touch wood, nor do I have, any life-threatening things at the moment." She smiles as she looks at Trev across the room. "He's in great shape, but as we always say, he's the sickest well person that we've ever seen."

Perhaps the biggest impact the round of illnesses had on Trev was that they convinced him to give up flying, and in particular, to give up flying the last in his collection of aircraft, his jet helicopter.

Trevor had graduated to helicopters in 1981. He and a group of his aviation friends in Sidney had decided to club together and buy a vintage Bell 47G3B1 helicopter, the "bubble" type used in the movie *M.A.S.H.* Trev, always looking for an edge, wanted to get the jump on the others without telling them. To do this he went to a helicopter air charter company in Desert Hot Springs and asked around about getting some flying instruction. The owners, Don and Elaine Landells, just happened to have been Canadians and knew some of the same people Trev knew back in Vancouver.

In fact, they hit it off so well Don decided to make an exception and assign one of his pilots, Steve deJesus, to train his new friend.

The lessons began on January 27, 1981, in a dual control Bell 47 similar to the one Trev planned to buy. He was, in deJesus's words, "a quick learner."

"Because he rides motorcycles, he's had a lot of good hand-eye-feet coordination so he was easy to teach. He picked it up pretty quickly."

Trev arrived back in Sidney with a tan, a smile and a secret. His partners, who knew nothing about his months of training in the clear desert air, were stunned at the speed with which Trev qualified for his licence. It was yet another example of Trevor working as hard at playing as other people did at working. It could also be viewed another way; as another example of Trev having an ace up his sleeve. He had learned from racing, from business and from life that success comes to those who look for and make their own advantages.

The helicopter itself was a case in point. It was twenty years old when it went into Vancouver Island Helicopters for a refit. It was brand new when it came out, in fact, better than brand new. Trevor had the shell gutted, polished, repainted, rewired, and refitted. The controls were customized, the stick was chromed, the "popcorn maker" and various covers were detailed. Custom upholstery was created with the Harley-Davidson logo for the seats. The instruments were an example of the extent Trev went to. Instead of merely being serviced and reinstalled, Trev had them pulled apart and their faces repainted and re-silk-screened. Outside, the Bell was lavished with a custom paint job in red, black and white, with pinstriping, the H-D logo and eagles.

The resulting chopper was a knockout in aviation circles, but it would have been familiar to anyone knowledgeable about custom motorcycles. What Trev had done, in effect, was to apply motorcycle restoration and customizing techniques to his new helicopter.

He was busy flying it too, as well as helicopters back in California at Landells' Aviation. Don Landells and Steve deJesus had been so impressed with Trev's skills as a pilot they convinced their insurance company to allow them to rent him a helicopter. He was the only one of their customers to get this special treatment. Because he could do this, Trev's guests in Palm Springs often got to savour this special treatment from their host, being whisked across the California countryside as if they were in a Hollywood movie.

Gussied up or not, the Bell with its piston engine was still an anachronism. As a result, Trev went out and bought himself his personal Jet Ranger helicopter. These babies, which go for around US $750,000, could be picked up for about half that on the used market at the time, so Trev probably put out around $400,000 for the purchase. Like the other, it went straight into Vancouver Island Helicopters where technicians lavished $150,000 on bringing it up to scratch. By the time they finished, it had "all the pilot toys on it, all the bells and whistles."

Still, it was ten years old, so Trev had Barry Hewko of Vancouver Island Helicopters buy it back and pick him up a nearly new Jet Ranger III in the United States instead. About this time, 1985, the owner of the company had a heart attack, leaving its future in doubt. Trev, a believer in putting money where his interests lie, bought a third of Vancouver Island Helicopters, and became a vice president. The price wasn't disclosed, but when he bought in, the company had seventeen helicopters and about forty employees.

The turning point was 1991. Trev has never explained the exact sequence of events, but most of the elements have already been touched on. He had committed to building his new sixty-footer at Canoe Cove and supervision of that project was taking all his time. He twice stepped up to death's door, damaging his confidence in his health. And the boat project went past $1 million, eventually reaching $1.3 million. As a result, Trev parted with his helicopter, lost interest in the flying business and sold his portion of the company.

It had been a good investment, and would have continued to

be had he maintained his financial interest. Vancouver Island Helicopters now has thirty-eight helicopters, a staff of 105 and has branched out into building medical evacuation interior conversions. The fact that he sold may mean he wasn't in it for the money, or it may mean, given the cost of the boat, that even millionaires need to sell old toys to buy new ones. In any event, Vancouver Island Helicopters was grateful for his support through a difficult period, as was Canoe Cove Manufacturing.

Both events point to a role Frederick Trevor Deeley has played throughout his life, that in the downsizing and layoff-prone '90s, should receive a larger degree of public recognition than it has. That role has been, to put it simply, job creation. From the introduction of Honda motorcycles, the creation of the Yamaha dealer network, the revitalizing of the Harley-Davidson business to his activities on Vancouver Island, Trev Deeley has always left behind him a string of new jobs. Literally thousands of Canadians, and indeed many Americans, are working today as a direct or indirect result of his efforts to provide the motorcycling public with high-quality personal transportation.

Many others are indebted to his public generosity: kids at a Rotary club "Field of Dreams" five-diamond baseball park at Victoria Airport he helped build with a $30,000 gift, businessmen who use a van he presented to the Sidney Merchants Association, and eye patients at Saanich Peninsula Hospital where he donated $100,000. The recipients, of course, have included his own family, who have been just as surprised and pleased as the general public. Ted Deeley, who had been an ice show performer for many years, returned to Vancouver and had some difficulty with his partner in a photography business. As a result, he had to start all over again, working out of his father's warehouse doing wedding photographs. Trev heard about his cousin's difficulties through his bank manager, Don Chatterton, who told him Ted had been wiped out. Without Ted knowing about it, Trev had Chatterton find out exactly what camera he needed to carry on his business.

About a month later, Trev and Joyce phoned Ted and asked him and his wife out to dinner along with Ray and his wife. When Trev arrived at Ted's house, he gave him a box.

"What's in this?" Ted asked.

"Just something to help you out," Trev replied. Inside the box was a brand new Hasselblad worth up to $10,000. Ted was deeply touched at the gift. It was totally unexpected.

For motorcycle buffs, Trev turned part of his Vancouver warehouse in Richmond into the largest motorcycle museum in Canada, with more than 200 vintage and classic machines of all makes, free to anyone to see and enjoy. It was an effort, he said, to give something back to motorcycling which had given so much to him.

Perhaps his largest act of philanthropy was for students at Fairview College in northern Alberta, who will use the facilities of the Trev Deeley Technical Training Centre which was built as a result of a gift of $700,000. The main role of the centre will be to train certified Harley-Davidson mechanics for dealerships across the country.

When he inaugurated the building in September 1993, he predicted a glowing future for the college and its graduates.

"It won't be long before there are 100,000 Harleys running in Canada. They all have to be serviced. Dealers we have now just simply can't handle the work we expect two years down the road. That's where a place like Fairview College is so valuable. This will pay off down the road."

No one in the audience, which included Jack Ady, the Alberta Minister of Advanced Education and Career Development; Agriculture Minister Walter Paszkowski and MLAs Glen Clegg and Gary Friedel and local and school officials, as well as staff and students, would have missed the direction in which Trevor, then seventy-three, was looking — down the road, to more Harley-Davidsons, and to more highly skilled, well-paying jobs.

The old hell raiser, who showered his racing opponents in dirt, out-finessed the inscrutable Japanese, helped save Harley-Davidson, and triumphed over parental abuse, personal tragedy, business reverses and ill health to become one of the most successful and best-loved individuals of his generation, was providing a message for the future.

Hope, confidence, and the joy of riding a big twin on an open road.

APPENDIX A

TREV DEELEY SHOULD be a beacon to young people wondering in the current dismal economic climate what to do with their lives. He succeeded where others, in the same industry, fell flat on their face. Why he did so was largely because of an almost pathological need to win the respect and admiration of his father, only sixteen years older than himself. In this, he ultimately failed, but in the process of failing he succeeded in business beyond his wildest dreams. This painful, bruising and often excruciating catalyst is not the kind of inducement anyone would wish for themselves, or their children. However, the method of his success is another matter. By looking at the basic ideas he used in business, we can identify concepts and principles that can be applied to any life and any career, pursuits far removed from the smell of Castrol R and high octane gasoline.

Spread the Risk

The first principle of Trev Deeley's success was that he correctly identified that the business he was in was "motorcycles," not B.S.A.s, Triumphs or Harley-Davidsons. He learned this from his grandfather, who was cut off from the supply of English bikes by the First World War and had to look around for another manufacturer to keep his shop open. Reliance on one brand was both risky and unnecessary. It was because of this attitude that Trev was open to the idea of importing Hondas from Japan. Had he thought of himself as the importer of a particular brand, he would have denied himself the opportunity of growing with the Japanese motorcycle boom. Observers looking at Trev's close association with Harley-Davidson today, might argue that he appears to have renounced this any-grist-for-the-mill approach. In fact, if Trev was actively in the business today, he would secretly be the importer of Triumph, Ducati, Moto Guzzi, Aprilia and MuZ motorcycles, and probably would be angling for Norton as well.

Use Objective Analysis

His father and grandfather rejected Honda out of hand, not because the first one they saw was badly made or deficient, but because it came from Japan. They didn't like or trust the Japanese for racial reasons and carried this prejudice over to Japanese products. One can argue they were conditioned by cheap Japanese tinware that flooded North America after the war, however that is hardly enough reason. Had they studied the conflict even superficially, they would have been struck by the depth and breadth of Japanese industrial technology. The point was that they didn't use objective analysis and neither did the English bike dealers in Trev's network. Trev was objective, and as a result, was successful.

Employ Parallelism

Trev never accepted that he couldn't do something, even when he was told not to. If he couldn't do it one way, he did it another. This never-take-no-for-an-answer attitude is neither gentlemanly nor sportsmanlike, but it certainly is a winning technique in business. Trev took on Honda even though B.S.A. didn't like it. He started his Yamaha business in direct conflict with his agreement with Honda. Later he made a verbal deal with Harley-Davidson almost a year before leaving Yamaha. Bad faith? No, good sense. The basic point is that in business, especially an import business, one's company must be protected against arbitrary actions from manufacturers, governments or Acts of God. Trev proved the best defence is a parallel plan, fully operational, in competition with the primary activity.

Harness the Power of Wholesaling

Wholesaling is the greatest way to leverage profits ever invented. It's so good, it has been the basis of a lot of nefarious pyramid schemes over the years. The basic lesson it teaches is that a company will make a lot more money with a small percentage as a wholesaler, than it will as a dealer selling for itself. The power of a distribution network, with dealers constantly beating the bushes for new customers, is enormous; at times, product seems to be drawn through the pipeline as if a giant suction is at work. A second benefit is that wholesaling, like widening the number of product lines carried, also involves risk sharing. In any group of dealers, some will necessarily be more successful than others. A distributor, one step back from the front line, can be insulated from the inevitable failures by the inevitable successes. Then, through coercion and example, he can try and get the weaker dealers to emulate the more successful. The importance of this concept, which played a key role throughout Trev's business career, can hardly be overstated.

Provide Credit

Fred Deeley Ltd. always provided generous credit terms to its dealership network and Trev Deeley carried this practice on with his dealers. The basic argument is that it's critical to have product in front of the customer, even if it costs you some money in carrying charges. In the long run, a successful distributor can push this process back onto the manufacturer, reducing or eliminating his own exposure, but even before this point is reached, it's still better to have the product on a dealer's floor rather than sitting in a warehouse.

Fulfill Commitments

This may sound simple enough, but you'd be surprised how many companies make enemies of their dealers and customers by failing to deliver on their commitments. Trev tried very hard to always live up to deals he made with his dealer network. This wasn't always possible, but his dealers always got the impression he was at least trying to help them with parts, product or whatever. Dealers interviewed for this book, put this attribute right at the top of the list. Trev, they said, was a straight shooter.

Support the Sport

Trev Deeley supported motorcycle racing as a rider and later as a team manager. It's easy enough to say he did it because he liked it. Too easy. Trev knew, like his father and grandfather, that racing both "improved the breed" and acted as a wonderful advertising medium. In addition, it kept his employees current with the most up-to-date techniques and products which they could then filter down to the customer base. The same concept applies to other fields, even those less obviously competitive.

A computer hardware company, for example, should always have demo models, using the latest hot processor, assembled by its own staff so that they can attract the most technically sophisticated customers, and also filter down the best of the new technology to the general public. How does such a company "support the sport"? Why, by supporting the local hobbyist computer bulletin board, by sponsoring local computer fairs, by getting involved in computer education. In business, Trev found, you only get something out if you first put something in.

Selection Beats Price

Certainly everyone likes a bargain, but when push comes to shove, parts availability beats price every time. Trev learned this lesson because he had a dealer network to serve and had to have every part in stock. Carrying a big inventory cost money, but it also drew customers in from far and wide who knew the parts they wanted would be available. When you can't complete a project because one little widget is missing, most people would do almost anything to get it. They will certainly pay ten or fifteen percent more if you have it in stock. At a time when huge super stores and factory outlets are roaming the retail landscape like modern-day dinosaurs, ready to devour little shops with a single bite, it's worth remembering that in every product line, most of these stores lack depth, especially in parts.

Mix Business with Pleasure

If there is any activity on which Trevor put his personal stamp, it was business socializing. From the earliest days, he has always made personal friends, wherever possible, with the people with whom he did business. One of the reasons John Davidson asked him to become the Canadian distributor of Harley-Davidson was the excellent impression Trev left on him years earlier when he was a H-D factory racer. He kept this impression when he became more wealthy by inviting H-D officials, and representatives of other manufacturers, out to B.C. for some fly-in fishing at a mountain lake or some cruising on his yacht along B.C.'s magnificent Pacific coast. Parties and gifts have often played a part in cementing good relations. On one occasion, for example, Trev gave Davidson the Deeley Number 1 Sales Ring, a gold ring with five diamonds in it that he still wears proudly to this day. Another time, Trev gave Harley-Davidson a bronze and gold eagle sculpture. The company was so pleased, it placed it on a pedestal in a place of honour in its lobby. Still other times, he has invited all his staff to lavish parties to recognize their achievements. People like this kind of attention. It's surprising more companies don't try giving it to them.

Know the Product

Have you ever met a company president who didn't know his own products? Of course you have. The business world is replete with executive pencil pushers who have a sharp eye for a profit and loss statement but know little or nothing about the products they actually make. Trev not only could read a balance sheet with the best of them, but he was also intimately conversant with his products, both from the standpoint of servicing and that of use under demanding conditions. Trev's expertise in running a distribution network was certainly appreciated when he joined the Harley-Davidson board, but it was his product and customer knowledge that had the biggest impact. A bike might have a perfectly good oil tank, but Trev would say, "It's just not right. It just doesn't look right," and the other members paid attention. You don't get that kind of respect without a lot of handshakes and dirty fingernails.

Keep Smiling

Sometimes this is the hardest lesson of all, to be optimistic in the face of one disaster or another that comes down the business pike and lands on your desk. It's much easier, and much more common, to let setbacks affect your mood and to let your mood affect your decisions. Trev Deeley didn't do that. When bad news came along, he would just smile, switch gears and think of another way to get around the problem. In a larger sense, even the failure of the British car industry in North America, the collapse of most English motorcycle makes, and the precipitous drop in Japanese motorcycle sales all were just rocks in the road for Trev to ride his career around. One gets the impression, viewing the twinkle in his eye, that – if the flesh were willing – there's still enough piss and vinegar in "Daredevil Deeley" to do it all over again.

APPENDIX B

THE TREV DEELEY Motorcycle Museum is one of the most comprehensive displays of motorcycle history in North America. It's located inside the head office and distribution centre of Fred Deeley Imports Ltd. at 13500 Verdun Place in Richmond, B.C., an industrial suburb of Vancouver not far from Vancouver International Airport. Visitors enter through the company lobby and then through a small steel door. What they see on the other side is a large room with dramatic orange neon accents that resembles Aladdin's cave — a veritable treasure trove of motorcycle memorabilia. In front is a revolving stand with a feature motorcycle, and beyond that are rows and rows of vintage, classic and historic motorcycles from scores of manufacturers around the world. It usually takes a moment to realize there are more motorcycles on a mezzanine level that runs around the room, and still more in a workshop at the back and in storage behind that.

From the littlest 1948 Whizzer — a 100 cc motor added to a Schwinn bicycle — to the legendary Brough-Superior — the marque ridden by Lawrence of Arabia — the museum has an eclectic collection of nearly 200 machines. Pride of place goes to Trev's favourite, a 1936 Harley-Davidson Knucklehead, but there are many other interesting offerings, including an Indian four, B.S.A. Gold Star, Hesketh V1000 and a collection of Italian-built Harley-Davidson roadracers. You can mention almost any make, from Triumph to

A.J.S., Zundapp, Ducati and Lilac and find it represented.

That so many are present is a reflection of Trev Deeley's widening objective as his museum grew. "The interest started with Harley. Then it went to B.S.A. and Triumph and then I could see the value of adding some Indians," he remembers. "Now my aim is to have a motorcycle of almost every make."

There is ample room to walk around and see the collection. The museum extends over 13,000 square feet of floor space in what was the original Yamaha Canada distribution warehouse. Most of the motorcycles carry clear explanatory cards giving the make, model and age and saying something about their place in history. Admission, for the time being, is free. One of the most interesting groupings are the early Japanese street motorcycles from the late 1950s and early 1960s. Visitors have the opportunity to compare European, British and American bikes with the first export Hondas. They can place themselves in the shoes of Trev's dealers and ask themselves what their reaction would have been to his sales pitch.

Besides Trev himself, the person most responsible for the museum is Trev's former racing opponent and long-time friend, Fred Pazaski. He was the first curator of the museum, restored many of the bikes on display and has been a tireless booster of the facility from the beginning. At the opening ceremony in 1993, Don James, CEO of Fred Deeley Imports Ltd., said the company was supporting the museum in an attempt to show the legacy of motorcycling, especially to young people.

"There's a little motorcycle in everyone," he said. "Our intention is to get people back into it."

There was applause for that remark, and for the president of Harley-Davidson, Jeffrey L. Bleustein, when he said Deeley's has contributed not only to Harley-Davidson, but to the whole sport of motorcycling. "Trev taught a lot of us much of what we know about motorcycling," he said. "He is one of the few people who can enjoy being a legend in their own time."

FRANK HILLIARD has had a lifelong romance with motorcycles, starting in 1957 when he bought his first two-wheeler, a Lambretta 150cc scooter. As a young man he rode across Canada and Europe by motorcycle and later toured the United States on a BMW R75/5 and a Kawasaki GPz 750. During his career as a professional journalist, he has bought and sold an eclectic mixture of machines from Ariel Leaders and BSA Gold Stars to an autobahn-burning Suzuki GS1100SZ. His interest in Harley-Davidsons began with a Harley test ride during Bike Week at Daytona and grew when he became an editor at *Canadian Biker Magazine*. It was here he first met Trev Deeley and became fascinated with Deeley's meteoric, and at times, miraculous race to the top of the business and social world in western Canada.

Frank Hilliard now lives in Victoria, B.C., where he can pursue his passion for riding classic bikes twelve months of the year.